THE JOB HU

THE JOB HUNTER'S GUIDE TO JAPAN

TERRA BROCKMAN

KODANSHA INTERNATIONAL
Tokyo and New York

For my mother and father

Distributed in the United States by Kodansha/USA Ltd., 114 Fifth Avenue, New York, New York 10011. Published by Kodansha International Ltd., 17-14, Otowa 1-chome, Bunkyo-ku, Tokyo 112 and Kodansha International/USA Ltd., 114 Fifth Avenue, New York, New York 10011. Copyright © 1990 by Terra Brockman.
All rights reserved. Printed in Japan.

Library of Congress Cataloging-in-Publication Date

Brockman, Terra, 1958-
   The job hunter's guide to Japan/by Terra Brockman—1st
    ed. p. cm.
   Includes bibliographical references
   1. Americans—Employment—Japan I. Title
HF5549.5.E45B755 1990
650.14'089'13052—dc20   90-30927

ISBN 0-87011-984-2 (U.S.)
ISBN 4-7700-1484-8 (Japan)

First edition, 1990

ACKNOWLEDGEMENTS

This is the kind of book that would have been impossible to write without the help of a great many people. The list of those who contributed is far too long to detail here, but I would like to sincerely thank each person who took time out of his or her busy schedule to tell me about their jobs and experiences in Japan.

Special thanks must also go to:

—my editors at Kodansha International who gave me this project,

—my colleagues at *The Daily Yomiuri* for their patience, advice, and encouragement,

—Ross Langford for his bitter humor and help on the advertising chapter,

—Bryan Harrell for help with the music section,

—Irene Olshewsky for providing much of the material for the chapter on Japanese corporate culture,

—Ross Long for reading and checking the information in the chapter on lawyers, and

—Tim Jackson for the brilliant dinners and nonstop optimism that kept me going.

CONTENTS

GLOSSARY

Baishu - acquisition, as in "mergers and acquisitions"

Bengoshi - lawyer

Eigo - the English language

Eikaiwa - literally "English conversation;" this is what foreigners are usually employed to teach at language schools in Japan

Gaijin - literally "outside person;" this word is generally used to refer to foreigners of European descent

Gaikokuho jimu bengoshi - licensed foreign lawyers

Gaman - endurance

Gambatte - "do your best," "go for it"—an exhortation commonly heard in Japan

Hajimemashite - "How do you do"

Kabushiki kaisha - a standard corporation with shareholders—usually abbreviated to K.K.

Kaisha - company

Kensetsu kaisha - construction company

Kohai - your junior in a company or a school

Meishi - business card

Seisha-in - a regular company employee—foreigners with this kind of contract get the same pay and benefits as Japanese employees

Sekkei jimusho - design office

Senpai - your senior in a company or a school

Shihonkin - share capital

Shokutaku - employee on a short term contract

Sogo shosha - general trading company

Yugen kaisha - a limited liability company

8

INTRODUCTION

It is no accident that the title of this book resembles Douglas Adams's *Hitchhiker's Guide to the Galaxy*. Like that idiosyncratic romp though a strange and wonderful universe, this romp through the fascinations and frustrations of working in Japan is also, perforce, idiosyncratic—based as it is on extensive interviews with foreigners of all ages, backgrounds, and personalities employed at an array of companies—Japanese and foreign.

Yet through all the differences, some constants emerge. As the intergalactic hitch-hiker Ford Prefect tried to persuade the ever-anxious earthling Arthur Dent in their travels through the cosmos, a profitable and productive sojourn is largely a matter of being prepared and not panicking. *The Job Hunter's Guide to Japan* has been written to provide the information about jobs in Japan that will prepare the job hunter and help lead to a rich, rewarding, and panic-free experience.

The first and last chapters provide an overview and some general comments on working and living in Japan that are applicable no matter what particular job you may be interested in doing. Each of the other chapters covers a specific job area and outlines the qualifications necessary to get the job, the best way to go about getting hired, what you can expect in terms of salary, working hours and working conditions, and what foreigners working in this field find to be its main frustrations and joys.

Thus, the book can be read cover to cover for an overview of the spectrum of jobs available and the pros and cons of each, or it can be used as a reference guide—if you are interested in jobs in advertising, turn to the advertising chapter; if you have been thinking of setting up your own business, turn to the chapter on entrepreneurs. If, after reading the chapter, you would like to investigate the job area more thoroughly, turn to the appendices listing professional organizations, suggested reading, and contact addresses and phone numbers for some of the companies that hire foreigners in each job area.

The history of foreigners working in Japan is fairly brief. In the late 1800s the Meiji government actively sought out foreign specialists who would introduce occidental scientific knowledge, culture, and literature to get Japan moving along the road from an isolated feudal nation to a world power. Engineers, zoologists, language teachers, and artists from the United States and Europe were invited to come to Japan and teach at universities and government institutes.

But then rising nationalism sparked by the military victories over China and Russia (1905) and the annexation of Korea (1910) returned most Westerners again to the status of persona non grata. It was not until after World War II, during the Occupation and into the 1950s, that large numbers of foreigners again began living and working in Japan.

During the 1960s and 1970s most foreigners who came to Japan were academics or travelers fascinated with some aspect of the Orient. They studied Japanese language, literature or culture; some steeped themselves in the arcane teachings of Zen Buddhism while others became devotees of the martial arts.

The eighties, however, saw the influx of a new breed of foreigner. As the roots of plants are drawn downward, so foreigners have been drawn to Japan in the eighties by the seemingly geotropic powers of the yen. Anyone who reads the newspapers or watches television knows that Japan is now firmly in the ranks of the economic superpowers. In addition to bringing Japan into the headlines, this fact has brought record numbers of foreigners to jobs in this thriving nation. The trend will almost certainly continue through the nineties and into what pundits have already dubbed "The Pacific Century."

While a job in Japan is not necessarily a ticket to a hot career on Wall Street, Fleet Street, or Madison Avenue, there are certainly plenty of interesting and lucrative positions available. This was brought home to me when I was sent to Italy on another assignment during the time I was researching this book. An American woman living there asked me what kind of jobs foreigners have in Japan and I said they are doing just about anything—working in banks, ad agencies, trading companies, law offices, schools, laboratories, multinationals, electronics companies, and in their own businesses. She was amazed. In Italy, she said, just about all a foreigner can do is teach or translate. While as recently as ten years ago the only jobs advertised in the English-language papers in Japan were for English teachers, now you see ads for computer programmers, translators, sales people, and engineers. An even broader spectrum of job possibilities circulates via the foreign community's grapevine.

Yet not all foreigners are created equal in the eyes of Japanese employers. Japan has become the land of opportunity for white, educated people from English-speaking countries on one level, and for the Third World labor force on quite another level. The white, educated foreigners get the white collar jobs while the Asians and Middle Easterners generally get the *kitanai* (dirty), *kitsui* (hard), and *kiken* (dangerous) jobs. Non-white, educated English speakers generally find it more difficult to land a good job because most Japanese view blacks, Hispanics, and even Westerners of Asian descent as inferior. This prejudice may gradually disappear as more Japanese have experience living and working overseas.

While the official policy of the Japanese government is to refuse a work visa to any foreigner if the job could be done by a Japanese, the policy is followed only sporadically for educated Westerners. Until recently the government also had a laissez-faire attitude toward foreigners (mainly Southeast Asians) who came to work in factories and in the construction industry without proper visas. The story of these people and the Japanese reaction to them deserves another book.

The subject of this book, however, is the work that the 200,000 or so skilled foreigners are doing. Since I have spoken to only a small fraction of this group, I make no claims of having done a quantitative study. Neither do I claim to have done an exhaustive study that covers every job currently held by a foreigner in Japan. Such a list would be far too long and not very informative. Instead, I have divided the book into chapters that reflect the fields in which the majority of foreigners are working. Within these chapters, I have tried to convey the qualitative experience of working in Japan by giving a balanced view of what foreigners in these fields do and how they feel about it.

Regardless of the kind of work the forigner does, he or she invariably finds that being a *gaijin* (literally "outside-person," a term used to mean "Western foreigner") has its positive and negative sides. On the plus side is opportunity—the opportunity to make good money merely by speaking in your mother tongue or the opportunity to change careers and get in on the whirlwind of new ideas, new technologies, new materials, and new concepts that swirl around Japan, particularly Tokyo.

There is also the opportunity to get "Japan experience"—a working knowledge of Japanese language, culture, and business practices that will, at worst, look good on a resume and, at best, help accelerate your career and raise your salary in your next job. Last but not least, working in Japan allows you to do any number of interesting and lucrative part-time jobs that you would probably never be able to do in your home country.

In my five years in Japan I have taught English to factory workers, to businessmen at a large corporation, and to students in cram schools, junior colleges, and universities. I have also given private lessons to a wide cross section of the Japanese population, from plastic surgeons to housewives. I have done some modelling jobs for print and television advertisements, narrated a video tape, and played flute in two orchestras. I have edited a local city magazine, worked for the largest newspaper in Japan, and I have had the opportunity to write freelance articles and this book.

But if the good side of working in Japan is opportunity, the bad side is discrimination. I have already mentioned the discrimination against blacks, Hispanics, Westerners of Asian descent, and non-Japanese Asians. But even white foreigners are subject to discrimination. Most *gaijin* need little prompting to tell their stories of being pointed at, stared at, refused service in restaurants and refused housing just because they are *gaijin*.

Yet it seems the opportunities outweigh the indignities because foreigners are coming in record numbers and infiltrating just about every job field, working at both foreign- and Japanese-owned companies. In relating the experiences of foreigners working for Japanese companies, the book also provides answers to

**Foreign Inbound Travelers and Registered
Foreign Residents in Japan (1988)**

(1,000)	Foreign Travelers	Foreign Residents[a]
Korea, Rep. of	516	677.1[b]
U.S.A	458	32.8
Taiwan	393	—
U.K.	150	8.5
Philippines	87	32.2
China	112	129.3[c]
Canada	59	3.5
Germany, F.R.	57	3.2
Malaysia	46	3.5
Australia	41	2.6
France	41	2.7
Total	**1,960**	**895.4**

a) As of July 30, 1989. b) Includes people from North Korea. c) Includes people from Taiwan and Hong Kong.
Source: Ministry of Justice, Japan.

questions like, "What is Japanese management and corporate culture really like?" "Is working for a Japanese company something to be welcomed or avoided?"

The answers to such questions are important even for those who may never set foot in Japan, for as this nation invests more and more heavily overseas, buying up land, factories, and companies, more non-Japanese will be working for Japanese companies and Japanese bosses. The experiences of those foreigners now working at Japanese companies in Japan will provide valuable firsthand knowledge that may serve to inform policy decisions in years to come.

This would be an important and valuable contribution because, for all the news reports coming out of Japan in recent years, it remains a country bathed in myth and misunderstanding. I hope that the voices of foreigners living and working here will fill in a few of the gaps and dispel a few of the misconceptions. And I hope this guide will provide useful information to help both foreigners living in Japan, and those thinking of coming here, find the job that will help them have an enjoyable, enlightening, and panic-free stay in this corner of the galaxy.

Terra Brockman
Tokyo, 1990

Author's note: Throughout the text I have used an exchange rate of ¥143 to one U.S. dollar. Based on this rate, ¥1,000 is approximately U.S. $7.00. I have also reluctantly used the pronoun "he" for "he and/or she."

1. OVERVIEW

It's pretty clear to me that Japan will be the economic power of the nineties and that anyone who has firsthand experience working in Japan will be a step ahead of the competition. That's why I'm here.

I had studied Japanese at university and wanted to try and put it to use.

I was traveling and ran out of money in Thailand. I had heard I could make good money in Japan so I came. It was so good I ended up staying.

I had just gotten divorced. I wanted to escape—start over somewhere where no one knew me.

After I graduated from university, I worked for two years as an industrial chemist—making dyes for flesh-colored girdles. I figured it was time for a change.

It was not so long ago that "working overseas" meant working in one of the major cities of Europe or North America. In the 1990s, though, it will mean Tokyo or Osaka as often as it means New York, London, or Paris.

With people coming to Japan from such diverse backgrounds and for reasons as dissimilar as those given above, it is not surprising that the "Japan experience" itself ends up being hard to define. Some foreigners find they get perks that their Japanese colleagues do not; others find they are treated as second-class workers and given only the most menial office tasks. Some find they have plenty of time to pursue outside interests while others succumb to the "salaryman" routine of work, cigarettes, and

15

booze fifteen hours a day, six days a week. Some feel accepted into the family-like atmosphere of a Japanese office while others feel more alienated each day.

And yet through all the contradictions and confusion, one thing is certain: more and more foreigners are coming to work in Japan. From 1976 to 1988 the number of entry permits given to foreign workers increased almost four-fold. The number of illegal workers coming into the country also skyrocketed in the eighties. So great was the influx that in December 1989 the Japanese government approved the first major amendment to the nation's immigration laws in thirty-eight years.

A booming economy and booming job market go hand in hand. Foreign companies are setting up offices in Tokyo to get in on the world's second largest market, and Japanese companies are looking for foreigners to help them internationalize still further. This translates into job opportunities for young people just out of university, for those in midcareer, and even for retirees who come to Japan and serve as consultants or start second careers.

Jobs in Japan often put people on the fast track as far as career development is concerned. A young Australian lawyer got a job in international law at a major Japanese trading company where she was able to work on huge international deals and get a broad range of experience that would have taken years to accumulate had she continued working in Australia. Architects, bankers, journalists, and many others report similar experiences.

The booming economy in Japan also means hefty salaries for those who find work. Because of the strength of the yen, the dollar value of salaries paid in yen nearly doubled from 1983 to 1989. This means that a job in Japan often pays at least twice the amount it would back home.

With all this opportunity to do interesting work and make money, one might ask why there are only 200,000 foreigners working in Japan.

One reason is the visa situation. By looking at the rules it seems almost impossible to get a work visa since if a Japanese person could do your job, you are theoretically barred from working in Japan. Theory and reality are two separate entities, though, and visas can usually be obtained if you are patient and jump through the right hoops (see appendix).

Another reason that foreigners nix the idea of moving to Japan is the common perception that this country resembles one of the circles of Dante's hell. Mention Tokyo and most Westerners think of tiny streets, crowded trains, and hordes of Japanese working late into the night for the greater glory of Toyota or Sony. There is some truth to this vision. The Japanese work more hours per year and take fewer holidays than any other industrialized nation. While their net earnings are fairly high, their purchasing power is low and their housing conditions poor.

**Trends in Hours (Actual) Worked in
Manufacturing Industry (1978-1988)**a)

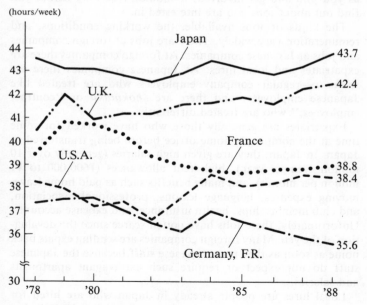

a) Production workers only.

Source: Bank of Japan, *Comparative International Statistics*, 1989.

But the factors that may be most responsible for keeping foreigners away from Japan are simply inertia and the fear of the unknown. Roosevelt's words are applicable—there is really nothing to fear but fear itself—and if you overcome the inertia and are willing to put as much effort into looking for a job in Japan as you would at home, there is no real reason that you should fail.

Personal connections are critical for getting work in Japan. Many foreigners who come to Japan with no connections begin by teaching English to get established and begin meeting people. Then after a year or so, they go on to find a job in their area of interest or specialty. Networking is the name of the game and any connection, no matter how tenuous, is better than none. It doesn't really matter whether you join churches, clubs, special interest groups, or professional associations. As long as you join and get involved, it shouldn't be long before you find out about jobs you are interested in.

The kinds of jobs available, the working conditions, and remuneration vary widely. There are jobs at foreign companies and jobs at Japanese companies. At foreign companies there are expatriates and local hires. At Japanese companies there are *seisha-in*—regular company employees who are treated like Japanese employees—and there are *shokutaku* or "contract employees," who are treated differently.

Expatriates are generally those who have worked for some time at the company's home office before being transferred to Japan. In Japan, they are given high salaries (generally over 10 million yen per year), high rent allowances (¥600,000 to ¥1 million per month), and many benefits such as paid home leave, moving expenses, language lessons, professional association, and club memberships, health insurance, and expense accounts. Unfortunately, these jobs have gotten scarce since the devaluation of the yen. Many foreign companies are sending expats back home as soon as they train Japanese staff because the Japanese staff do not expect or require such extravagant apartments and salaries.

Local hires are people already in Japan who are hired for short one- or two-year periods. They are usually given modest salaries (around ¥300,000 a month) and few benefits. There have

Living Expenses in Chief Cities of the World
(As of November, 1988)

(yen)

	Tokyo	New York	London	Paris
Bread (1kg)	363	329	174	492
Beef (100g)	353	110	100	122
Milk (1ℓ)	198	99	105	109
Sugar (1kg)	308	163	148	146
Eggs (1kg)	288	218	372	415
Onion (1kg)	202	132	199	77
Business Suit[a]	57,420	36,328	38,809	39,686
Shoes[b]	9,424	9,433	8,408	8,260
Gasoline (1ℓ)	121	36	88	108
Permanent	5,783	7,689	9,588	7,937
Laundry Expenses[c]	884	978	1,096	1,205
Electricity (250kw/month)	5,844	4,249	4,004	3,438
Gas (550,000kcal/month)	6,808	3,383	2,580	4,162
Taxi (5km)	1,190	609	685	482

Exchange rate: ¥128/$1.00.
a) Winter clothes. b) A pair of men's shoes. c) Suit.
Source: Economic Planning Agency, Japan.

been a few cases of foreigners who have special skills being hired locally but given salaries and benefits that approximate those of an expat. There are also rare cases when a local hire will move back home and be hired by the head office. These, however, are definitely exceptions.

JOINING THE JAPANESE

The KAISHA Society, a non-profit professional association made up of more than 150 foreign nationals working at Japanese corporations, organizations, and academic institutions, surveys its membership regularly. In their 1989 survey, nearly 30 percent of the respondents were female. The average age of the women was 26.6 while that of the men was 30.3. Fifty-eight percent of the men found that the reality of working in a Japanese company met their expectations. Only 10 percent of the women responded similarly, while 47 percent said that it was "below expectations" and 40 percent said it was "completely different" from their expectations.

Nearly all of the respondents (80 percent) reported annual salaries of between three million yen and seven million yen. Most (41 percent) receive a straight annual salary with no bonuses. Benefits included: paid sick leave (32 percent), paid home leave (28 percent), moving expenses from the home country (34 percent), language lessons (38 percent), professional association memberships (34 percent), non-company housing costs (46 percent), expense accounts (40 percent), pension plan (40 percent), and health insurance (76 percent).

All respondents held undergraduate degrees, with 29 percent holding master's degrees and 11 percent holding some kind of professional degree.

Sixty-two percent were recruited and/or interviewed for their current position while in Japan and 36 percent in their home country.

When asked what they considered the main factor responsible for their employment, most cited their personality. This was followed by their academic background and previous work experience. Japanese language ability was the most cited factor that was "not considered."

Nevertheless, 85 percent of respondents said they spent most, half, or some of the business day communicating in Japanese.

The respondents had been with their organizations for an average of 23 months. Eighty percent said they planned to use their Japan work experience to gain a position with a non-Japanese company in the near future. Only 13 percent said they might stay with a Japanese company for more than 10 years.

Although there is a wide variety of jobs available in Japanese companies, most still relate to English—either teaching, writing, or rewriting it. Even lawyers and personnel managers are often asked to proofread and correct English correspondence. There is rarely such a thing as a job description in Japanese companies, and the more flexible you are, the better you will get along with your Japanese colleagues.

While being a native speaker of English used to be the only real qualification needed to get a job with a Japanese company, this is rapidly changing. In July of 1989 the Sanwa Research Institute surveyed about 200 small companies. In contrast to the KAISHA Society survey in which most respondents said Japanese language ability was not critical, 76 percent of the companies said that they required non-Japanese employees to speak Japanese.

Foreigners working at Japanese companies report two basic contract patterns—*seisha-in* and *shokutaku*. A 1988 survey found only about 20 percent of foreigners working as *seisha-in*. The remaining 80 percent were *shokutaku*, short-term contract workers brought in to perform a specific task like developing software or teaching English. These positions pay substantially more than what an entry-level Japanese would make (about ¥300,000 per month as compared to ¥150,000 to ¥200,000 for a Japanese employee).

However, the Japanese employee has "lifetime employment," bonuses, and advancement possibilities that the foreigner generally doesn't. A few companies offer these kinds of *seisha-in* positions to foreigners, but they are only a good deal for those who are planning to stay in Japan, because starting salaries and benefits are low.

The main complaints of foreign workers at Japanese companies are the lack of advancement opportunities, the lack of praise for a job well done, and the feeling that they are always outsiders. These factors usually lead most foreigners to leave after two or three years. Edward Seidensticker, a respected translator of many works of Japanese literature, lived in Japan for fifteen years. He left because "They [the Japanese] are not like other people. They are infinitely more clannish, insular, parochial, and one owes it to one's self-respect to preserve a feeling of outrage at the insularity. To have the sense of outrage go dull is to lose the will to communicate; and that, I think, is death. So I am going home."

These words were written in 1962, but they have been echoed

by countless foreigners countless times every year since then. Being constantly treated as an alien species leads to alienation and isolation and a kind of "*gaijin* paranoia" that makes one feel unimportant, utterly dispensable in the Japanese scheme of things.

Luckily there is a kind of "*gaijin* power" to balance the paranoia. It is the power to challenge and experiment with the system and it comes from being outside the rings of duty and obligation that bind the Japanese.

THE BIG PICTURE

Whether you are sent to Japan by your company, are recruited, or venture here on your own; whether you intend to stay a year or a lifetime, to do modelling or money management, there are quite a few good reasons to make the move.

Remember, though, the eighties have already attracted a lot of highly qualified people with a good command of Japanese, who possess impressive credentials and have specialized knowledge. The bottom line, according to a ten-year Japan resident, is that if you want to find a good job in Japan, you must be prepared to invest the same amount of time and energy that you would back home. Research the possibilities, make the connections, and when you sign a contract, remember that adaptability and commitment are critical.

In the following chapters people who have worked in various fields relate their experiences of finding jobs and working. There is no secret to success—no one path to any job—but the information in the coming chapters will give you an idea of what's out there and how to get it.

2. ENGLISH TEACHING

People complain of the constant routine, the travel, the same daily pattern. They are legitimate complaints, but . . . it takes a real cynic not to respond to the effort and the sincere interest people show you. It's usually hard not to end up liking the people around you and trying to make the best of the short time you have with them. . . . It's a fun experience, a learning experience.

A 32-year-old Australian woman teaching at public high schools through the Japan Exchange and Teaching (JET) program.

Classes have leapt the rails of reason. Each now has 15 to 20 percent more students. Just when forty-five seemed manageable, they've all become over sixty. Far from remembering names and faces, I'm hard put to know if I'm speaking in the right room. Even after four weeks they all seem to be strangers.

I've come to hate teaching English so much that I cannot conceive of its pleasures until my clenched teeth relax a bit on the weekends.

A 36-year-old American man teaching at a national university

I'm teaching the whole spectrum of Japanese society: teenagers who want to understand the lyrics to pop songs and ones who want to pass exams, businessmen who want to improve their professional status and ones who need English because they do business abroad, housewives who want to get out of the house and ones who want to get out of the country, even retired old men. They come from different backgrounds and are at different proficiency levels and so I'm always think-

*ing about new methods, new curricula, new ways to make learn-
ing English easy and enjoyable for each of them.*

*Unfortunately, most teachers here are not that interested in
whether the students learn English or not. A lot of them are
not teachers at all. As far as I'm concerned, if a person
doesn't have some kind of TESL (Teaching English As A Second Language) qualification, he shouldn't be here."*

A 28-year-old British man teaching at a private language school

These excerpts from letters and conversations of English
teachers in Japan reveal teaching here for what it is—a Dickensian experience that can be the best of times or the worst of
times.

The best of times could be that rarest of birds in Japan, a class
of lively, inquisitive students who never fail to engage, stimulate,
and delight you with their questions and comments as they learn
about your language and culture, and you learn about theirs. Or
it could be the special students who become your friends and
take you to their favorite bars, their homes, and on outings
around the country.

Sometimes the best part of your job is the richness of the experience of living in a foreign country—of seeing another pattern of thinking and living, of relying on the kindness of
strangers to perform small favors like explaining the intricacies
of the Japanese garbage separation system and gift-giving pro-
tocol.

The worst of times could be waking up at six in the morning to
ride packed trains through gray flannel fog and icy drizzle to the
class that is waiting, silent and sullen, to be dragged through the
next hour or two of Pinteresque dialogue—full of pregnant
pauses that, often as not, miscarry. Or it could be suffering
through the sweat and grime of the deadly summers and dealing
with the Scrooge who manages your school—a squeezing, wren-
ching, grasping creature who sees you as just another imported
raw material to be used for profit, squeezed dry and sent back
whence you came.

Still, if you are a native speaker of English and want to work
in Japan, English teaching is the easiest, and often the only, job
to get when you first arrive, *sans* money, *sans* connections, *sans*

everything. If you are aware of the alternatives, search carefully, and ask a lot of questions, you can find yourself a job that will let you have more of the good times and fewer of the bad.

SUPPLY AND DEMAND

Ever since Japan opened its door to the West in the Meiji period, there has been a great demand for language teachers, and English is still by far the main foreign language that the Japanese study. In fact, until the 1980s, if a native English speaker were working in Japan you could safely bet that he or she was teaching English. This is no longer the case, as other job areas have opened up to foreigners, but the business of English teaching has continued to grow and the demand for teachers has yet to be met.

There is also a much lower but growing demand for teachers of subjects other than English at international schools and universities, but because the vast majority of foreign teachers teach English, this chapter is devoted to those jobs.

To get that full-time teaching job with an employer who will sponsor your work visa, the only qualification the immigration officials insist on is a university degree—any university will do, any degree will do. Without a university degree, it is entirely possible to piece together part-time jobs that will more than equal a full-time one, but unless you have a work visa, you will be working illegally. (See appendix for details).

The great demand for teachers who are native speakers of English is due in part to the Japanese attitude toward foreigners and in part to the Japanese education system. The attitude toward and treatment of foreign workers has not changed much since the Meiji era when Japan began importing foreign specialists. By and large, foreigners are still considered an infinitely renewable resource to be obtained and exploited. This attitude virtually guarantees that most foreign teachers will quit after a few years, creating a constant need for new ones.

The Japanese education system is also responsible for the constant demand for English teachers, even though foreign language instruction, generally in English, begins for Japanese children in junior high school. By the time young people graduate from high school, they will have had six years of

English. It is one of the truly amazing feats of the much-lauded Japanese education system that six years of language study produces very few people who can manage anything more complex than "hello" or "good morning."

Amazing it is—but also easily explainable. What is taught in the schools is something called *eigo* (English). This is a rather abstract academic discipline, something like mathematics or Latin. It consists of memorizing a set of complex grammatical rules and constructions and being able to regurgitate them upon command. Instruction in *eigo* is aimed exclusively at giving students the necessary information to help them do well on the *eigo* part of the college entrance examination. So students who are confused by a spoken "How are you?" can often answer questions on the most obscure points of grammar and often understand (and use) archaic forms of English that would stump most native speakers.

As Japan finds itself doing more and more business overseas, it has begun to realize the shortcomings of *eigo*. It will be quite some time, however, before the sluggish educational establishment decides to change the college entrance exam. Until that time, there will be hundreds of thousands of Japanese who have studied English in school but cannot communicate in the spoken language. Of these, there will be thousands who study it for work reasons or as a hobby or social activity.

Enter the native speaker who teaches *eikaiwa* (English conversation) rather than *eigo*.

WORK AND WAGES

With a college diploma in hand, the well-informed native speaker can choose from a myriad of possible teaching jobs—from one in a rice paddy village in the mountains to one in the *Blade Runner* worlds of Tokyo, Osaka, or Nagoya; from one that requires ten or fewer teaching hours per week to one that requires forty or more; from one paying a subsistence-level salary to one paying megayen; from teaching casual conversation to housewives to preparing students for study abroad.

As the jobs vary dramatically, so do the teachers. While most are in their twenties, there are also a fair number in their thirties and forties and a sprinkling of retirees in their fifties and sixties.

Teachers' backgrounds also vary widely—a few are professionals trained in teaching English as a second language, but most are amateurs. ''Amateur,'' however, does not necessarily mean ''unprofessional.'' Many amateurs are dedicated and enthusiastic, and able to teach English as effectively as professionals.

The amateurs are often drawn to Japan because they have heard that it is easy to find high-paying teaching jobs that require no experience and no training. Others come to Japan on tourist or cultural visas and end up doing some English teaching to finance their stay or to line their pockets for later.

While it is true that teachers' wages are high when translated into dollars or pounds ($14 to $35 an hour), they are not so high when you take the cost of living in Japan into consideration. You will probably be making two or three times what you could at home, but you will also be spending two or three times as much each month on three-dollar cups of coffee and 800-dollar-a-month apartments that are cold in the winter, stifling in the summer.

The first job many teachers get in Japan is with an English teaching company. Those who want to make as much money as possible fill the gaps in their schedules with private students—preferably doctors, lawyers, and executives, who are often willing to pay 10,000 yen an hour for the prestige of having a private lesson with a native speaker.

These plum private lessons are not so easy to pick up though. It will most likely take a year or more before you land one. And even when you do, you will probably have to travel a couple of hours to get there and back, so hour for hour it is not as lucrative as it first appears.

Those who are really serious about making a lot of money and are not so interested in experiencing Japan will piece together regular work, part-time work, and private students. It is not too difficult to take home over half a million yen a month if you are willing to teach ten to twelve hours a day, six or seven days a week. But after a few years of this sort of routine, most people burn out. In the past, teacher burnout was usually followed by a trip home. Recently though, as Japan has opened its markets and become more and more international, other nonteaching jobs have become available to foreigners. Those who stay for more than one or two years, and study Japanese, often find that they take on more and more rewriting and translation work and eventually can land jobs in financial institutions, advertising agencies, and elsewhere.

One of the most commonly-heard stories from long-time foreign residents of Japan is that they came to Japan to "teach for a year." It was to be a year of money making or learning or fun. Then, with the swiftness and ease of a film dissolve, that one year turned into five or ten.

The reason for this phenomenon is that after one year many teachers find they have paid off school loans and are starting to make money, learn the language, make connections and friends, and feel comfortable living in Japan. They then find a better teaching job to do for "just another year."

What happens in many cases is that the English teacher, without realizing or intending it, has used those first few years of teaching to become marketable for other jobs in Japan. Language ability, a working knowledge of the culture, and connections with foreigners and Japanese often become the ticket to jobs in the teacher's area of interest or expertise.

This was what happened to a young American who taught English in Kyoto for ten months just to save money in order to travel. In those ten months he saved 10,000 dollars and then traveled the world for a year. Upon returning to the U.S., he finished his bachelor's degree in Asian studies and then returned to Japan. This time he found a teaching job in Tokyo, but soon became dissatisfied as he realized he was just marking time and not advancing toward any goal.

"I didn't want to stay in Japan forever, so I decided I'd better look for more serious work here—something related to business, since that was my minor—something that would be valuable for my future career. I went to an agency specializing in placing bilingual beople and because my Japanese is pretty good, it didn't take too long to find this job I'm doing now—researching the best way to introduce my company's products into the Japanese market. It's long hours and hard work, but I'm sure it will come in handy when I'm ready to go back home."

While in the past this movement from English teaching to

another job in Japan seemed to happen due to the brittleness of certainty and the queerness of fate, now it more often happens by design. People come to Japan and teach only as long as it takes to make the contacts, learn the language, and find a job that suits them better.

FINDING THE FIRST JOB

There are two ways of finding your first teaching job in Japan: while still in your home country or after you come to Japan. Those who dislike taking risks prefer the former. The advantage to doing it this way is that you won't waste time and money looking for work and will have someone to help you get settled in. You also enter the country with a working visa and avoid having to change from a tourist or cultural visa. Switching from any visa category (except the 'working holiday' type, which is only available to Australians, Canadians, and New Zealanders) to a working visa always involves a major tussle with red tape and sometimes even requires that you leave the country, returning on your new visa status.

The disadvantages of getting your first job while in your home country are that it will take a lot longer to find a job since the vast majority of schools and companies do not recruit from overseas and the Japanese do not like to hire people on paper qualifications alone. Also, the working conditions and remuneration you settle on overseas may seem fine from an overseas perspective, but often turn out to be less than optimal or downright miserable once you get to Japan.

What you are looking for is an organization that will sponsor your work visa and pay a decent guaranteed minimum salary (around 200,000 yen a month) for a reasonable number of teaching hours (about fifty-five a month), plus a decent hourly rate (¥3,000 to ¥4,000) for hours that you teach over your guaranteed minimum. If you are very lucky you may be able to find one that will also be willing to help you find an apartment, pay the key money (a nonrefundable "gift" to the landlord for agreeing to let you stay in his apartment), get a phone, open a bank account, and pay your health insurance and your transportation to and from work.

A school that does not offer to help you get settled in should not be automatically disqualified. More important to avoid are the organizations that do not guarantee you a minimum monthly salary. A British man employed by a school with this policy made only 60,000 yen one month while he was paying 50,000 yen a month in rent. Also watch out for companies that do not reward teachers who renew their contracts and those that do not have a sliding pay scale that increases with a teacher's educational level and experience. These policies indicate the organization is not interested in keeping its staff happy and may actively discourage contract renewals in order to keep teachers' salaries as low as possible.

THE JET PROGRAM

One of the safest jobs to get while still in your home country is one with the Japan Exchange and Teaching (JET) Program—the most ambitious experiment in international education ever undertaken by the Japanese government. It was established in August 1987 to promote English language teaching and international exchange within Japan. In 1988 about 1,400 people from six countries (U.S., Canada, Britain, Australia, New Zealand, and Ireland) participated.

To be eligible to participate in the JET Program, an applicant must be a native speaker of standard English, a citizen of one of the six above-mentioned countries, and be under age thirty-five with a university degree and an interest in Japan. Information and application materials can be obtained from Japanese embassies and consulates in your country, and applications can only be made from overseas. The one-year renewable contracts run from the beginning of August to the end of July and applications should be made the autumn before the year you intend to participate.

Administered by the Japanese government, this program eliminates most of the uncertainties involved when you accept a job overseas because the contract conditions are clearly defined and quite reasonable. About 95 percent of the JET participants are Assistant English Teachers (AETs) who are assigned to public schools throughout Japan—from large metropolises to remote mountain or island villages. Their duties vary but generally they assist Japanese teachers at their base school and travel to other schools in the area for regular and "one-shot" visits. The salary is about 3,600,000 yen a year.

Because the AET is not in charge of the class, he or she does not usually have a chance to significantly affect the way English is taught in Japan. Nevertheless, most AETs feel they have a positive effect.

One Australian woman said, "Just by being there—in the school and in the community—I could interact with Japanese people, most of whom had never spoken with a foreign person before. And I could expose Japanese teachers to new ideas and teaching techniques and give them encouragement and support.

"The experience was also very beneficial for me. I became proficient at public speaking and at putting people at ease. I learned some Japanese and I got a comprehensive introduction to the variety of people, places, and customs of this country."

On the other hand, AETs often complain that some Japanese teachers seem threatened by them and only want to use them as human tape recorders—voices for the students to imitate. They also complain that the one-shot appearances are useless from an educational point of view and that they function primarily as professional *gaijin*—a creature not so different from a dancing bear.

The 5 percent of JET participants who are not AETs are Coordinators of International Relations (CIRs). They must have a functional command of Japanese and their duties include assisting with international activities carried out by local governments, as well as teaching English to government employees. Like the AETs, some CIRs feel that most of their duties are insignificant. An American woman said, "I am considered one of the tools in Japan's 'internationalization' and sometimes I am used to that end, but mostly I am just wheeled out for show."

Others, however, feel that their mere presence contributes in a grassroots way to the internationalization of Japan by allowing the Japanese to glimpse non-Japanese ways of thinking and working. A Canadian man stated that these glimpses are "of paramount importance to Japan's long-term goals of integrating itself into the larger picture."

OTHER JAPAN JOBS FROM HOME

It will take a bit more searching to find other teaching jobs while you are still in your home country. Although schools do hire year-round, most hiring is done to prepare for the school year which begins in April. Contracts usually begin around April 20, so many schools do most of their recruiting in March.

The main types of jobs available include those at English teaching companies and schools, at language lounges and salons, and at public and private colleges and universities.

English teaching companies generally specialize in either teaching at their institution or sending teachers out to teach at client companies. Language lounges and salons provide a relaxing place for students to meet their friends and practice their English in a nonthreatening (i.e. non-school-like) environment. The college and university jobs range from cushy, highly paid numbers with six-month holidays to those where you are just another civil servant and must clock in six days a week all year round except for national holidays and a three-week vacation.

Because the English teaching business usually means big money, and because where there's big money there will be smooth operators hungry for a piece of the action, all potential positions must be researched thoroughly, especially those that you might accept from overseas.

A good place to start looking while in your home country is at meetings and conferences of professional teachers of English to speakers of other languages (TESOL). Some Japanese companies and schools send recruiters to conferences such as the annual TESOL conference in the U.S. in March. The monthly TESOL newsletter also lists job openings overseas and is usually available at university libraries or by subscription.

If you get a chance to talk to representatives of a school or company, be sure to ask a lot of questions about what will be expected of you. Some organizations hire exclusively from overseas so they can get people who don't know the ins and outs of teaching in Japan and who will therefore sign contracts that seem reasonable to a neophyte but that a veteran teacher would reject in seconds for reasons such as no minimum guaranteed salary or unreasonable time demands or few weekends and holidays.

AN OBJECT LESSON

A couple who found themselves in this situation were interviewed in Los Angeles by a very friendly man, the owner of a small school in a small city in western Japan. He offered them each a two-year job which paid 200,000 yen for fifty hours of teaching per month plus a rent-free apartment near the school.

"We couldn't believe our luck—a job where we'd work in a month what most people work in a week and no commuting time to boot. It sounded too good to be true."

It was. What the hapless couple found upon arriving in Japan was that although they only had to *teach* fifty hours a month, these hours were scattered over six days a week and from 8:00 A.M. to 9:00 P.M. In between they were expected to counsel students and prepare lessons and teaching material.

"We came to Japan to see the country and to save money to travel in Asia. But we had absolutely no time for travel. During the major national holiday seasons in August, April/May and December/January the school offered intensive courses for businessmen who were on *their* holidays, so we had almost no holidays at all and no time to teach privately for extra money."

Had the couple been offered such a job while in Japan, they would have had other jobs to compare it to and other foreigners to consult.

The other way to find a job while still in your home country is through mass mailing. Feed the addresses in the back of this book (and from advertisements in the current issue of the TESOL newsletter) into your computer and fire out a lot of letters. To save them from becoming instant *gomi* (trash), personnel managers advise you to say that you *will* be in Japan around a certain date and plan to stay for at least a year. Saying that you are just "thinking about" working in Japan or only plan to stay six months will result in sudden death for your application. In your letter be sure to ask if they will be sending a representative from their school to your country for recruiting purposes and indicate your eagerness to be interviewed in person or over the phone.

When you get interested replies (consider yourself lucky if you get a 10 percent response), send a copy of your diploma, transcripts, and letters of recommendation. A follow-up phone call to schools that responded (or even those that didn't) will impress personnel directors.

But the fact is there is not much to worry about if you come to Japan without a contract in hand. Unless you are a seriously different unit, you *will* find an employer who will sponsor your work visa and allow you to live and work legally in Japan. Because the Japanese tend to think that all foreigners have a fairly high "weirdness quotient," even folks who might have a difficult time getting work in their home countries seem to have little trouble finding teaching jobs in Japan, as long as they possess a set of conservative clothes.

The main urban centers—Tokyo, Osaka, and Nagoya—are where the jobs are concentrated. However, if you find city life abhorrent, there are countless small and medium-sized towns with many English schools that would dearly love to get their hands on a real live foreigner to beat out the competition. It will take a little longer to find work in the smaller towns and villages, but it is an option worth considering—especially for those who want to learn Japanese and become a part of a Japanese community (or at least as much a part as a foreigner can). The pay in the countryside is not spectacular (around 160,000 yen a month), but the cost of living is somewhat lower and since you will be one of the few foreigners around, there will be abundant opportunity for part-time and private work.

Those who are driven mad by quiet will feel more at home in the buzzing hives of activity, the cities of Japan. If this is the case, it would be best to begin your search for gainful employment in Tokyo or Osaka. Depending on who you talk to, Tokyo is the more cosmopolitan, more stimulating city—or it is more crowded, cold-hearted, and impersonal.

Check the advertisements in the English-language daily newspapers. The Monday edition of *The Japan Times* has the most extensive job listings, but it is worth glancing over the others, *The Daily Yomiuri*, *The Asahi Evening News*, and *The Mainichi Daily News*, as well. When you call, be sure to sound enthusiastic. If they haven't filled their position yet, and if the hours and pay suit you, take the trouble to visit their office and deliver your resume in person. Remember that it is usually your personality more than your resume that will get you hired for a teaching job in Japan. By coming into the office, you will be demonstrating your keenness to get the job and will have the opportunity to show off your charming, cheerful personality.

It will be worth your while to corner a few of the foreign teachers (out of management's earshot) and find out how they feel about working at the school. If you're feeling bold and loquacious, you might also try to find out where they like to go after hours and plan your nocturnal activities accordingly.

You'll want to find out which schools have good reputations and which ones don't, as well as gather information about schools that may be hiring. It may take a while, but chances are that you will at some point bump into someone who is leaving the country soon or knows someone who knows someone who will be, and you may be able to step into his job.

In the meantime, keep checking the classifieds and also make some calls to the schools listed in the appendix. These organizations fall into two basic categories: those that teach mostly in-house classes and those that send teachers out to teach at client companies. Both generally provide the teacher with set curricula to follow, although individual schools may encourage the teacher to use his or her own material. The in-house type are preferred by those who dislike traveling, while the in-company type are better if you appreciate the freedom of not having to work in an office.

Teaching in-company means the teacher travels to the client company (often large firms like Nissan, Sony, or Matsushita). Pay is usually around 3,000 yen an hour the first year and you generally teach about fifteen hours a week. Given that the large English teaching companies like OTC, Time, and Interac employ 100 to 300 foreign teachers, there is a fairly high turnover rate and chances are they will be needing new teachers sooner than they think. Don't be discouraged by, "Sorry, we're not hiring." Drop by the office anyway, leaving your resume and a number where you can be reached.

If you find yourself running into a lot of brick walls, consider working in a smaller city for your first year. You will increase your chances of getting hired if you let personnel managers know that you don't mind working in outlying districts such as Hiroshima, Okayama, Sapporo, or Miyazaki because schools with branches in these places often have difficulty finding people willing to say goodbye to the bright lights of the big city. You will probably learn more Japanese and make more Japanese friends if you are not in the large urban areas where most of the *gaijin* are.

A typical day in the life of an in-company teacher might involve getting up at six-thirty to get to a company across town by eight o'clock. In a classroom or conference room, ten to twenty bright or bleary-eyed students will await you. They may be factory workers or executives or general office staff. Your mission is to coach or cajole them in spoken English for the next one or two hours. Depending on the level and motivation of the students and the attitude and energy level of the teacher, the class may be stimulating or stifling.

After your morning class you will probably have at least a few "free" hours until your afternoon or evening class. Prime time for teaching is from five to nine in the evening and you will almost always have one or two classes during this time slot. To the uninitiated, one class in the morning and one in the evening seems to leave the teacher a lot of free time. However, depending on the location of the client company, the hours can (and usually do) dwindle away as you find yourself spending long stretches on crowded trains during rush hours.

Especially during your first year at a company, you tend to be a virtual slave to the needs of the management. If the company sells a new course and you are not teaching on Friday nights, you will have to teach it even though it conflicts with your Japanese class or a private lesson or your private life. After you build up some seniority with a company, you can usually make some arrangements with the management to always have, say, Wednesdays off, but this will probably not be possible in the first year, and most teachers find it difficult to fit in outside interests.

One hidden benefit of working at client companies is that you can get to know people in positions of power who may later turn out to be the ticket to a job with a Japanese or foreign company based either in Japan or overseas.

Whether the class is in business English or daily conversational English, the emphasis is always on the spoken language.

You will not be teaching English grammar per se. Some of your students will already know the difference between the subjunctive and the passive, between flaunt and flout. Your job is to translate the vocabulary and grammar knowledge acquired during their six to eight years of formal language training into conversational ability.

If you are lucky, some of your classes will consist of people who often travel abroad on business trips. They are usually lively, and interested both in improving their English and in learning about the teacher's country and culture. Lessons with these students can be very interesting and after a while it can be like meeting with friends, rather than going to work.

An American who has taught at client companies for a large English teaching company in Tokyo on two occasions for a total of about four years says that teaching in client companies has "all the benefits of a real job—regular salary and respectability—with none of the strings or hassles—like going into an office every day and dealing with bosses and office politics."

He also found it easy to quit his job and then begin it again. After his first two years of playing music and teaching, he decided to go back to California and try to make it in the real world of rock and roll.

"But it was tough. I got tired of applying for food stamps and living in dirty apartments. After a year and a half I looked at my alternatives and it seemed that Japan would be the best place to do what I want—play music, make a decent living, and travel.

"Sure I complain about things now and then—boring classes, problems with the office staff—and I hate wearing a suit and tie. But it's all right really. There's a lot of freedom. You just have to show up at the client company and teach for an hour or two—after a while you can do it on automatic pilot. When the class reaches optimal cruising altitude you give them pair-work assignments like making up a dialogue using certain grammatical constructions and pretty soon the class is over and you walk out a free man."

In-house teaching operations generally expect a higher level of company loyalty from their employees and in turn sometimes offer greater benefits. You are often required to be physically present in the school eight hours a day, five days a week, even though you may only teach four hours a day. During the rest of the time you are expected to prepare for classes, help with placement interviews and tests, and be available for "free conversation" with the students. Many schools will offer Japanese classes outside of work time as a service for their teachers.

Because of the greater amount of time spent in contact with students and fellow teachers, there can be a greater sense of camaraderie in such establishments and more opportunity to meet and work with Japanese people. But there can also be a greater degree of war weariness or a seige mentality, depending on the management. The monthly pay is usually around 250,000 yen, and sometimes there are annual bonuses.

The only critical qualification for getting hired at either of these kinds of organizations will be a university degree. People with training in teaching English as a foreign language (TEFL) are often preferred, especially by the better schools. But only about 20 percent of the staff of most large organizations have had such training.

An administrator of one large school said that although they say in their advertisements that they prefer TEFL experience so as to appear a reputable organization, they in fact hire mostly non-TEFL people, because they find them more enthusiastic and trainable. They have also found that in general their students prefer teachers trained in business or engineering rather than teaching because teacher and student can then communicate intelligently on more topics of mutual interest. Theater and other arts majors are also smiled upon because they are often outgoing and natural entertainers—an important quality in teachers anywhere, but particularly in Japan where students tend to be reticent.

An English woman who had also taught English in England, Italy, and Malaysia found her Japanese students different in the way they "absorb everything without a sound. Nothing gets reflected back so it's like talking to blotting paper. They never ask questions, never query, never argue. Sometimes I think they'd be relieved if for once I would stand with my back to them writing on the board all day."

Personnel managers know they need a teacher who can deal with and hopefully break this reserve. What will sell you to a school will be your personality (bright, cheerful, lively) and your attitude (cooperative, adaptable). A few years back, white skin, blond hair and blue eyes were also *de rigueur* because the Japanese had a very narrow view of a foreigner as a white person from northern European stock. This feeling is still around, but as the Japanese have become a bit more sophisticated, dark-haired, dark-skinned foreigners are now being hired by most companies in the urban areas.

This does not mean that life is easy for blacks or those of Asian descent though. Former Prime Minister Yasuhiro Nakasone's slip in September 1986, when he declared that America's intellectual level was lower than Japan's because American society had too many blacks, Mexicans, and Puerto Ricans was a reflection of the widely-shared Japanese view that dark-skinned people *are* inferior. Foreigners of Asian descent also face problems since they are "invisible *gaijin*"—they look Japanese, but they don't act Japanese and this makes for uncomfortable feelings all round.

YOU ARE WHAT YOU WEAR

The other important factor in getting a teaching job in Japan is sartorial. If you glance around a crowded Tokyo train in the morning you might think you got caught in a commercial for a new laundry soap. Every shirt collar is blindingly white, every suit spotless, every dress unwrinkled and every pair of shoes shiny and unscuffed. You would be wise to follow suit and place yourself in a fairly conservative set of nice clothes. This usually means ties for men and skirts for women.

But, as you button the starched collar of your new shirt, remember Thoreau's warning against all enterprises that require new clothes. English teaching schools and companies in Japan, large and small, are almost always run by entrepreneurs, not educators, and their primary (often only) concern, is making money. It follows that your duties as a teacher are less to actually teach and more to have lively, fun classes for the students (clients) who will then cheerfully continue pouring their yen into the school's coffers.

Newly-arrived teachers often find the business aspect of teaching in Japan disconcerting. But it is important to remember that, business or not, the students can, and often *do*, learn English, while you can and often do learn about Japan and the Japanese. Since the money-making aspect is the owner's top priority, you will often find that you have considerable autonomy in the classroom.

But unless you don't mind ripping off students, you should investigate the salons and lounges carefully. Some are on the level and some are not. The ones that are OK don't require students to sign long-term contracts and do provide a structured lesson designed to draw out the English hidden away in the brains of most Japanese. The others are often lonely-hearts language schemes which specialize in separating unsuspecting students from their money.

Reputable salons often have a call-in system and a drop-in system. The drop-in time is for watching videos or for unstructured conversation with a native speaker. But members who are more serious about learning and practicing English call in to schedule a lesson with other members at a similar proficiency level. The teacher presents a lesson and the students practice the grammar and vocabulary they have just learned. The idea is to provide a low-anxiety, non-classroom atmosphere so that the students can relax and speak freely. While this would not be a very efficient way to learn a language in most countries, it works well in Japan, where most people have a high level of book-knowledge of English and only need to become comfortable putting that knowledge into practice. But not all of the clubs and salons are interested in teaching the members anything.

One school put out an advertisement that became a focus of controversy within the foreign community. It featured a Japanese woman, her long hair being blown away from her lovely face, leaning toward a handsome foreign man who was tipping her chin up, his lips just inches from hers. In the upper corner of the poster, a blond, chubby Cupid was shooting his arrow toward the young lovers. The copy next to the Cupid said, "Let's master English conversation," and the copy under the romantic couple said, "Just because you're touching, doesn't mean you're communicating."

A person who wants to really teach English and not just

engage callow youths in idle conversation will find it easy to spot and avoid such schools.

HIGHER EDUCATION: MORE MONEY, MORE FRUSTRATION

Those with master's or Ph.D's in teaching English as a second language often look for positions at colleges or universities. Japanese universities, however, bear little resemblance to Western universities because the most difficult test, the entrance exam, has been passed before students attend the first day of classes. Combined with the fact that *entering* a university virtually guarantees *graduating* from it, this means that from the moment the passing results are received, the students are on a four-year holiday.

The brief hiatus between the grind of exams and the grind of a job is their one and only chance to truly relax and enjoy themselves. The students are keenly aware of this and even the most enthusiastic teacher can seldom get them to take their classes seriously.

When fifty to 100 students are herded into large lecture classes and their physical attendance guarantees that they will pass the course, this makes for universities with very little academic inquiry or intellectual stimulation.

Still, university positions are much in demand because they offer very nice salaries (starting at around seven million yen a year) for very little work (about eight to ten teaching hours per week for about thirty weeks a year). Because these jobs are cushy, they are not easy to find. You will definitely need personal connections.

There are basically two types of positions: visiting foreign lecturers and regular faculty members. The visiting foreign lecturer jobs are the norm. Visiting lecturers are paid very well and are expected to be more or less aloof. Thus they can avoid the political wranglings of the mini-feudal system found in most universities.

Regular faculty members are rarer, but some universities do employ foreigners on the same contract basis as regular Japanese faculty. Under this system, the foreigner is expected to participate in all aspects of university life including interminable faculty meetings and low starting salaries.

Under either system, teaching duties generally amount to instructing classes of about sixty students for about eight to ten hours per week. A few universities with special language programs like International Christian University and Sophia require their foreign teachers to teach about twenty hours a week and classes are smaller and more manageable.

Other than the light teaching load, the main attraction of university jobs is the long vacations. Professors at private universities can take up to six months of holiday a year, but teachers at national universities are considered government employees. As such they are entitled only to national holidays and two weeks of vacation per year, even though the two terms are only fifteen weeks each. The remaining weeks of the year are to be used for research.

During the five months of unofficial holiday time, some universities require teachers to sign in every day, whether classes are in session or not, while others will have the office secretary sign the faculty members in automatically. In some cases, if a teacher wants to leave town he must turn in an itinerary listing the academic institutions and activities he will be engaged in and a phone number where he can be reached. This makes it difficult, but not impossible, to sneak away for a week at a hot spring resort. As with so many things in Japan, these sorts of rules and regulations are "case by case," and it would be a good idea to find out which case it is before you sign any contracts.

It is possible to get jobs with two-year colleges by answering advertisements, but four-year universities do not usually advertise. If they do, the "open" solicitation for applicants is generally for the sake of propriety.

To get the insider information that a job is available and the all-important recommendation from an insider, you will have to be in Japan. Many teachers spend a year or two teaching at companies and cultivating friendships with university professors, foreign and Japanese, who then tip them off and introduce them to the search committee when a position becomes available.

While the vast majority of university positions are filled by foreigners who are living in Japan, it is possible to get the job from overseas if you have some kind of connection. A man who was finishing his Ph.D. in comparative literature had a dissertation director who knew people in Japan, among them the dean of a university in Osaka. When a position opened up at the university, the dean contacted the professor who then told his graduate student. Since the man was working in a steel mill while finishing his dissertation, he figured any move would be a step up and accepted the job.

He characterized the three-year visiting lectureship as "brutal." His students were noisy and disrespectful and had absolutely no interest in learning English or anything else as far as he could tell.

Other university teachers find that although most students are not interested in learning, a few are. Some teachers set up small discussion groups for these students and find that these sessions are stimulating and rewarding. One teacher who has been teaching in various situations in Japan for twenty-five years says these small groups are "the only way to find some satisfaction from teaching at universities. This is where I am rewarded professionally and personally. I know that at least the students who come to the discussion groups will learn some English and something about Western culture."

Whether you do it for a year or for the rest of your professional life, teaching English in Japan will be an experience you will never forget. Good luck, or, as the Japanese would say, *Gambatte*!

3. TRANSLATING, WRITING, AND EDITING

An American negotiator needs to know what the Japanese pundits are saying in the domestic press about the latest round of trade talks.

A foreign brokerage firm must submit its reports to the Ministry of Finance in Japanese.

A Japanese company wants to market a product in the U.S. and needs advertising copy that will appeal to Americans.

The Japanese government is making a promotional video and needs a native English speaker to narrate it.

Where do hundreds of people like this turn for help? To the language brokers—the translators, interpreters, writers, rewriters, editors, and narrators who are the unsung heroes of international commerce and cross-cultural communication. An extension of the first wave of language professionals—the English teachers—this new wave is meeting the many language needs of the ever more complex international web Japan is spinning itself into. Multimillion dollar deals, technology transfer and trade agreements, and thousands of other transactions, large and small, are dependent upon these traffickers in foreign tongues who often slave away, unseen, at home or in cubbyhole offices, to help Japan in the complex and multifaceted task of becoming part of the international network of the twenty-first century.

Language brokers can be found interpreting, translating, writing, rewriting, editing, and proofreading for newspapers, magazines, and publishing companies, as well as for a host of other firms, from trading companies to heavy industries to banks. After a few years working for a company, many English brokers go on to set up their own companies to provide writing, translating, editing, proofreading, or book packaging services—often to their former employers.

■ INTERPRETERS

Taking what one person says in one language and putting it into another in such a way that the purpose, intent, and nuance of the original is maintained is no mean task. It is particularly difficult between Japanese and English because the very function and philosophical starting points of the two tongues seem to be at cross purposes.

From a Western point of view, English is an adventure in the clarification of thought and Japanese an exercise in obfuscation. Where English seeks to define, delineate, explain, elucidate, and clarify, Japanese seeks to blur and obscure in order to retain vagueness and ambiguity, thereby preventing disagreements or (God forbid) confrontations.

Like the ghost of Hamlet's father, the Japanese language often eludes the best weaponry of Western minds. Rapier wit and the cut and thrust of hardnosed bargaining or intellectual debate are worse than useless in Japan where harmony, at least surface harmony, must be maintained at all costs. If a confrontation is provoked, the party who did so generally loses in the proceedings.

BRINGING EAST AND WEST TOGETHER

A good interpreter is the bridge that facilitates communication and understanding between Japanese and Westerner. It takes years of language study and exposure to both cultures to produce a good interpreter. The best are often those who grew up bilingual and bicultural.

While there are many Japanese nationals serving as interpreters for business and government, there are very few foreign nationals who work exclusively as interpreters. One reason is that bilingual foreigners usually find they have more prestige and higher salaries if they work as securities analysts, marketing advisers, or TV personalities. Another reason cited for the dearth of foreign interpreters is the Japanese view that their language is so "unique," so full of nuance and subtlety, that it cannot possibly be completely understood by anyone who is not Japanese—never mind that the Japanese language has borrowed the word "nuance" from the French to articulate that concept.

An American who became fluent in Japanese after a year in a Japanese high school, two years in a Japanese university, a year working for a Japanese travel agency, and a year translating for a Japanese newspaper said that the few times he served as an interpreter convinced him never to do it again.

"It is much easier to find Westerners tolerant of imperfect English than it is to find Japanese tolerant of imperfect Japanese," he explained. "The Japanese people I was interpreting for made me feel so small, so incapable, so horrible if I made the slightest mistake, that after I finished the job I felt like going home and hanging myself."

Another reason for the lack of foreign interpreters may be that it takes a certain kind of self-effacing personality to be a good interpreter, and Japanese tend toward this character more than Westerners. An Australian translator and part-time interpreter explained, "We are tools—tools that exchange one language for another. And the better the tool, the less aware people are that they are using it. In an ideal situation, the tool is invisible." She noted that interpreters are almost always women because a good interpreter must have what are perceived as the "feminine" qualities of patience, endurance, flexibility, and intuition.

A bilingual foreigner in Japan will have any number of job areas to choose from. The ones who choose to be interpreters find there are two basic paths to follow—to be primarily a freelancer, or primarily a company interpreter. For hustlers and those who want the freedom to format their daily and yearly schedules, freelancing is the better deal. However, it is very difficult to get a working visa based on freelancing unless you are married to a Japanese national or can find a company willing to sponsor your visa.

If you have been assiduous in maintaining relationships, a former employer or someone you have worked part-time for will often agree to sponsor your visa, even though you will not be working full-time for them. Although this is illegal, some companies will do it as a favor for you. In return, you are usually expected to give their work priority over any other jobs you may have.

Working full time for a company has the advantages of security and a sponsor for your visa. As is usual in Japan, the best way to find a job is through personal connections. If you have none, your best bet would be to send a resume to and visit branch offices of various foreign companies and large translation/interpreting services such as Simul International or Japan Convention Services (for a complete listing, see appendix).

Most of these companies charge their clients about 80,000 yen a day for the services of an interpreter. The interpreter, however, is generally on a base salary of about 300,000 yen a month. A few quick calculations will show you who is raking in the yen. It was reported that Japan Convention Services, one of the largest of Japan's approximately 700 translation/interpretation firms, recorded earnings in excess of five billion yen in 1988.

Working with a company is a good way to get your foot in the door, get experience, and make connections in the business, but the really big money can be made through private jobs, where 50 percent or more of the fee will not go to the parent company. Those who manage to work around the visa regulations and do mostly or all freelance work can do very well financially and have the added bonus of being able to take vacations when and for as long as they please. Of course it takes some time to build up the contacts that will let you go solo, but once you have them, and if you keep your fees somewhat below those of interpretation companies, you will find no shortage of work in the big cities of Japan.

■ TRANSLATORS

Translation is an undeservedly low-status job in Japan. An American who has been doing it for nearly fifteen years said that too often the client seems to think that it is a job that any monkey could do by sitting down and mechanically exchanging each word for its English equivalent—as if the much-vaunted nuance and subtlety of the spoken language were not present in its written form.

Unlike other low-status jobs, however, translating work can be very lucrative. One translator who has been working in Japan for five years makes thirteen to fifteen million yen a year—as much as the expatriate bankers and brokers. Like many others, he is a freelancer who works out of his apartment, communicating with various offices by telephone, fax, and modem. He admits that he works virtually all the time—often seven days a week. But he has also taken long vacations in Australia, California, and Europe.

His workload has increased steadily and substantially over the years—a fact he attributes to the rapid rise in the volume of business that Japanese firms are doing overseas. There are countless manuals, leaflets, brochures, annual reports, and advertisements for Japanese companies and products that must be put into the language of the countries they are destined for.

THE ACCIDENTAL TRANSLATOR

An accomplished translator working at a newspaper and doing freelance work at home said, "I don't understand how people become translators. I studied Japanese at college. Someone gave me a job. I botched a lot of things and gradually improved. The only way to be a good translator is to do it. The only way to do it is to get a job. The only way to get a job is to fake your way into it—find someone who's gullible enough to hire you, then cut links with them before they get too mad at you."

Although that man became a translator largely by design, many others fall into the profession more or less by accident. Michael came to Japan ten years ago on part of a trip around the world, began teaching English, got a Japanese girlfriend, and found the years zipping by with alarming speed.

He had learned spoken Japanese on his own with some help from his girlfriend and after he had been teaching for about five years, he noticed that most of his friends were moving into translating or starting their own businesses, while he was still only teaching. So, out of embarrassment, he began studying *kanji* (the Chinese characters in the Japanese language) on his own and a friend started passing on translations that he was too busy to do. With the help of his friend, his girlfriend, and several dictionaries, he learned the trade little by little and began doing more technical work, translating manuals for video and fax machines.

As he became better and got more work, he dropped most of his English classes, keeping only those that he enjoyed and that paid well. By agreeing to teach one evening class a week for the company that sponsored his visa, he was able to keep them as his sponsor.

THE EUROPEAN CONNECTION

Mario, an Italian, first came to Japan to study for a year at a Japanese university. He has been working as a translator in Japan five years now, but about 80 percent of his work is translating from English into Italian. This is because generally a Japanese company will want something translated into five or ten European languages and it is very difficult to find people capable of translating the Japanese original into, say, Polish or Serbo-Croatian. However, if you translate it from Japanese into English first, it is much easier to find someone to translate the English into a European language.

The problem is that the initial translation is almost always done by a Japanese whose English ability is minimal. Mario says, "Many times the translations are word for word so you get sentences without verbs and bizarre words that haven't been used since the sixteenth century. My job is often to try and imagine what they mean, but the bottom line is junk in-junk out— and most of the time I get junk—70 percent of what I get has been translated badly into English."

For this reason, it is not enough to be fluent only in English and a European language. Japanese ability is necessary even if you are not translating directly from the Japanese original because you will probably have to ask to see the Japanese original to figure out what the intermediate English translation means.

There is also a large and growing market for people who can translate from Japanese or Japanese-English into Chinese, Thai, Hindi, and other Asian languages.

THE SPECIALISTS

Some of the more interesting and lucrative work is translating material that is in your area of specialty. An Australian woman had been teaching genetics at a Melbourne college when she took an interest in Japanese and started attending night classes as a sort of hobby. But the more she learned, the more she wanted to learn.

Because it was "like the carrot in front of the donkey," she ended up getting a B.A. in Japanese and went on to do a postgraduate diploma in Japanese newspaper reading. "It was very demanding and also fascinating," she said, adding that finally it became an obsession.

She answered an advertisement in *The Japan Times* placed by a company that needed a translator and editor. They interviewed her over the phone and gave her the job, which involved translating a variety of business documents and rewriting material that had been translated by the Japanese staff.

While working for this company, she was approached by some English language magazines to write articles on recent advances in Japanese biotechnology, so she began reading all the Japanese scientific and industrial newspapers and magazines and then writing articles for English publications. "It was very demanding because I had to end up with a higher level of writing than is usually required in straight translation work. But I liked it because it was interesting and a good way to use my Japanese. In fact I liked it so much I left my company and became a freelancer."

Before quitting, though, she made an agreement with her employers that she would continue to be available for assignments if they would continue sponsoring her work visa. Because they were on good terms with each other and they valued her work, the agreement presented no difficulty. This shows once again how important it is to be sure and maintain good relationships in Japan. Unfailing geniality and flexibility are keys to a successful stay, no matter if you are translating or teaching or striking out on your own.

Quid pro quo arrangements are ubiquitous among translators because there is no such thing as a freelance translator as far as the Immigration Bureau is concerned. This means that most of the translators in Japan are in legal limbo. On paper they are company translators or English teachers or Japanese students. As long as it looks OK on paper, there are rarely problems.

WORK AND WAGES

All translators agree that there is no shortage of work for those who can translate from Japanese to English, but they also warn that you can't expect to freelance from day one. Usually people work in a company for a year or so to make contacts and build relationships.

As with interpretation agencies, translation companies naturally keep a good percentage of the fees in their pockets. An average agency will pay a native English speaker ¥2,500 to ¥3,000 to translate a page of Japanese into English—slightly more if it is specialized work such as electronics or scientific material. A good translator can do twenty to thirty pages a day, so the money can be quite good. However, it can be even better. If you are freelancing you can charge from ¥4,000 to ¥5,000 a page and work at home.

Because there is a huge demand for quality translations, translators can often choose their jobs after they become established, weeding out the tedious and low-paying jobs and working for only one or two clients. A major advantage to working for only a few companies is that the material tends to be similar. Often you'll have to translate a set of manuals for a line of products like fax machines or cameras, which are all basically the same. Once you've translated the manual for the first model, you have virtually completed the job except for the distinguishing features of each model. An Englishman who has been in Japan nine years and now works for two major clients says this is the best kind of work because, "all you have to do is go back to your original document, make a few changes, and print it out again. This is very cost effective—it lets you do translations by the kilo rather than the page—of course, you still charge by the page."

ADVICE FROM THE PROS

All freelance translators who have had any success say that to freelance you have to realize that you are in effect running a small business. This means you need office equipment—at the very least, a word processor, a fax machine, and a telephone. A modem is also very useful to receive and send jobs.

An experienced translator says, "When you go for an interview, the first question is 'Do you have a fax?' and if you say no, the interview is over, whether it ends then or not.''

With a fax and telephone, even beginners are able to find work. One experienced translator says he knows people who have to look up nearly every word they translate, but they still get work.

After getting set up with adequate equipment, another translator advises developing an area of specialty because ''being able to translate general everyday Japanese will get you nowhere in the long run. It's becoming more and more a specialist's world.'' She is working as both a translator and a translation coordinator for a small company. When the company lands a job, they send it to her, and she consults her list of translators and their specialties and assigns it accordingly.

Another factor encouraging specialization is that most of the work translators in Japan do is of a fairly technical nature. Often it is written to communicate between one engineer and another and may be in a sort of shorthand that would be incomprehensible to a nonspecialist. One translator with an engineering background said that because Japanese sentences often omit the subject, a nonspecialist wouldn't have a clue as to the meaning of many technical documents.

Because of the deadlines a translator must deal with, organization and self-discipline are at a premium. Most translators find that they hear ''get it done'' more often than ''do it well.'' After you are established and have links with certain agencies, you will probably start getting large jobs of 300–400 pages from major corporations like Toyota or Toshiba. One translator got 300 pages to do in two weeks and told the translation company that he'd like a little more time so that the client company would end up with a decent translation. They told him that was *muzukashii* (literally ''difficult'', but a polite way of saying ''impossible'') and that he should just do the best he could. So he worked on it every day for ten hours and by the last day he said he was so groggy he couldn't see straight, but it was done on time and he was rewarded handsomely for his less-than-perfect effort.

A New Zealander doing translation work in Tokyo for six years says, ''The thing that used to annoy me intensely and bugs the hell out of most translators is when a non-native speaker edits your translation or rewrites and makes complete nonsense out of what was perfectly understandable English prose. It seems like there's always at least one person at a translation company who thinks he knows English better than any native speaker and he tampers with everything that comes through just to show how knowledgeable he is. This used to annoy me but now I just laugh and let it slide—after all, they're responsible for the final product—not me.''

A LOOK AHEAD

The profession has come a long way from the scribes of centuries past who spent years painstakingly translating ancient Chinese law and Buddhist and Confucian teachings into Japanese. Now foreigners are turning Japanese into English and other languages at a furious pace.

Although computerized translation systems are being developed, they present no immediate threat to the livelihood of human translators. All of those with whom I spoke said that as far as they could see, the translation industry is booming. No matter if they had been working one or ten years in Japan, they said their workload had increased greatly and many were turning extra work away or passing it on to acquaintances.

■ FREELANCE WRITERS

Like freelance translators, freelance writers have to treat their work as a small business. And, as in translation, if you're good and put in your time making connections and maintaining relationships, there is plenty of work to be found—even for novices.

Japan often serves as a training ground for beginners, people who have thought about trying their hand at writing but for whatever reason haven't yet begun. Japan is not a bad place to begin since there is not too much competition and it is fairly easy to get both Japanese and other foreigners to speak with you. The Japanese are usually flattered to be the subject of *gaijin* interest, and the foreigners just like to talk and help each other out in any way they can.

If you are a competent writer, it is fairly easy to get your work published in Japan because the standard of writing in the English-language publications is generally not that high. It is also not too difficult to get your work published overseas because Japan is a hot topic nearly everywhere, and most newspapers and magazines are hungry for Japan news—even from unknowns and even if the piece needs to be edited heavily.

Unless they are independently wealthy, however, most nascent writers teach English to provide a steady income while they try to get their work published. Not only does teaching keep you fed and sheltered, it is also one of the best ways to make connections and learn about subjects you may want to write about. Because as a foreigner you are a guest in the country, and as a teacher you are held in respect, you can often meet vice-presidents, chairmen, and other hotshots in the world of business that you wouldn't have access to in the normal course of events.

An Englishman teaching and writing in Tokyo said his teaching jobs are invaluable sources for interviews and information. "They think I'm teaching English when I walk in and say, 'Right. Today let's have free conversation. The topic is kickbacks in the food industry. Do you know what a kickback is, Mr. Tanaka?' And before I know it I've got another article half-written. If I need more information about something I'll call up some of my students and they'll either tell me what I need to know or introduce me to someone who does."

But while many people have published articles here and there in Japan, not so many have been able to translate this into a ticket to serious journalism. This is largely because the *pro* of being able to get things published relatively easily is linked to the *con* of getting little or no constructive criticism on your writing. The neophyte can tap away blithely on his or her word processor for years, turning out humdrum material that is publishable in Japan—but probably nowhere else.

Yet for those with talent and perserverance, Japan can be a ticket to the "real world" of journalism. A young woman from England began by sending interesting snippets she learned from her English students back to tabloids like *The Sun* and *The Star*. She gradually moved from writing about the peculiarities of the Japanese ("Knickers Nicked In Japan"—about the risks of hanging women's underwear out to dry) to serious pieces on the Japanese royal family for *The Times*.

"REAL" JOBS IN WRITING

For those who aren't up to the hustle of a freelance career or don't want to teach English for their monthly paycheck, there are quite a few jobs that involve writing, rewriting, editing, and proofreading.

For those interested in journalism, there are four English-language daily newspapers, *The Japan Times*, *The Asahi Evening News*, *The Daily Yomiuri*, and the *Mainichi Daily News*, and four news services, Kyodo, the Associated Press, Agence France Presse (AFP), and Reuters, which are often looking for people with good reporting, writing, and/or editing skills.

As with all jobs in Japan, an introduction or personal connection is a good way to begin. To make those connections, get involved in organizations such as the Society of Writers, Editors, and Translators (SWET), the Forum for Corporate Communications (FCC), or any of the other professional organizations listed in the appendix. In this field, though, just getting in the door may not be good enough.

One editor at a major English language daily newspaper complained that "anyone can call himself a writer here. It doesn't mean a thing. You can't even trust diplomas or clippings—they can be faked or not a true reflection of the person's ability."

For this reason, most jobs in Japan that require writing skills will also require job candidates to take a writing and/or editing test, and employers base their hiring decisions almost exclusively on the test results.

The test is usually similar to what you would be doing in the job. If you are to rewrite translations from Japanese, you will be given such copy to rewrite. If you are to edit annual reports, you will be given part of an unedited one. In this way writers with egos larger than their talents can be weeded out. If you go to a job interview, be prepared to back up your sparkling wit and shining resume with a demonstration of your skills.

Finding a job is not necessarily a sure thing—even for those with demonstrable ability. An American with six years' journalism experience—five in the U.S. and one in Thailand—wanted to work in Japan, but had no idea if he would be able to find work. His experience in the U.S. had been in political reporting, but he knew that business stories were the hot item in Japan and was somewhat apprehensive since he had little experience in that area.

After sending out resumes to all of the wire services and foreign bureaus of newspapers and magazines in Tokyo, his fears were confirmed. He found that the journalism people in Tokyo were weighting Japanese language ability far more heavily than journalism experience.

"They seemed to figure that if they could get someone who was bilingual and had at least minimal writing ability, they could teach them the journalism. Just having journalism experience behind me didn't seem to be enough."

So he changed his approach and set about renewing his contacts with newspapers in the U.S. He found that "they were all dying for copy from Japan because they sense it's a really big story. The problem was the money—they would pay in dollars and that just won't cut it if you're living in Japan. Non-yen payment is almost nonpayment."

Because the yen doubled in value against the dollar during the eighties, the dollar equivalent has halved. This means that in 1984 every 100 dollars you earned translated into a respectable 30,000 yen. In 1989, with the yen at around 140 to the dollar, however, every 100 dollars gave you only about 15,000 yen—or the price of a decent dinner for two in Tokyo.

This journalist ended up working part-time for an English-language paper in Tokyo and part-time for a newspaper in the U.S. The American paper paid him in dollars—a retainer plus a per-piece rate—and the Japanese paper gave him the yen income that he needed to survive.

An American woman with nearly ten years of journalism experience in the U.S. worked out a similar scheme in which she contributes to papers back home on a freelance basis, and gets her yen income from working as an editor and reporter for a news service in Tokyo.

With both academic and practical training in journalism, she admitted being shocked when she first began working in Japan. She had thought that Japan, being the high-tech capital of the world, would have offices with the latest computerized systems. Instead she found herself at a desk with a red pencil, wire service copy, and a typewriter that didn't work.

"It was Dickensian—filthy and disorganized, with stacks of yellowing paper piled up on the desks and from the floor to the ceiling, and cockroaches climbing into your coffee before you had even finished it."

Her job involved editing articles that had been written or translated by the Japanese staff, and researching and writing her own pieces. She found that both editing and reporting were different in Japan and that, in general, the journalistic standards she was used to didn't apply. Checking facts was just not done in most cases and plagiarism was a totally alien concept. One day when she was editing a Japanese reporter's feature story, she wanted to check something that she found confusing. When she asked to see the reporter's notes, he showed her an article in an Australian newspaper that he had virtually copied with no acknowledgements. Even more surprising to her was that no one in the office seemed to have any problem with this, least of all the person who had done it.

Editorial control and reporting are also quite different in Japanese journalism. One reporter said, "In America, a good editor will give you rope and encouragement. If you stray too far, he'll tug on the rope a little. Here there's no one holding the rope."

Foreign reporters find that it takes four or five times longer to do stories in Japan because everything has to be done in person. This can mean spending hours on the trains criss-crossing Tokyo. The interviews themselves often take longer than they would elsewhere as well, since there are many pleasantries which must be expressed before and after the business at hand, and answers to questions often involve a good deal of beating around the bush.

Things are made even more difficult by the fact that foreign reporters are still barred from most of the *kisha* (reporters') clubs. Bernard Krisher, former Tokyo bureau chief for *Newsweek*, related in his book, *Japan As We Lived It*, his experience of trying to get a comment from the prime minister's office on the day John F. Kennedy was assassinated. When he called and politely asked the prime minister's secretary a few questions, the secretary refused to tell him anything because he was not a member of the club covering the prime minister.

JOINING THE JOURNALISTS

While there is a fairly good chance of being hired by a Japanese English-language daily or a news service in Tokyo, there is not a lot of hiring of resident foreigners by bureaus of foreign newspapers and magazines. Nearly all foreign correspondents are sent by the home office. Only rarely will a bureau hire a writer locally. The exceptions are bilingual foreigners with proven writing skills. Trilingual foreigners (Japanese-Chinese-English is perhaps the best combination) also have a good chance of being hired.

If you have your eye on a job with a foreign newspaper or magazine, you might try submitting "specials" to the bureau chief. If your work is accepted and printed, you may eventually persuade them to hire you—either in Japan or back home. There has been at least one case of a man submitting freelance stories to his hometown paper which, after a few years, decided to let him open its Tokyo bureau.

If you do not find work at a newspaper or news service right away, do not be discouraged. Most practicing journalists say if you really want to work as a writer in Japan, go about it systematically. If possible, start in your home country and make the rounds of the publications you would like to submit articles to. Introduce yourself to the editors you would be sending material to, tell them you are moving to Japan, and ask what topics they would like you to cover for them. Doing this before you leave home will save you a lot of international phone calls, time, and effort.

Upon arriving in Japan start making connections with other foreigners in the field and visit the AP, AFP, Kyodo, and Reuters offices as well as the offices of the four English language dailies. The turnover rate at all of these is fairly high, so even if there is no opening, take the writing or editing test and keep in touch.

A Tokyo correspondent for *The Asian Wall Street Journal* characterized himself as a dinosaur, one of the dying breed of reporters in Japan who does not speak Japanese. The good old days when a good writer would be snapped up seconds after landing in Japan are pretty much over (if they ever existed at all). With Japan becoming a hot news item, the market has tightened up and more and more editors feel that it is easier and more efficient to train a bilingual person to write than to spend time teaching a monolingual journalist Japanese. However, there are still some dinosaurs alive and well in Tokyo because of the extensive background material in English from sources such as JETRO, the American Chamber of Commerce in Japan, the Foreign Correspondents Club, the American Library, the Japan Foundation Library, and the Japan Foreign Press Center in the Nippon Press Center building. They are also able to function here because of the growing number of Japanese who speak good English.

One newly arrived journalist said, "When I call a company, it's amazing to me how, sooner or later, if you stumble around and work your way through the switchboard, you'll get someone who speaks English and he can set you up with an appointment with someone who can talk knowledgeably on whatever topic."

The wisest plan for those wanting to start a writing career in Japan is to start out with another source of income, then slowly build up contacts, sources, and markets in Japan and overseas. What will happen is that as you spend time working and living in Japan, you will build not only contacts, but also your understanding of the country and this will help you write more knowledgeably and sensitively.

Although not all writers are interested in writing public relations pieces, this can be a good way to start earning money and making connections. The work is usually unadvertised, but is definitely available. One journalist admitted to doing such work but said, "Everytime I do it I cringe. You're like a lawyer with a brief. You are pitching somebody's company and when you're trying to be a journalist, that puts you in an uncomfortable position. But the work is there. A lot of it comes through the press club and gets passed around. Often it's writing or rewriting of brochures or company reports."

Some writers find that they like the PR and advertising work more than the hard journalism and move into that field. But if you want to be a journalist, and if you have some Japanese ability, it should not be too difficult to get a job with one of the wire services or newspapers in Tokyo and do freelance work on the side. In this way you can make connections with the journals or newspapers in Japan or back home that you would like to work for in the future.

Like people in so many other professions in Japan, the journalists often stay longer than they initially intended because of the many opportunities to do exciting and important work. One reporter said he came here because he was impatient with the pace at his newspaper in a medium-sized U.S. city. "If I had stayed there and gone the conventional route—working my way up from the police beat to city hall to city desk and then trying to talk them into sending me here—I probably would have never come. You've just got to take the risk, jump in, and sink or swim."

As Japan becomes more and more a global center, it will not be so difficult for writers to keep afloat on the constant stream of news that is generated daily.

■ REWRITERS, EDITORS, PROOFREADERS

The many businesses in Japan that sell their products and services overseas must produce advertisements, brochures, manuals, catalogs, and other material in English. There is also a great deal of routine correspondence that must be done in English, as well as the odd paper or speech for engineers or CEOs to present overseas.

Much of this material is first translated into rough English by a Japanese translator. Foreigners are then needed to rewrite it into the kind of English a native speaker would use. Such rewriting is a necessary facet of many companies' business.

Rewriters are also an important link in the work of the English language newspapers and some magazines that translate articles by Japanese writers. The *Mainichi Daily News*, *The Daily Yomiuri* and *The Asahi Evening News* are all associated with major Japanese newspapers and many of the articles are translated from their Japanese editions. It is the rewriter's job to turn what is often a rambling, circular sort of piece into a standard news article with a clear lead and logical progression.

The same companies that need rewriters often need editors and proofreaders to get the rewritten material into its final form. In a small company, the rewriter is often the editor and the proofreader all rolled up into one. In other cases, the editor takes the rewritten material and edits it for style and length, and then the proofreader checks the rewritten and edited work before it goes to press.

PUBLISHING

Editors, copy editors, and proofreaders are also needed by the English-language publishing companies in Tokyo. Since these companies are relatively small and have a rather small foreign staff, the proofreaders and copy editors are often hired on a part-time basis while the editors tend to do a little of everything—from finding books to publish, to manuscript editing, to design, to copyediting, to proofreading, to publicity. Also, because much of the work being published in English is translated or written by non-native speakers, the editors sometimes serve as rewriters and must spend far more time with a manuscript than their counterparts back home.

While this wide variety of tasks gives editors the opportunity to learn a little about a lot of things and to gain experience in many areas, it can also lead to a feeling of scatteredness and exhaustion. Being responsible for a project and having to steer it through the Japanese corporate maze can be a frustrating, even frightening, experience. However, being involved in attempts to interpret and explain a wholly foreign history and culture can also be very rewarding.

Like the English-language newspapers, some of the publishing companies have a fairly high turnover rate. Others have found editors who have made Japan their home and therefore hire only the occasional part-timer. Publishers naturally prefer people with prior editing or publishing experience and good Japanese language skills.

4. FINANCE

*Japanese banks have something American banks don't—
money.*

An American working at a major Japanese bank

Just down the two-level expressway from Roppongi, Tokyo's
disco mecca, is Ark Hills, an architectural wonder of glass and
chrome which houses posh offices, fancy restaurants, a glitzy
hotel and several waterfalls. Here, gray-suited Westerners with
money on their minds and in their healthy bank accounts are a
common sight. They work for the likes of Salomon Brothers,
Nikko Securities and Citicorp. Now and then some slip out of
their plush offices to slurp down Hobson's Ice Cream at the franchise in the Ark Hills complex.

Across town, in the financial districts of Otemachi and
Kabuto-cho, serious white-shirted Westerners bend over their
desks in the offices of Sanwa Bank, Fuji Bank, Nomura
Securities, and the Industrial Bank of Japan. Late in the evening
they go out with their colleagues or clients to nibble on *yaki-tori*
(grilled chicken on bamboo skewers) or indulge in some sushi.

Both of these scenes are new. Less than a decade ago, a
foreigner working for the Industrial Bank of Japan was as
unknown as Hobson's Ice Cream, Western money men and
women were a rare sight anywhere in Tokyo, and Ark Hills was
just a gleam in the developer's eye.

The change began in 1981, when the barriers to foreign participation in the Japanese financial scene first began to fall.
More restrictions were lifted in 1984, and the number of
foreigners working in finance in Japan skyrocketed. The foreign
firms rushed in, pulled by the extraordinary gravitational field
that was exerted by the mighty yen.

At the same time, the growing internationalization of finance led Japanese institutions to seek out foreigners who could help them with their overseas endeavors. The lucky foreigners who happened to be in the right place at the right time were able to get a variety of high-paying jobs, mostly on the strength of their Japanese language ability. These people gave rise to a number of rags to riches (read English teacher to banker) stories that still enjoy currency both in Japan and overseas. The stories have found their way into the collective unconscious of dissatisfied English teachers throughout the archipelago, and have even made their way overseas. Both foreign and Japanese institutions receive calls and resumes—two or three a week—from foreigners who figure it's their time for a piece of the pie.

But a piece of the pie now only comes to those who have planted the tree, picked the fruit, made the crust, and shoved the whole thing in the oven. The golden days when any Japanese-speaking foreigner could walk into any bank or financial institution—foreign or Japanese—and be hired on the spot are over.

A familiarity with language and culture is no longer enough. An economist at Salomon Brothers, drinking champagne in his palatial apartment in Roppongi near the American Embassy intoned, "It's a dust to dust situation here. That translates as English teacher to English teacher. Five years ago a little language ability got you a good job. If that's all you've got now, you're not cost-effective and they'll boot you out."

The boom in employment in the financial field peaked around 1985, and now nearly all of the bankers, analysts, and brokers who work at foreign companies are, like the Salomon Brothers economist, sent to Japan from their company offices overseas. Many foreigners working at Japanese institutions are also sent here from overseas branches.

Some of the lucky ones who got hired in the mid-eighties have carved a niche for themselves and have a secure position. But many others are being let go as more highly qualified people come pouring into the country. This new wave is coming to get in on the Japanese "economic miracle." This "miracle" has become a cliche, but that makes it no less real and its consequences no less significant.

Japan left the 1980s as an economic superpower. The Tokyo

Stock Exchange roared through the decade on the longest and most dazzling bull market the world has ever seen and the per capita income of a Japanese now surpasses that of an American.

Barring a dramatic crash of the Tokyo Stock Exchange or another killer earthquake (judging from the past, Tokyo is due for one), most pundits agree that, financially speaking, Japan is where it's at. A few dissent, but most also agree that Japan's role in the financial world will become greater in the coming years.

While this means more jobs for foreign money men and women in Japan, it also means more competition for those jobs in the financial field as more qualified Westerners seek entry into this crucial market.

WHAT IT TAKES

A highly qualified person with a good chance of getting a job in the financial field will:

Be proficient in Japanese—spoken is most important, but written will be a big bonus; have something specific to offer—an area of expertise and/or experience; and be creative, energetic, and adaptable.

Once you land a job, you can look forward to:

A comfortable salary (lavish ones are becoming rare) and good benefits; a working knowledge of Japanese financial practices; and valuable experience in the Japanese financial scene that can lead to good jobs in your home country.

However, you will have to put up with:

The Japanese way of doing business; little free time; and little to do in it.

There is such a variety of jobs available in the financial field that it is hard to generalize or clearly define them. In this age of the financial service company, distinctions between banks, investment banks, and brokerage firms have blurred. In the Japanese institutions the outlines are even fuzzier as there is really no such thing as a job description.

Investment banks have a wide variety of activities. They act as intermediaries, bringing together people who want to buy and those who want to sell, matching those who want to loan with those who want to borrow. Their clients are generally large corporations and governments that want to build their net worth by raising capital through mergers and acquisitions and other means. Many of the jobs at investment banks involve researching and preparing for these kinds of deals.

A woman who was transferred from the London office of such a bank said her job here involves analyzing the needs of the client and making recommendations. Her clients are usually large multinationals that come looking for advice and assistance on acquiring a firm or selling one of their own.

Investment banks also generally have a large sales division that buys and sells equities. One equities broker at an investment bank said it was his responsibility to develop and maintain the bank's relationship with their institutional clients by offering ideas that would help the clients meet their financial goals. Like an analyst, he had to have a thorough knowledge of the strategies employed by institutional investors as well as an ability to sell stocks and securities.

There are quite a few research analysts in Tokyo since they are employed by just about every kind of financial firm—bank trust departments, brokerage firm research departments, and insurance companies. They gather the information that others rely on to make buy, sell, or loan decisions. The bottom line is that they must generate orders—get clients to buy or sell stocks and bonds.

An analyst in her first year at a major British bank spends most of her twelve-hour workday at her desk—researching and analyzing annual reports, quarterly reports, and reading industry journals. In a year or two she expects to be doing more work away from her desk—attending analysts' meetings, industry conferences, conventions, and trade shows.

Most analysts specialize in either a country or an industry group. Sometimes a firm is looking specifically for someone who knows the electronics industry, and other times it will want someone with a broad knowledge of, say, the West German market.

As an analyst you are expected to know all there is to know about the companies or industries in your area of specialty. This includes history, management, products, markets, competition, and finances. You are also expected to be able to analyze and synthesize the information in order to predict the future prospects of the companies.

To do this, you must have quantitative skills to read and understand the many graphs and tables in financial reports, as well as highly developed writing skills to generate the frequent comprehensive research reports on the companies or industries you follow.

Brokers, bond traders, and equities dealers are all basically salespeople. They spend the day listening to the analysts and reading their reports and then calling up clients to persuade them to buy or sell a particular item in their portfolio.

Securities markets went global during the eighties due to advances in telecommunications technology and the worldwide deregulation of the industry. Since the Tokyo markets were deregulated in 1981, hundreds of foreigners have come here to work—many of them for the twenty-five foreign brokerage houses that now have seats on the Tokyo Stock Exchange.

"What it takes," according to a young Australian woman who attended a Japanese high school and now works as a broker for a securities company, "is an innovative, creative, aggressive person with a world outlook. It doesn't really matter what you studied at university—economics or business helps, but not that much.

"An equities dealer," she explains, "is basically a salesperson. A good salesperson is always aware of things affecting the sales of the product. With equities, you have to be aware of more industries. You have to always keep your mind and your eyes open and look for new things.

"For example, when I was in Japan three years ago, I didn't see Kraft Parmesan cheese anywhere. Now it's in every pizza and spaghetti place around.

"It's all these little things—you notice them and file them in your brain and they come in handy when you're talking with a client."

After studying Japanese in Australia, she spent a year teaching skiing and tennis at a resort outside Tokyo. She then returned to Australia and was hired by a Hong Kong-based securities company. After a year of training, she was sent to Tokyo because of her familiarity with the language and culture.

While a few years ago it was standard practice for a company to hire you and then train you in the language and in the specific field in which you were to work, now most companies prefer to save their time and money by choosing new employees from the ever-growing pool of foreigners who already know Japanese and have experience.

A bond broker predicts that soon foreigners will be replaced by Japanese who speak English since they do not demand extravagant salaries, bonuses, and housing allowances. Foreign establishments can pay a Japanese two or three times the going salary paid by a similar Japanese establishment and still save money since the salary will be substantially less than the standard expat package.

QUALIFICATIONS

Since the field of finance encompasses a wide range of jobs, from computer whiz kids to M & A experts, the qualifications for jobs also vary considerably.

One twenty-six-year-old Australian investment analyst working for a British firm advises, "if you want a job here, you really have to do your homework. Know exactly what position you want, what you can offer the company, what industry you want to get into, and the important issues in that industry.

"When a person comes to us for a job interview and we ask, 'What do you want to do?' and he says, 'Whatever you want me to do,' we show him the door pretty quickly."

Although there are some exceptions, nearly all foreigners working in finance in Japan are fairly proficient in Japanese. At the British securities company, W.I. Carr, all of the foreigners in the research department are fluent in spoken Japanese and all but two can read it fluently as well. A young woman working there as an analyst found it fairly easy to get a job in the financial field on the strength of her language ability alone.

Most institutions generally say they are "not hiring," but insiders say that if a qualified person comes by, someone who will be an asset, the company won't let them pass by and get a job with the competition.

JAPANESE FIRMS

Working at a Japanese financial institution is another story altogether. If you are hired as a regular "lifetime" employee (*seisha-in*), you will work long hours. The pay is very low, the living conditions the same, and the benefits few. Even if you are hired on a short-term contract (*shokutaku*), the pay will still be about half that of an expat working at a foreign institution.

But if you can survive for two or three years, you gain a very marketable experience: a working knowledge of the ins and outs of the Japanese financial world and contacts in it. The trend seems to be for foreign employees at Japanese companies to leave after a fairly short time to work with a foreign institution in Japan or abroad where their knowledge and connections can be put to use.

A young man who had worked for a European commercial bank was introduced to the director of mergers and acquisitions at one of the Big Four Japanese securities houses (Nomura, Yamaichi, Nikko, and Daiwa) by an American woman working there. The director wanted to "internationalize" his department and wanted to do so by hiring young foreigners "unspoiled" by previous work experience in Japan.

Of the five foreigners hired at that time, he was the only one hired as a *seisha-in*. "I have no idea why I was singled out for the honor," he said with an ironic smile. "It seemed like an arbitrary decision." He hazards it may have been because he had spent a year at a Japanese university or because the woman who introduced him was also a *seisha-in*. What it meant was that his contract was the same as that of a Japanese employee—a single sheet of paper with a half-dozen lines containing a minimum of information including the employment period (only a starting date was given), the section that was employing him, the hours he was expected to work (8:40 A.M.–5:00 P.M. Monday through Friday and Saturday 8:40 A.M.–12:00 noon), and his salary, a pitiful 166,000 yen per month. This salary is at the low end of low salaries for foreigners in Japan—substantially less than most English teachers pull in—and only slightly more than the starting salary for Japanese company employees. That he had two years of experience working for a bank in Europe did not seem to matter and he was given the salary of a regular twenty-five-year-old Japanese employee.

Like the regular employees, he was "allowed" to do thirty-five hours of overtime a month. This meant he was paid for thirty-five hours even though he routinely worked sixty to eighty hours of overtime a month, as did his colleagues. The overtime pay boosted his monthly income to about 217,000 yen. In addition he got a bonus every six months that was equivalent to up to six months' salary. The bonuses in Japanese companies fluctuate with business and sometimes decrease, rather than increase. After two years, he received almost 1.5 million yen as his winter bonus.

His company paid 70 percent of his housing costs, but only up to 100,000 yen a month. Although his local taxes were zero the first year, they quickly climbed to about 6,000 yen a month the second and 28,000 yen a month the third, and he found that even with no entertainment expenses whatsoever, he could hardly make it from one month to the next.

The one bright spot in the whole deal, he thought, was the twelve days off that he was allotted each year. "I thought, well, that's not too bad and I planned out a schedule using Sundays and national holidays so that I could take a nice three-week vacation back home. I presented this plan to my boss, and he sucked a lot of air in through his teeth and looked uncomfortable and finally told me he was sorry, but the company never gave anyone more than ten consecutive days off. Not only that, but he also casually mentioned that my sick days were considered part of my twelve days' holiday and I'd better save a few 'just in case'."

Later on he noticed that most of his Japanese colleagues would come in to the office even when they were sick and should have been home in bed. When he asked them why, they said it showed "fighting spirit" and dedication to the company. He also saw that his company handed out care packages of medicine twice a year to encourage employees to take cold tablets, throat lozenges, stomach pills, and the like to keep them coming in to work no matter what.

From his talks with foreign employees in the other Big Four securities companies, he found that his situation was typical and so he stuck with it for two years. At the end of that time he returned home and soon found a German bank that was more than willing to hire him and send him back to Japan on an expatriate package.

While Japanese language ability, keenness, and doing your homework are critical for getting a job with a foreign firm, many foreigners feel that good English skills, adaptability, and a modicum of foolhardiness are required for a job with a Japanese institution.

Jobs with Japanese financial concerns range from general work as English resource people—proofreading, editing English communications, and gathering information from English sources—to specialist work in mergers and acquisitions, foreign exchange and other fields.

The easiest way to get any job in Japan is through personal connections. If you can be introduced by someone already working in the organization or by someone with a relationship to the organization, you are a giant step ahead of the competition.

INTERVIEWING

Getting hired at a Japanese institution can be a long drawn-out process. There are usually a number of interviews that, according to one veteran, seem designed to test one's patience more than anything else.

A young man from Ireland who came to Japan after graduating from university first worked for a large Japanese multinational as an engineer in microelectronics. After working with the company in technology transfer for two years, his project group grew and he found he couldn't get along with the new people so he started looking around for a new job.

A friend who was leaving a Japanese commercial bank introduced him to his boss and then he began a series of five interviews. He was surprised by the amount of time his interviewers seemed willing to waste on light personal topics of conversation at the expense of not having time to get to the business at hand—his qualifications and suitability for the job. Only later did he realize that, to the Japanese, light personal conversation *was* the business at hand because it is the way they sound out the candidate's character and his potential in terms of a long-term personal relationship.

THE *GAIJIN* NICHE

Since *shokutaku* employees usually stay for less than five years, they have virtually no chance for advancement—even if they decide to stay in Japan. One American employee at a Japanese bank said that, while foreigners can fit into a sort of *gaijin* niche for a year or two, he doubts whether they can ever fit in the long term. "Although the Japanese give lip service to internationalization, deep down they see themselves as unique. So unless you were born in Japan of Japanese parents, you'll never really fit into their little club."

Foreigners working at Japanese banks or securities houses have a variety of experiences, ranging from operating as insiders to being on the periphery.

The experience of the periphery may be more common but many foreign employees of Japanese firms feel that this situation, while true in the past, is changing because Japan has no choice but to become truly international.

THAT'S ENTERTAINING

When you do land a job in the financial world in Japan, either at a foreign or Japanese firm, you will not have a lot of time to sit back and congratulate yourself. Without exception, every person I interviewed in this field spends about twelve hours a day at the office. And office hours can be extended late into the night if part of your job is entertaining clients.

One of the oft-repeated statistics about Japan is that more money is spent on business entertaining than on national defense. While some foreigners enjoy this and others loathe it, entertaining is a necessary part of business in Japan.

"What you've got to realize," said an investment banker, "is that even if you're the most famous company in the world, you've got to build a friendly relationship before the Japanese will start talking to you.

"London is always calling me saying, 'Find out what the problem is and why it's taking them so long to reach a decision.'

"If I meet with them during the day, I won't find out a thing. But if you go out at night and pour two or three beers down their throats, it has the effect of about sixteen pints and you can find out a few things—enough to pacify the London office for awhile anyway.''

The long hours are not without their rewards—in salary or in contacts and experience. By all current indications Japan will continue to be one of the world's main financial centers in the coming decades. There are some points to argue, but as far as money matters are concerned, the facts speak for themselves:

—In April 1987 the Tokyo Stock Exchange replaced New York's as the world's biggest and richest, with as many as 3 billion shares worth about 3.8 trillion dollars being traded in a day. Its capitalization has jumped 15 percent from 1980 to 1989 so that it now accounts for about 42 percent of the capitalization in the world's stock markets.

—Whereas thirty years ago not one Japanese bank was listed in the world's top fifty, today nine of the world's ten largest banks (ranked by assets) are Japanese.

—Japanese financial institutions have a one-third share of Britain's international banking transactions.

These and other facts are a clear indication of the growing importance of Tokyo on the world financial scene and of the strength of Japan in the global economy, and have led many economists to conclude that this is where the future lies.

If you want to find work in the Japanese financial scene, planning and perseverance are necessary. First, you should learn at least some Japanese. Then acquire experience or expertise in a particular area and send out resumes, or make the connections that will land you a job with a bank or other financial company (Japanese or other) in your country or in Japan. There are thousands of foreigners working in Japan right now to prove that, with a little planning and a healthy dose of perseverance, it can be done.

5. COMPUTERS

Everyone knows the Japanese are good at making hardware, but not everyone knows how lousy they are at making good software. To produce good software, you need real creativity and that kind of thinking just isn't allowed in the Japanese educational and business worlds.

The young American computer whiz who said this has worked with a number of computer companies in Japan, both Japanese and foreign, and was echoing the sentiments of most foreign computer specialists in this country.

The Japanese have heard such words again and again in recent years and are now taking steps to catch up in this and other perceived areas of weakness. Rather than try to change the monolithic education system, they have decided to inject creativity into their projects through the hiring of foreigners.

Even without the help of foreigners, Japan has become the second largest computer industry and computer market in the world. It has reached this level of prominence through incremental improvements on existing technology and through various government-sponsored R & D programs that have provided support, direction, and assistance. The computer industry has been identified as a growth sector of the Japanese economy and is expected to exhibit high growth into the 1990s.

But this may be too much of a good thing. A recent MITI (Ministry of International Trade and Industry) report found that if the demand for computer software continues to grow at its present pace, 85,000 systems engineers and programmers will be needed in 1990. In 1988 there were about 43,000, and only 60,000 were expected to be available by 1990. This leaves an astonishing 25,000 unfilled jobs.

To meet the twin and sometimes overlapping needs of more creativity and more workers in the future, many major Japanese electronics and engineering firms are shattering their traditional "Japanese only" employment practices with the tacit aid of the Immigration Bureau. Officially, only foreigners who are performing work that Japanese cannot do are allowed to work in Japan, but the bureau has been looking the other way and freely handing out visas to foreigners with degrees in computer science or electronic engineering.

Computer scientists and technicians are coming to Japan through various programs—governmental and private—to work in a wide spectrum of companies and institutes.

Sometimes the foreign talent is put to good use; sometimes it is not. Three young Americans who had studied artificial intelligence systems at top universities were recruited in the U.S. by a small printing company, which had just decided to diversify into computer-aided design and artificial intelligence. After arriving at their new workplace, the Americans discovered that the company had no idea what it was getting into.

"The guy who interviewed us wasn't even the boss and didn't really know what was going on. But it seems that one day he had a brainstorm and said, 'Let's do computers—they're the wave of the future.' And he leaps off to America and hires qualified specialists who will magically transform chaos into order."

Although this man's starting salary of about 35,000 dollars wasn't that much better than what he could make in the U.S., he took the job because he wanted to travel and because, "I was sick of hearing my friends bitch and whine about the Japanese. I figured I'd go see for myself what they were up to—pick their brains while they were picking mine."

But the situation he found himself in was far from the smoothly functioning Japan, Inc. that he had heard about and imagined before he came. During his interview, he had been led to believe that there would be a new department set up and ready to roll. What he found was "no machines, no manuals, no nothing—well, there were desks, and chairs so we could sit at the desks. And that's what we did for a few weeks until the manuals came. Then we read manuals for two or three months until the computers finally came."

A similar experience was reported by an American who had ended up in the computer business after some time in the music world. He was working as a systems specialist for an American company in New York that made international banking software, but wanted to move to Asia. When the day came that one of his interviewers casually mentioned there was a position open in Tokyo, he found himself blurting out, "I'll take it."

The interviewer looked at him like he was crazy because, "you gotta realize, in New York nobody wants to go to Tokyo. That's why these jobs, when they do exist, stay open for a long time. People think Tokyo is all screwed up. They think the language is wrong, they can't adapt to the culture—you know, the problem is, basically, it's not America."

The company, a brokerage house, was having trouble finding a qualified systems programmer to be stationed in Tokyo. While many were attracted at first by the mystique of the Orient, when it actually came to pulling up roots, saying goodbye to house and car, friends and family, not many were willing to go through with it.

But this man was different. "I've always wanted to do something like this and for me it's been an adventure."

An adventure, of course, comes complete with surprises and he has had his fair share. The position, doing systems programming for an American brokerage house in Tokyo, turned out to be "the worst job I ever had in my life. They lied to me about everything. Instead of doing this big project they'd described to me, I was basically office help. But I wanted to be in Japan, so I looked at it like an entry-level job where you do a lot of dirty work, get lied to, abused and kicked around, but you make your connections."

Through his connections, he was offered another job as EDP manager at a foreign bank. He is very happy there how and has no intention of returning home in the near future.

The demand for foreign expertise in the high-tech fields is so great that it is not too difficult to find work even without any personal connections. One Canadian came through Japan on a tour of the Far East. He stayed only one week because it was so expensive and then went on to Hong Kong. On his way back to Toronto, he had a stopover in Tokyo and so, just for the hell of it, leafed through the English yellow pages and sent off unsolicited letters to all of the computer companies. Two days later he had a response from a franchise of an American company and had a job.

The job, however, turned out to be not very satisfying. "All they really wanted was an office *gaijin* to deal with the *gaijin* customers. We were selling computers like they were TVs—just put one in a box, tell the customer to plug it in when they get home, and send them away."

Since he was more of a technician than a salesman, he soon started looking for a new job. After about six months he was recruited by one of his acquaintances to work at a Japanese company. It was a small company that was only selling modems, and not very good ones at that. The acquaintance who had recruited him was a very good salesperson and with her expertise in sales and his in the technical side of things, they soon turned the business around.

"We proceeded in the first six months to raise sales figures about fifty-fold. This increase was mainly because they were selling modems for ¥20,000 to ¥30,000 each and we got them to sell computers for over a million yen each."

His time with that company turned out to be quite an education in both Japanese business practices and the way Japanese deal with computers. The thing that hit him first was that the industry was "one of the biggest price-fixing rings in the world." Because the company was using the exchange rate of three years ago (¥250 to U.S.$1), it could rake in enormous profits by selling U.S.-made machines that would go for about 2,000 dollars or less in the U.S. for the yen equivalent of $9,000 to $10,000.

He also learned that maintaining an orderly system was more important to the company than making a lot of sales. Every day in the morning meeting, he and all of his co-workers would stand in a circle and listen to the boss tell them to work hard. But either they weren't listening or he didn't really mean it because when the two foreigners started picking up new business selling and installing systems as fast as they could, the company reacted unexpectedly.

"They appreciated the fact that we were helping them make money, but we were screwing up their system. There wasn't time to get fifteen people to put their *hankos* (personal seal) on every piece of paper and to fill in the incredibly detailed reports like they used to.'' So again, he began looking for a new job.

Since he was getting attractive offers from various securities houses, he felt his prospects were good, and quit to move on to greener pastures. The very next month, though, the American stock market crashed, the job offers disappeared, and he found himself in a state of unemployment—not a very comfortable place to be, particularly in Japan.

DOING IT YOUR WAY

But he had made enough connections in his previous jobs that people knew him and respected his abilities. Soon after his entry into the ranks of the unemployed, a friend told him about someone who needed a certain program designed. He did it, enjoyed it, and then somebody else wanted something done, and somebody else. Things snowballed rapidly, his name started being circulated informally, and, before he realized it, he had become an independent computer consultant.

He describes his work simply: ''I help people use their machines. That's the skill that's lacking here. Sure you can find Japanese to help you plug in your machine—and maybe install a piece of software on a basic level. But it's really hard to find people who can design a complete system, customize software for the person's particular needs—that kind of messing around.

''The Japanese produce machines in the old-fashioned sense of the word—little things you fit together and that work in a certain way. But as for extending the use of that machine . . . no, it's just not done. Japanese firms still use computers mainly for word processing and a little databasing. There's a Japanese version of Lotus 1-2-3 but it's hardly used at all.''

This means that it doesn't take an expert to be a consultant. Unfortunately, some unscrupulous foreigners with just a smattering of computer know-how have seen this as a quick way to make big money.

''They don't want to share their information with anyone and are deathly afraid of anyone stealing their business. I think they're also afraid that someone will find them out. I inherited some business from a guy who left the country and I couldn't believe how he was ripping people off—selling software packages at the Japanese retail prices—four to five times the U.S. prices—even when the software was just a copy that he had got from a friend.''

Although the field is wide open and there is plenty of money to be made—even ethically—there are not many independent consultants in Tokyo. The reason is simply that a visa for such a job does not exist, and you must either do it as part-time work while holding another job that provides your work visa, or incorporate yourself as a company.

One person who decided to start his own company spent six months scrambling to get all the necessary papers and sponsors and information. But when he presented it all to the immigration officials they refused to grant him the visa. He said, ''But I have all these customers, all these projects; I'm providing a service that people need.'' And they said, ''Sure, you can do your business, but you can't get a work visa based on it.''

What it came down to was that the immigration officials insisted that his projected sales in the first year had to be 100 million yen. They knew as well as he did that this was impossible for a one-man company, and so he found himself back at square one.

Unwilling to give up, he found a small company that would agree to employ him on paper when in fact he would continue to work as a consultant. This got him a six-month working visa, but then immigration officials began nosing around his sponsor's company, so he took an impromptu vacation to Hong Kong and came back on a tourist visa to look for work. Some banks and securities houses have expressed interest, but he will probably be a ''local hire.'' He is not too happy about that because it means lower pay, and few holidays. But for now, he feels that the secure visa such a job offers is worth it.

For those who are thinking of going solo as a consultant, one of the easiest ways is to marry a Japanese national. With a spouse visa you can go ahead and open a small business, one which would not get you a work visa with the Immigration Bureau, but which will give you a good income and the freedom to do as much or as little work as you like. Another way is to set up your company overseas and then come to Japan as a "representative." Alternatively, you can buy a "paper company" in Hong Kong and come as its representative. Because of Japanese officialdom's greater respect for organizations than for individuals, some say this is the way to go. Be warned though, that if your bogus company is found out, you will probably be deported and not allowed to come back for some time.

FRUSTRATIONS

Nearly every foreigner experiences some level of background frustration in Japan, and the computer people are no exception, whether they are working in an office or on their own. One person working in an all-Japanese office complained that he was always left out of interoffice socializing. He tried to change the situation, but found it impossible and finally accepted it and socialized with his own circle of friends outside the office. Another person had to learn to deal with the fact that no one in the office was willing to take responsibility for making a decision and no one would ever take any authority in telling other people what to do.

Nearly everyone advises learning Japanese. Says one three-year veteran, "It's to my eternal shame that I don't speak Japanese. A lot of foreign companies are sending their foreign expat staff back home because it's just too expensive to keep them here. To replace them, they're hiring local Japanese staff and training them. Often they'll put someone in charge of the computer system who has never touched a computer before. After I've designed and installed some new software, these are the people I have to teach, and of course, it's a lot better if I can do it in Japanese. Without a doubt, you're a giant step ahead if you speak Japanese."

If you are able, by hook or by crook, to become an independent consultant, you can look forward to spending about 30 percent of your time researching and reading all of the publications to make sure you know what you're supposed to know, 30 percent of the time doing administrative things—keeping the books and banking, and 30 percent doing what you get paid for—consulting.

One successful programmer said, "Getting a good job is a matter of good luck, good planning, and good relationship building.

If you network and build relationships and know how to present yourself to and work with Japanese, you will have no problem getting a job here. Sure, you'll have to put up with a lot of politics and baloney, and you can always find something to complain about. Some folks are miserable here. I think some come because it's one of the best places to be miserable—there are so many things to bitch about if you want to. There are personality clashes, power plays, no-exit situations . . . but if you want to come, come, by all means. You can make a hell of a lot of money and learn a lot too.''

6. LAW

In California, if you're not a lawyer, then you're a therapist. In Japan, you could hold a national convention for practicing psychotherapists in a phone booth, and a meeting of all Japanese lawyers in a fair-size public bath.

A lawyer from California working as a trainee at a Japanese law firm

The relatively low number of Japanese therapists and lawyers reflects a culture which has always abhorred confrontational behavior, and considers mental or emotional problems a character defect. But as Japan assumes a major role in a world characterized by confrontation, litigation, and mental instability, she is finding herself in need of the expertise of these and other foreign professionals. Once before, in the 1870s and 1880s, the Meiji government imported foreigners, mainly engineers and scientists, as *oyatoi gaijin* to help Japan catch up with and participate in the modern world.

These "hired outside people" were just that—hired temporary help with no real prospects for future advancement. "Outsiders" by literal definition, they had little hope of being accepted into the culture and were tolerated only because they were needed.

Some would argue that not a lot has changed in the Japanese feeling toward the foreign "hired help." Others find they are genuinely welcomed by the Japanese. But welcome or not, foreigners are now working in many fields in Japan, and one of those fields is law.

LAWS OF LIFE

One of the basic laws of modern life seems to be that when

money reaches a certain critical mass, lawyers spontaneously appear. Now that Tokyo has the most heavily capitalized stock market in the world in dollar terms and the Osaka stock exchange ranks third behind New York, the critical mass has been achieved and foreign lawyers have come.

They fall into four general categories:

1) licensed foreign lawyers (*gaikokuho jimu bengoshi*),

2) "trainees" at Japanese law firms,

3) teachers and researchers at universities and research institutes, and

4) corporate lawyers in various companies, Japanese and foreign.

Although the history of foreign lawyers working in Japan extends back to the Meiji era, the current set-up, which includes *gaikokuho jimu bengoshi*, has only been in effect since 1987. Prior to the second world war, the Japanese had consistently admitted qualified foreign lawyers to the bar. With or without formal admission, the foreign attorney's right to provide commercial counseling services was undisputed.

Then, during the Occupation, a lawyers law was passed, Article 7 of which expressly permitted foreign lawyers to practice in Japan. This resulted in a number of American-style firms opening in Tokyo to provide a broad range of legal services, from routine counseling and drafting of documents to corporate registration and administrative agency filings.

But in 1955, Article 7 was repealed and foreign lawyers were barred from setting up offices. They could only come to Japan and work as "trainees," assisting domestic lawyers, or fly in and out of Japan to work with their Japanese clients.

As the Japanese economy continued to grow, and Japanese overseas investment skyrocketed, the demand for international legal services increased and lawyers from large law offices in the U.S. or Europe made ever-more frequent trips to Japan, sometimes spending nearly half of every year in the country without having a permanent office to work from.

This lack of an official way for foreign attorneys to set up a practice in Japan was a thorn in the side of many lawyers and politicians and became one of the liberalizations sought by the U.S. during the trade negotiations of the 80s. Both Japanese and foreigners alike felt the passage of a law allowing foreign lawyers to open offices was inevitable, given the emergence of Japan as a center of international finance, but it took many years of sometimes acrimonious debate before the legislation was enacted on April 1, 1987.

What this "Act Providing Special Measures for the Treatment of the Performance of Legal Business by Foreign Lawyers" actually allows for is less impressive than its name. The extensive restrictions detailed in its twenty-eight pages are testimony to the reluctance of the Japanese legal establishment to allow the foreigners in. Many feared that if foreign lawyers were admitted they would soon overrun the quiet, consensus-oriented Japanese house.

The act stipulates that only those lawyers who have practiced for five years in a state or country that grants equal treatment to Japanese lawyers may apply to the Ministry of Justice for a license to set up an office. Applied to the United States, this means that only lawyers from New York, California, Hawaii, Michigan, New Jersey, and the District of Colombia are eligible.

After a license is granted, the foreign lawyer is able to provide only a narrow range of legal services. He or she is expressly prohibited from a long list of activities, including representing any party before a court or other public office in Japan and employing or establishing a partnership with Japanese lawyers—even though Japanese law firms may hire foreign lawyers as "trainees."

ONE STEP FORWARD . . .

Although the general reaction of observers, both Japanese and foreign, was that the law was a step in the right direction, i.e. in the direction of openness and internationalization, some have questioned this assumption.

An American professor of law believes that because of its many limitations, the 1987 statute represents a setback for Japanese and foreign lawyers as well as for the international business community in general. He feels that, "Until Japan truly opens, the best international legal services for Japanese and American clients involved in trans-Pacific commerce will continue to be offered by American firms in the U.S., particularly those on the West coast that have in increasing numbers begun to include Japanese *bengoshi* (lawyers) as full partners.''

Other lawyers, however, maintain that none of the restrictions is a serious obstacle to successfully practicing law in Japan. While a *gaikokuho jimu bengoshi* may not appear in court, most of the legal work in Japan is not litigation but business-related transactions and contracts. While the foreign lawyers are not allowed to practice Japanese law, few are qualified to do so and they are in demand precisely for their foreign law expertise. While they may not form partnerships with Japanese lawyers, most have found their Japanese colleagues more than willing to work with them on an informal basis.

Proof that the restrictions are not prohibitive can be found in the fact that dozens of foreign lawyers sought licenses as soon as the law was promulgated. Most of them were partners in large multinational firms based in New York or Los Angeles that had already built up a base of Japanese clients in the years prior to the enactment of the statute.

After the initial rush, however, the numbers quickly fell off and the Ministry of Justice admitted it was somewhat disappointed in the turnout. Two years after the law went into effect, there were only 46 individual lawyers, representing 33 firms—26 from the U.S., six from the U.K., and one from France.

Getting certified to practice in Japan turned out to be the lowest hurdle for many. It was followed by the *real* problems: finding office space, rent money, and office staff, and finding out about what lawyers do in Japan and how they do it.

The licensed lawyers find they have little trouble filling their days with roughly the same sort of business negotiations and documentation of financial transactions that they would be doing in their home jurisdictions. The difference is that they are usually representing Japanese clients—big names like Nissan, Toyota, Sony and Hitachi, as well as smaller banks and trading companies. These companies often need foreign expertise on technical money matters and trade problems. One British firm specializes in assisting its Japanese clients with every stage of transactions. It advises on strategy and negotiations, drafts documents, consults with both the client and the other side, and drafts and redrafts until both sides are satisfied.

Much of the foreign lawyers' work is with Japanese investors wanting to increase their property portfolios. The lawyers assist them in making real estate investments and advise them on tax codes and zoning restrictions. Many also advise Japanese companies on how to avoid trade law violations and will represent companies accused of unfair trade practices.

Although the licensed foreign lawyers are doing work similar to what they would be doing at home, they are doing it in Japan—and cultural factors naturally affect the legal environment. One of the most obvious differences between Japan and most Western countries is the number of legal professionals.

In Japan there is one lawyer for nearly 7,000 people, while in the U.S. the figure is one for every 360. Some people have hypothesized that this apparently low need for lawyers stems from the Buddhist teachings of mildness and forbearance. This sounds plausible enough at first glance—except that the Judeo-Christian tradition embraces similar teachings ("If any man will sue thee at the law, and take away thy coat, let him have thy cloak also." Matt. 5:40) that seem not to have had much effect on lawsuit-hungry Americans. The numbers, however, do reflect a society that is less argumentative than most Western ones and places greater importance on maintaining at least a surface level of harmony.

For both cultural and non-cultural reasons, the Japanese tend to shy away from litigation. On the cultural side, the assertion of a right which causes a confrontation tends to be considered childish and a sign of weakness in Japan whereas non-assertion of rights tends to be considered a weakness in the West.

An American would not feel uncomfortable asking a smoker to extinguish his cigarette (or would feel he should not)—particularly if they were in a no-smoking area. To *not* assert one's right to clean air would be seen as immature and weak. But in Japan no matter what obnoxious behavior another person may be engaging in—from smoking to fondling women on the subway (the ubiquitous *chikan*)—a "mature" response is to *gaman* (endure, put up with it) rather than object and cause a confrontation.

There are also non-cultural reasons why the Japanese do not like litigation. Often it is because they know that the case will drag on and on through the slow judicial process. Suits against companies polluting Lake Biwa near Osaka, for example, have been in the courts for over 20 years. Most Japanese agree that even if one wins a lawsuit, the cost in time and money is likely to be greater than the benefits.

NOT INSCRUTABLE, JUST HIGHLY MUTABLE

In areas other than litigation, the lawyer's work in Japan is also influenced by cultural factors. The Western idea of a contract as a final and legally binding document, a stable element in a changing world, is still not fully accepted by the Japanese. Japanese culture in general is more situational than Western cultures. What is "right" or "wrong" can change with the situation, and business relations, as well, are seen as fluid and subject to change.

Traditionally, written agreements were seen as unnecessary and a sign that the two sides did not trust each other. Although the Japanese have acquiesced to the Western idea of written contracts, they still like to write them flexibly, allowing for altered circumstances. Quite often, after a contract has been signed, the Japanese side will ask for changes due to changed conditions such as a rise in the price of oil. Such a request would strike most Westerners as absurd since it nullifies the point of drawing up the contract in the first place.

The Japanese way of managing and making decisions also leads to a different way of using lawyers. Before Japan became immersed in trade with the West, lawyers were considered relatively unimportant in business and were involved peripherally, if at all, in decision making. Even now, and even in large international transactions, the foreign lawyer may only be consulted for general advice at the outset.

The businessmen who come to see a lawyer are usually middle managers. They ask a few questions and gather the preliminary information the lawyer offers and return to their company. The lawyer's advice then becomes just one of the many factors to be digested in long meetings over many months. Because the lawyer is not kept informed of the progress of the discussions, the final decision that is reached is often not the best one. But once it has been so laboriously reached by consensus, it is very difficult, if not impossible, to change it. Lawyers have found this lack of an intimate relationship with their Japanese corporate clients and the diffuse nature of the decision-making process one of the biggest obstacles to giving effective advice.

After becoming accustomed to the Japanese business style, life in Japan becomes somewhat easier—but not a lot. One of the most difficult aspects of working as a licensed foreign lawyer is that you are in effect working two shifts—one during business hours in Japan and another during business hours in your home country.

"We're still the tail, not the dog," said an American lawyer from a California law firm. "From the moment I wake in the morning until late at night I'm on the phone to the U.S. There is always the unrelenting pressure of an eighteen- or nineteen-hour day."

But if you can survive the pressure, there are many benefits of living and working in Japan: career acceleration, a healthy salary with good benefits, and an affluent lifestyle in one of the world's safest countries. The foreign licensed lawyers are not considered a branch office of their firm by the Japanese, but they are treated as expats just the same and have salaries and benefits comparable to those of expats in banking and finance.

A young British lawyer whose firm had had an informal relationship with a Japanese firm for fifteen years prior to the passage of the new law, asked to be transferred to Japan when one of the partners obtained his foreign lawyer's license. He found that the range of transactions passing through the office in Tokyo was far broader than what he could have expected in London, and, although he has to work twelve-hour days to keep on top of things, he sees the experience as a big plus because he is getting more experience more quickly than he would have in a normal career progression.

INS AND OUTS

Most of the licensed lawyers stay for two to five years. An American explained, "Most lawyers here are experienced senior partners, not junior researchers, and our function is to dispense on-the-spot advice. We're successful here because of our expertise and our ability to give advice quickly. If you stay longer than five years, it becomes hard to give accurate advice. You lose your effectiveness as you lose touch with what's happening back in your home jurisdiction.''

Although it is likely that more and more foreign law firms will be sending their lawyers to Japan for short-term work as business between Japanese and foreign companies continues to expand, most foreign licensed lawyers predict that not many more of their brethren will take advantage of the new statute and set up offices. The main reason is that it is extremely difficult for an office in Tokyo to turn a profit. Most of the larger firms with a good number of Japanese clients have already sent one or more of their partners to be licensed. But smaller firms with a smaller base of Japanese clients find startup and operating costs prohibitive. Many observers even predict that some of the larger firms will be forced to abandon their Tokyo offices and will go back to serving their Japanese clients from Hong Kong or Singapore as they did before the passage of the law.

FOREIGN LAWYERS AT JAPANESE LAW FIRMS

The 1987 law did not affect the foreign lawyers working for Japanese firms. The practice of hiring a foreign lawyer on a fixed contract as a ''trainee'' began in the Meiji era, but has expanded considerably as Japan has become immersed in international business. The 200 or so trainees currently working at Japanese firms have widely varying duties, depending on the firm and the personal relationship between employer and employee.

An Australian working at one of the oldest and most prestigious Japanese firms admits that trainees are limited in what they can do because their primary function is to be of assistance to the Japanese partners. This is no great problem in his mind, though, because ''in any law firm in the world, until you become a partner yourself, your work is to assist the partner.''

A difficulty for some trainees is that they feel they have stepped off the promotion ladder. Back home, they would be moving up through the ranks and looking at partnership in five or seven years. To keep up with your colleagues, one foreign lawyer advises, it is necessary to assiduously maintain contacts at home so that you can fit back in when you return.

But this is not always a concern. A Canadian attorney who came to Japan on her own says she "stepped out of a position in Canada where I could move vertically but not horizontally. Working in Japan opens a lot of doors and has expanded my opportunities horizontally."

But not all lawyers are so adaptable or land in good situations as these two did. Many feel frustrated with the *sensei* (teacher) tradition in which your elders are your teachers and you have to endure lengthy lectures on how to do even the simplest tasks. This is also part of the *senpai-kohai* (senior-junior) relationship in which juniors are expected to be quiet, humble, and respectful. Most Westerners have no experience of dealing with such a rigid hierarchy, and don't like it because they want to feel on equal standing with others in the office. One British lawyer commented, "I find it all rather amusing. Of course, others find it infuriating."

An Australian who had spent five years living in Japan studying Zen before he went to law school said the feelings of frustration come from not understanding how to function within the Japanese system. "If you're going somewhere and you run into a wall, you don't keep batting your head against it, you assess the wall and climb over it or walk around it.

"Some people just don't understand the system. They don't understand that there is flexibility in the system if you understand its power and control parameters."

FINDING YOUR PLACE

Ways of finding work with a Japanese firm vary as much as the firms themselves. Some have a relationship with certain foreign law schools or firms and get their trainees from that pool. Others rely on their current trainee to introduce them to their next, and others are open to whoever comes along.

Most major Western firms have contacts with one or more Japanese firms, and exchanges of personnel for fixed time periods are quite common. One trainee recommends, "If you're working for a firm that is interested in Japan but has no connection with a Japanese firm, try setting up an exchange yourself. From a strategic point of view in law firm planning, a firm naturally wants connections with others overseas. Often they cannot find anyone willing to drop everything and go off to another country for a year or more so they are pleasantly surprised when someone takes the initiative and starts a relationship.'' This was what he did and found that both his home firm and the Japanese firm were pleased with the outcome.

Another man first came to Japan when he was still a law student at Harvard to do a three-month internship with a small Japanese firm. After he returned to finish his degree, he thought he would like to work another year or two in Japan. During his first stay he had learned that you should never be so rude as to directly ask a superior for something, so he wrote asking his former employer if he knew of any Japanese firms needing a foreign trainee. The soft sell had its desired effect and they wrote asking him to come work for them again.

Although connections like this are undoubtedly helpful, they are not absolutely necessary. A woman who came to Japan with absolutely no connections found work within a month. She attributed her success to being in the right place at the right time. But it was more than that. It was a matter of doing the right things in order to end up being in that place at that particular time.

Upon arriving in Japan she called all the foreign lawyers she could get phone numbers for and told them she was looking for work. Once that information got into the grapevine, it wasn't long before various trainees were introducing her to their bosses and colleagues. From these contacts, she was able to get a job replacing a foreigner who was returning home.

Her background and experience in international business transactions and intellectual property rights, patents, and joint ventures also made her very marketable. In fact, a background in international commercial transactions is a prerequisite to getting hired with one of the major Japanese firms. If you're from a small firm in the American Midwest that deals in criminal and family law and have never been exposed to commercial transactions, there's probably not much for you to do in Japan.

While experience in commercial law is necessary, prior Japan experience and knowledge of Japanese is not. One lawyer felt that his firm chose him precisely because he knew nothing about Japan and therefore didn't have any negative preconceptions and was more malleable. Since ninety-nine percent of all legal documentation and advice for international transactions is done in English, Japanese language ability is not critical.

Nevertheless, for one's personal development and career growth, the benefits of understanding the language and culture cannot be overestimated. While this knowledge may not be used overtly by the law firm, it will enhance your ability to contact people, to understand others in your firm, and to generate work—all of which are part and parcel of the purpose of working and living in Japan.

THE VAGARIES OF VAGUENESS

On average, Japanese law firms are much smaller than their Western counterparts and a larger proportion of their work involves international transactions such as joint venture agreements, licensing, and patents. The job of the trainee is often to assist the Japanese lawyers by preparing and checking English communications and documents relating to the transactions.

A recent law school graduate said, "At first I thought it'd be easy—just sticking in articles and plurals. But it's a lot more difficult than that. Often things are expressed very vaguely and I have to guess what it means and then write it out and get it checked. It's never quite right and we go back and forth and back and forth until I draft something that is clear enough to be understood in English and vague enough to be appropriate in Japanese."

In addition to his primary function of checking English, he sometimes researches points of American law, but feels that the main reason he was hired is because the partners wanted someone to practice their English with and because his presence lends an international air to the office.

Many foreign lawyers working as trainees become frustrated when they realize they have opted out of the promotion line back home just to check English and be a sort of office mascot. One trainee complained, "I'm so much *not* a part of things here. There's no place to advance to. I'm never going to be made a partner (not that I want to be), but it's strange. I feel they respect me for my skills, but at the same time have contempt for me. It's like, 'We've learned your language and how you do business, but you don't know our language or how we do business and still you have it so easy just because you're white and American.' "

While many trainees find themselves assigned to duties usually handled by legal assistants in the United States, others manage to find employers willing to give them more responsibility. To get into a firm where you'll do more than proofread, you need to do more groundwork. The key to finding these jobs is planning and presentation.

A foreign lawyer in his third year at a large Japanese firm where he is given a lot of responsibility says dozens of letters come in every year inquiring about jobs. The people that are chosen, he says, are those who "present themselves well and offer something to the firm, either by way of experience or expertise or through the connection they can provide to a major firm overseas."

With the growing importance of the European Community and the integrated European market in 1992, he says that lawyers from France or Germany who speak English should have good prospects. He also feels that anyone with three to five years' experience in commercial law who wants a job in Japan in two to three years' time has "a very good chance of getting a good one—it's very simple really if you plan ahead, make yourself marketable, and make the contacts."

He recommends that a foreign lawyer stay about three years because much of the first year is spent getting used to things and getting your productivity up. He feels that to accumulate a knowledge of Japanese law and business customs and contacts, anything less than three years is not cost or career effective.

At Japanese law firms the hours can vary tremendously depending on the projects underway, but twelve-hour days are the norm.

"It's a macho thing to stay after the last trains," one young American said. "Japanese lawyers, even more than most Japanese businessmen, think of themselves as hard workers and make a great show of working late as proof of their dedication."

A number of foreigners have noted that, for the average Japanese businessman, being at work is more like being at home than being at home is. They come in to the office, put on their slippers, have a cup of coffee, read the newspaper, and ease into work. Lunch and dinner are delivered to the office and it's all very relaxed and cozy.

However, what's cozy for a Japanese is often crazy for a foreigner. After a few months, intense claustrophobia often sets in and many foreigners complain that they never get out in the sun, never get out of town, and never get any exercise.

On the other hand, a foreigner has a great deal more freedom than his Japanese colleagues to take time off or leave work early. One trainee said, "I don't have to prove my loyalty or anything so I don't have to stay so late or come in on holidays and weekends like they do. Also, I find that some of the associates will speak to me more freely than to anyone else since I'm outside of the hierarchy and outside of office politics."

One woman who worked for a year as a trainee for a Tokyo law firm decided she wanted to stay in Japan a little longer, but not in Tokyo. She spread the word around her office and one of her acquaintances, a Japanese-American lawyer, introduced her to a professor at Kyoto University who then offered to sponsor her so that she could do research at the Kyoto Institute for Comparative Law Studies. In this job she is researching, editing, and rewriting a book on Japanese business law. She also works part-time at a firm in Osaka.

She said that before she came to Japan she had read many books that made disparaging remarks about "sexist Japan," and had expected that she would have to fight to be taken seriously. She was pleasantly surprised to find that this was not the case, and is now encouraging other women to come to Japan.

There are quite a few foreign lawyers doing research at the Kyoto institute and at universities throughout Japan. One lawyer who had studied in Japan when he was a university student recently came back on a Fulbright scholarship to study Japanese consumer rights and patient rights. He expects to publish a book from his research into these areas.

FOREIGN LAWYERS IN CORPORATIONS

A small but growing number of foreign lawyers is working at large corporations in Japan. With the tremendous growth in the Japanese industrial and financial sectors, the Japanese have found that they need foreign lawyers on hand to work effectively on international transactions. Even companies that get 95 percent of their revenues from sales within Japan are hiring foreign lawyers because they have long range plans to break into the international market.

An American lawyer was hired at a large translation and interpretation company for both his legal expertise and his editing skills. He had been editing law textbooks in the U.S. and had come to Japan, not so much for career advancement as for the experience.

When he was first hired, he did quite a lot of work that had some connection with law, but as time went on, he did more and more rewriting and editing of translated documents with little or no relation to legal matters. Perhaps because of his law background, though, he was given many of the most important jobs, such as rewriting official speeches to be given by the prime minister and other high government officials on their overseas trips. He finds the work stimulating and interesting because of its variety and says he has no regrets about coming to Japan.

An Australian lawyer who had practiced as a solicitor for three years in Melbourne decided to come to Japan primarily to learn Japanese, and also, possibly, to work. His main motivation was the skyrocketing Japanese investment in Australia—the rate of increase in real estate investment alone has been 1,800 percent over the past three years. He thought that figures like this obviously meant that people who spoke Japanese would have more options than others. "I thought if you go back to Australia after two years in Japan, you can't lose."

When he first arrived in Japan he enrolled at a Japanese school and studied full-time for six months. Although he wanted to continue, he was running low on funds and so, through a friend, got a part-time job with a law firm and for the next three months went to Japanese class each morning for three hours, worked at the law firm for five hours, went home, did his homework and slept.

Because this routine was wearing him out and he was still low on funds, he decided to look for a full-time job. His main source for contacts and job information was the Roppongi Bar Association (pun intended), a group of foreign lawyers working in

Japan who meet once a month to socialize and exchange information on jobs and changes in laws.

In the association's newsletter he saw an advertisement from a Japanese firm that wanted a foreign lawyer. At the interview he spoke in Japanese and felt that his efforts in that area plus his attitude were what landed him the job. He felt that the firm was searching for someone who was flexible and willing to adapt and fit into a Japanese company. Although some of the other candidates had very good qualifications, degrees from Harvard or Ph.D.s, he felt that he was hired because of his personality and willingness to speak Japanese.

The company employs some foreigners from Asian countries, but he is presently the only Westerner in the whole corporation and, although there are quite a few stresses associated with this fact, he feels it gives him valuable insights into the workings of Japanese companies and Japanese society.

"Everything is incredibly regimented. They have bells. They ring at 8:15 and if you're not busy at your desk, well, no one says anything, but they notice and it's a minor sin."

He also found that he had absolutely no privacy in the office. His boss and colleagues were forever looking over his shoulder, even reading his mail. But he says, "You've got to remember that this is business as usual in Japan and you just have to get used to it because there's no alternative."

He finds his work itself more general than his work in Australia—mostly contract law and liaison work for mergers and acquisitions. But he finds the experience valuable for what it is teaching him about the workings of a Japanese company. "The Japanese look at life as a battle, a continual struggle. It's always '*Gambatte*!' this and '*Gambatte*!' that. Their expansion plans are like battle plans and they can mobilize a lot of people, a lot of brainpower, a lot of resources, and get things done a lot faster than we can."

His salary and benefits are "reasonable, higher than my Japanese colleagues get, but about half of what expatriates get." He was aware of the high cost of living in Japan, but thought that the salary would make up for it. "The general perception of people in Australia is that you can save $5,000 or $10,000 a year in Japan, pick up a lot of girls, have a lot of fun—people think coming to Japan is an easy option. I did too. I thought I'd be able to save a lot of money. Well, it's not and I'm not. I've known a lot of people who have come here and gone into shock over the prices and have gone straight back home.''

He says his salary in Japan is about the same as his Australian salary was, but that the money goes five times further in Australia. Overall, he says his standard of living has fallen drastically.

For this and other reasons, he says, ''I couldn't stay here forever. It would drive me up the wall. I don't think many people can handle living in Tokyo after they get into their thirties. I find living here a big strain—in a small apartment, dealing with the crowds, the long commute, the long work hours, people always looking over your shoulder. . . . But I view it as an investment—not only for work in the future—but because of what I'm learning about Japanese people and society.''

FUTURE OPPORTUNITIES

Most lawyers agree that their ranks will slowly increase over the coming years because as long as Japan remains a center of international finance and an exporter of capital, the Japanese will need foreign expertise in international business transactions.

However, the difficulties in setting up permanent offices will keep the number of licensed foreign lawyers fairly low. At the same time, the constant rotation of people in and out will mean that the opportunity is always there.

Since foreign trade and other international transactions require extensive English-language documentation, opportunities for foreign lawyers in Japanese firms will also increase. A survey of Japanese companies conducted by the Association of Japanese Corporate Legal Departments revealed that nearly 60 percent supported the activities of foreign trainees and over 30 percent expected to be using their services more in the future.

The emergence of Tokyo as one of the major business centers of the world is also accelerating the need for international business law advice within corporations. In all areas, then, opportunities for foreign lawyers will increase. Since most lawyers come on a temporary basis, there will be a continual pool of opportunity which will expand gradually.

Although the number of foreign lawyers in Japan will probably not increase dramatically, some believe that they will have a disproportionately large effect on the way business is done in Japan. The old way of doing business—through influence peddling and kickbacks—is bound to change more quickly as foreign lawyers come to Japan because the foreign lawyer will work with evangelical zeal to correct perceived inequities.

To succeed as a lawyer in Japan, then, remember what an American baseball player in Japan said—leave your pride at home, be willing to adapt, and don't expect to play by the same rules. An Australian lawyer offered a further piece of advice: "Just remember the basic concepts of being successful in your early years as a lawyer: shut up, do as you're told, and work hard. It doesn't really matter what you say to people, it's what you do that counts. If you follow that, you'll do all right here."

7. SCIENCE

Science is a jealous mistress.

My father used to say this to explain the long hours he spent working in the laboratory. The only meaning of the word "mistress" that I understood then was that of the nursery rhyme, "Mistress Mary quite contrary . . ." And so it was that I thought I might come across a frilly-skirted girl whenever I went to his lab to help him by carefully lining up the clean flasks in the old wooden cabinets behind the smooth-sliding doors.

I know now what kind of mistress he was talking about, and, listening to the tales of foreign scientists working in Japan, the image of Science as a jealous mistress, sulking prettily in the corner of a laboratory, makes even more sense now than it did then.

THE CHANGING ROLE OF RESEARCH

In the fast-paced modern world, scientific research has become valued, not so much for its role as an instrument of public welfare, but as a means to guarantee economic and political security. And so Science sulks because she has been compelled to share her bed with politics and money. Perhaps no country has managed to carry off this *ménage à trois* more efficiently and with more aplomb than Japan. Politics is the orchestrator as the government targets key strategic industries such as biotechnology, computers, robotics, and new materials, and pours R & D money into them. Economics is the motivator since the development of new applied technology spells success for Japan in the world marketplace. And the scientist is the facilitator—a tireless, uncomplaining third party utterly faithful and loyal to the interests of the other two.

98

Science, politics, and economics find themselves between the sheets in nearly all developed countries now—partly as a response to Japan's postwar competitiveness. In broad terms, Japan's success was predicated on certain government-targeted industries carrying out intensive applied research that built on the basic research achieved in other countries. Japanese research aimed for market-specific applications, and quickly moved Japan ahead of the pack in developing and marketing products. As the trade imbalance loomed ever larger, some Western politicos cried 'foul' and began accusing the Japanese of taking a free ride on Western basic research.

This is probably an overstatement and would be a difficult assertion to prove in any case because of the overlapping of non-competitive basic research and competitive applied research. Until very recently, basic research has been open, free, and non-proprietary, while applied research was the stuff that patents were made of.

However, because of the shrinking time lag between the two, it is no longer so easy to distinguish between them and mark the point when one becomes the other. A theoretical physicist's experiments with nuclear spin soon become the applied technology of magnetic resonance imaging; biologists' basic research into the molecular mechanisms of bacterial viruses has spawned the burgeoning biotech industry. This blending of traditionally separate areas makes it difficult to separate basic research, which all nations should share, from developments with a particular "owner."

The swiftness with which one can become the other seemed to catch the Japanese by surprise in the early eighties and jolted them into action. For example, when Stanford University and the University of California at Berkeley patented the process for producing biologically functional chimeras—organisms made of tissues of different genetic origin—Japan suddenly became aware of how far it was behind the U.S. in biotechnology. This resulted in a group of fourteen companies active in biotechnology forming a consortium in 1981 to negotiate with the government for larger subsidies for biotech-related R & D. And in 1982 MITI established a Bioindustry Office to promote and coordinate development of Japan's biotech-related industries.

Similarly, only four days after American researcher Ching-Wu Paul Chu conducted successful experiments in super-conductivity at temperatures above that of liquid nitrogen in 1987, an association of electronics companies, and university and government labs was formed to organize the industry. According to Japan's equivalent of *The Wall Street Journal*, the *Nihon Keizai Shinbun*, the purpose of this association was "to get a jump on the West in applications and commercialization for a huge new market."

But not only is Japan jumping into applied research with feverish intensity, the goverment has also seen the wisdom of pouring similar amounts of money into basic research. The stinging words of M.I.T. researcher and Nobel prize winner Susumu Tonegawa, "Had I stayed in a Japanese university, I may not have been able to do this kind of work," spurred Japan to develop basic research capabilities equal to or better than those of the West. Shogo Kurachi, president of the Research and Development Corporation of Japan, was quoted as saying, "The fact that there has not been a single major contribution by Japan in basic scientific and technological inventions has further exacerbated trade friction . . . It is an inevitable fact that the Japanese economy must be supported by advanced science and technology, and therefore it is imperative that the Japanese people themselves strive to create and nurture original and basic scientific and technological innovations."

One part of that striving is sending Japanese scientists overseas and another is bringing Western scientists to Japan. From the Japanese point of view, the purpose of both exchanges is to help Japanese scientists learn how the West encourages independent thought and to pick up more detailed knowledge of Western technologies. The opening of Japanese laboratories to foreign scientists also met a demand of some in Western political and scientific circles who claimed that the bulk of Japan's leading science was being conducted behind closed *fusuma* (the sliding paper doors that separate rooms in a Japanese house). The demand was that Japan draw the door aside and let foreign scientists into their labs as freely as the West has done for most of this century.

The Japanese complied with more alacrity that most had imagined—with foreign researchers welcome in both the public and private sectors. The Japan Society for the Promotion of Science offers 50 post-doctoral fellowships each year and a parallel program sponsored by the Japanese Science and Technology Agency supports another 50 young researchers each year at any Japanese national laboratory except those affiliated with universities. In addition, the U.S. National Science Foundation and the Agency of Industrial Science and Technology (a section of MITI) have agreed that the agency will provide access to its research institutes each year for up to 30 U.S. scientists and engineers. (See next page for details.)

In the private sector, there are literally hundreds of private Japanese companies wanting to host foreign researchers. The Tokyo Office of the National Science Foundation put together a directory of over 100 Japanese companies willing to do so. The companies are divided by industry and cover 1) automobile, shipbuilding and other transportation equipment, 2) ceramics, cement and glass manufacturers, 3) the construction industry, 4) the chemical and pharmaceutical industries, 5) the electrical and electronics industries, 6) the food and beverage industry, 7) fisheries and forestry, 8) iron and steel works, 9) machine manufacturing, 10) non-ferrous metals, 11) petroleum and coal products, 12) paints, surface coatings, and ink, 13) precision machinery, 14) private research laboratories, 15) rubber, 16) textiles, and 17) utilities.

Most of the firms say they prefer researchers from their midtwenties to mid-forties, but a fair number are open to scientists of any age. Most specify a preference for stays of six months to two years, but a few would like commitments of three to five years. Many of the laboratories also expressed a willingness to provide travel, housing, commuting and other subsidies to visiting foreign researchers.

Since 79 percent of Japan's R & D expenditures are accounted for by the private sector, this should be where most foreign researchers are. Unfortunately, many of the positions go begging. Some speculate that many researchers doubt that the Japanese are at the cutting edge of research, or they are dissuaded by the high cost of living and modest accommodations in Japan—not to mention the language barrier.

AIST Laboratories: Researchers and Budget
The Agency of Industrial Science & Technology consists of the following facilities, located at Tsukuba unless otherwise noted.

Name	Researchers	Budget*	
		yen	dollars
Electrotechnical Laboratory	559	¥8,989	$70.2
National Chemical Laboratory for Industry	282	3,658	28.6
National Research Institute for Pollution and Resources	248	3,727	29.1
Geological Survey of Japan	243	4,429	34.6
Mechanical Engineering Laboratory	219	3,085	24.1
Government Industrial Research Institute, Nagoya	191	2,420	18.9
Goverment Industrial Research Institute, Osaka	172	2,442	19.1
National Research Laboratory of Metrology	128	2,066	16.1
Research Institute for Polymers and Textiles	104	1,675	13.1
Industrial Products Research Institute	103	1,423	11.1
Government Industrial Development Laboratory, Hokkaido	74	1,096	8.56
Fermentation Research Institute	71	1,085	8.48
Government Industrial Research Institute, Kyushu	70	903	7.05
Government Industrial Research Institute, Chugoku	40	682	5.33
Government Industrial Research Institute, Tohoku	39	509	3.98
Government Industrial Research Institute, Shikoku	34	466	3.64
Totals	**2,577**	**¥38,655**	**$302.00**

* Budget figures are for Japan fiscal year 1988, in millions of *yen* (middle column) and millions of dollars (right-hand column, at ¥128/US$1.00, the IMF average rate in 1988).

A recent survey showed that approximately 6,830 Japanese scientists went to the U.S. in 1988 while only about 120 Americans went to Japan—many of them for short stays of three months or less. This is a pity because a great deal of high-level applied science is taking place in the R & D facilities of Japanese private industry. An engineer working at a major electronics manufacturer said that his experience in Japan was valuable not only to him personally, but also to his colleagues back home who could get a glimpse of the projects the Japanese were working on and what advances they were making.

While individual researchers have been a bit slow off the mark, foreign governments and industries have gone ahead and set up their own programs. The Industrial Development Authority of Ireland launched a graduate scholarship program in 1984. In 1988, 90 Irish computer specialists came to work for a two-year stint at Japanese computer and electronics companies including Nippon Software Co., Ricoh, and Mitsubishi Electric Corp.

Although the men and women who participated in the program were expected to return after two years, many of them were offered permanent jobs in artificial intelligence, development of new word processors, facsimile machines and various kinds of software, and so have stayed on.

Quite a few foreign laboratories have also moved to Japan. Between October 1985 and February 1987, 17 research centers owned or partially funded by foreign companies were built in Japan and another 17 are currently in the planning stages.

Companies like DuPont, Monsanto, Hoffman-LaRoche, BASF, and Hoechst have set up R & D centers in Japan because of the size and increasing openness of the Japanese market. They want to meet the strict requirements of Japanese users and promote quality control and user-oriented products. They also want to develop products which are specifically designed for Japan and Japanese regulations. The firms are particularly interested in areas where Japanese technology is the world standard and are looking to transfer such technologies through joint research.

The experiences of foreign scientists working at private and government research laboratories in Japan reveal that, while language and culture barriers are often significant impediments to communication, an effective transfer of scientific knowledge and technology in both directions is usually achieved.

An American currently doing research at one of Japan's main national laboratories said he had never entertained the idea of going to Japan, and was taken by surprise when his boss suggested it. "I considered it for a nanosecond or so, and then I told him no and thought that would be the end of it."

But it wasn't. The U.S. institute was involved in a joint project with Japan, but all the personnel exchange was into the U.S. lab. The Japanese side had repeatedly expressed their desire to have a reciprocal exchange, so the project leader again asked this man and he again said no.

"It wasn't so much that I didn't want to go to Japan in particular, it was just that I had an established research program going and I didn't want the hassle of moving anywhere—what would I do with my house, my car, my stuff?"

But finally, because it was monetarily very attractive (800,000 yen a month plus housing, transportation, and insurance), and as a favor to his boss, he accepted a one year assignment.

A Canadian woman working in a Swiss institute felt honored when she was invited to work in Japan, but also had misgivings. "Back home all I heard were horror stories like, 'It's all men and it's work, work, work and they won't let women do anything important and it's going to be awful and you're going to hate it' and on and on."

But from the moment she arrived she found the stories false. "This place isn't a backwater. They have big name people coming through all the time giving lectures. It's a lot more international and exciting than where I was working before."

The slowdown in productivity that many foreign researchers experience is usually due to the language barrier and culturally based differences compounded by the fact that they are minicelebrities and must be on call to speak with visiting dignitaries.

The Canadian researcher explained, "This is a federal institute and gets funded by the government. We're all from prestigious international research centers, so when a government minister comes around to visit, we have to stop what we're doing, put on our lab coats if we're not wearing them, and line up to shake his hand. As they introduce us they say which country we're from, and the minister goes away thinking, 'Wow, this is a really good place,' and they get more funding.''

The fact that foreign scientists add to the institute's prestige is reflected in the center's brochure which has foreign faces in virtually every photograph. There is also a chart showing that more and more foreigners are coming every year. Although public relations often seems to be the main reason they are brought over, the real reason is for scientific exchange—they generally teach some technique or procedure and learn others. But this is invariably easier said than done.

Most Westerners get their first hint that things will not be the same when they first walk into their lab. Many labs, particularly those in private institutions, look like any Japanese office: a big room where everyone works amid ringing phones and other people's conversations. An Englishman working in a private lab said that the first time he walked into the lab he thought, ''How am I supposed to function in this chaos?''

He was expecting a private office or at least a quiet corner where he could sit and think and work. While the background noise distracted him at first, he found he got used to it in a few months and then began seeing some advantages: ''We're all a team here working on developing a particular technology and it's important to know what each part of the team is up to. This openness in terms of physical space lends itself to more open communication between people and seems to facilitate teamwork.''

But the same Japanese desire to do everything in an open way can lead to problems. Another Englishman in a government lab said that he feels like the lab is a little socialist state with no one owning anything.

''It's the 'let's share, let's all be together' attitude that really gets to me. You just can't do that in science. They share everything—even little bottles of chemicals, little pots of things. You have a little contamination in one, and then everyone's experiment is gone. Or you run out of something, then everyone's run out of it. You can't go and borrow some from so and so because he doesn't have it either. It's all communal. I don't like all this togetherness. I'm used to having my own block of materials, so that if I screw up I don't screw up everybody else.''

An American agreed that experiments that would be very straightforward and simple to do back home can turn into major productions in Japan. "It's awful because you don't know the most basic things, like where something is, a piece of glassware for example. So you ask someone and they get all flustered and they have a little powwow to figure out what it is the *gaijin* really wants. And then once they've figured it out they don't know where it is, so they go and ask someone else and then you've got a whole train of people running up and down the hall trying to find you something."

A QUESTION OF COMMUNICATION

Many difficulties foreign scientists encounter are related to the language barrier. Very few of the Westerners speak Japanese and since most stay less than one year, they figure it is not worth their time to try and learn.

Although most Japanese scientists have some proficiency in English, they are usually much better at reading than speaking the language. So when a problem comes up, it often takes a long time to solve it.

A Canadian researcher said, "You can't speak at normal speed and you have to keep checking to make sure you've been understood. I ask a question, then I ask the opposite question and if I get 'Yes' both times I know something is wrong, so I start over and rephrase things until I'm sure we understand each other." An American said that the biggest drawback to working in Japan is that he can't brainstorm with his colleagues. "We just can't have an off-the-cuff conversation and that's where you really learn things."

But the Canadian woman said that she had very few problems with communication, partly because she began studying Japanese a year before she came and has continued.

The difficulty in communicating and the unfamiliar surroundings often conspire to create a feeling of dependency. One Englishman spoke with frustration of the time he had just used the last drop of an enzyme and then discovered there was none in the freezer and he'd have to wait three weeks for the new shipment to come in from the U.S. "Normally I just order my own things, but here I'm dependent on somebody else to order it and they may be a little delinquent and forget about it, and so the last drop is gone and everyone's screaming and running up and down the stairs looking for more.''

NO NINE TO FIVE

Other foreign scientists report difficulties stemming from different work patterns. At government labs, as in most Japanese companies, the official work hours are 9:00 A.M. to 5:00 P.M. In practice though, 5:00 marks the midpoint of the workday. The unofficial hours are about 10:00 A.M. until 9:00 or 10:00 P.M. six days a week. One British scientist said he was glad he was divorced because his wife would never have accepted this lifestyle.

The Canadian researcher also had some difficulty at first because she felt a lot of pressure not to go home too early.

''I sit beside the section chief and he knows exactly what time I leave. I felt if I wanted to go home before eight o'clock I had to give some excuse. It really bugged me so I talked about it with the section chief and the department head. I said, 'If I've done my work and I'm tired, I'd like to go home around six o'clock and they said, 'Yes, of course, you *should* go home.' And I said, 'But I feel bad doing that because others stay so late.' And they said, 'No, no, it's good. You should go home at six o'clock.' ''

After the meeting she talked with some of her colleagues and they too encouraged her to leave at a reasonable hour. Her impression was that they too would like to go home early but can't because of peer pressure.

Although the usual work week is six days, Saturday is often very relaxed. ''We get the ping-pong tables out and have a good time,'' said an Irishman at a government lab. ''Not much work gets done, but they seem to feel they have to show up. I think that's changing though. I hope it's changing because they really don't seem to enjoy themselves generally. When you look deep down, I just can't believe they really enjoy their lives. They work all the hours God sends them, and the one day they have off they're dog-tired. Even at work they're always yawning and falling asleep at the bench, nodding off at their desks.''

OPINIONS ABOUT JAPANESE RESEARCH

As far as the science goes, most foreign scientists were very impressed and felt that the Japanese scientists are technically very good, very diligent, and conscientious. In a recent survey by the American Chamber of Commerce in Japan that questioned ninety-six American scientists who were working in Japanese labs, there was strong disagreement with the statement, "There is very little important research underway in my field in Japan." The survey also found that the longer respondents had been in Japan, the more likely they were to disagree.

The importance of Japanese research was confirmed when most respondents also agreed or strongly agreed with the statement, "It is essential for leading researchers in my field to keep abreast of Japanese scientific and technical information."

There was mild agreement with the statement that "Japanese research in my field involves incremental advances rather than major breakthroughs in knowledge."

However, a Canadian scientist said that in his experience 99 percent of Western scientists work in just the same way as the Japanese: they slowly pick away at some problem and make slight advances. The only difference he saw was that in the West, about 1 percent of the researchers are the truly brilliant ones who stimulate the rest, give them direction, and open new fields. In Japan he feels that this 1 percent is more like 0.01 percent because the educational system squeezes most creativity and innovative thinking out of people.

A researcher at IBM has pointed out that small advances on existing knowledge are nothing to scoff at. "Incremental improvement has given us better resolution screens and quieter and better quality printers each year. It has given us jet engines with double the thrust per unit weight . . . and light bulbs that are fifteen times more efficient than Edison's."

However, some foreigners find it difficult to cope with the reluctance of their Japanese colleagues to try new things. One American said, "If it's not been done before, they don't want to do it. I came up with a new idea for an experiment and they said, 'That's not been done before. Will it get results?' And I said, 'Hey, how can I know until I try?', and they looked real worried and didn't seem to want to waste time on it."

Many other foreign scientists observed that much of Japanese research is repeating other people's work with different systems.

"It's valuable work, but it won't push them into the forefront of biomedical research," said one biochemist. But he admitted that their method works very well in some fields like biotechnology where you can take research done somewhere else and apply it to fermentation or drug design. "They do very well building on what's been done before."

Some foreign researchers have complained that they have difficulty being taken seriously because they have no position in the established hierarchy of the lab. An Englishman in a private lab said, "Even though we're treated like hotshots in some ways, they still won't believe our results unless they can verify them. I was having some problems and thought that one of the counters might be calibrated wrong, but they insisted it was OK. They have absolute faith in machines. They only believed me after one of them ran into similar problems."

In the American Chamber of Commerce in Japan survey, only about one-third of the researchers reported any difficulty in carrying out their assignment. Two-thirds of the respondents said that their assignment was to carry out joint research. It was the only answer to the question, "What is the primary purpose of your visit?" given by 53 percent of the respondents. Teaching the Japanese was given as an answer by 28 percent (the only answer for 9 percent) and learning from the Japanese was the listed purpose of 22 percent (the only answer for 4 percent).

One of the main reasons for conducting the survey was to determine whether the presence of foreigners in Japanese laboratories was a net plus for the U.S. in terms of scientific information received versus that transmitted. When asked to respond to the statement, "I learned more from the Japanese than they learned from me," about half of the respondents neither agreed nor disagreed, indicating that the exchange of information was about the same in both directions. About 20 percent felt that the Japanese benefited more than they did and only 12 percent thought they had learned more than they taught.

Of the 22 percent who said "learning from the Japanese" was one of their objectives in coming to Japan, about half felt they received more information than they transmitted. In the group that strongly agreed that they had learned more from the Japanese than vice versa, all had stayed more than three months and two-thirds had at least some Japanese language ability. This supports the common sense conclusion that longer stays and greater language proficiency will result in the foreign scientist learning more from the Japanese.

The survey showed that most of the respondents were clearly in the role of a teacher since 96 percent said they presented seminars and the average number of seminars was 7.7 with an average attendance at these seminars of 300.

Most researchers found themselves exchanging not only scientific information, but also cultural and lifestyle information with their Japanese colleagues. "Most of them have never been out of Japan," said an English researcher. "They're not a very adventuresome bunch, but they are really curious about the West and very open to any Western ideas."

Some were also asked directly or indirectly to teach English to their colleagues. One American woman had noticed that people at work seemed to gravitate toward her whenever they had some time to kill in order to practice their English and ask her questions about her country. So she offered to teach an English class twice a week. Her ulterior motive was to create an opportunity to ask all the questions she had about Japanese culture and habits under the guise of teaching English.

She also finds that she is sometimes asked to look over English manuscripts and is happy to because it gives her a chance to peek into other projects going on at the institute.

In general, the foreign women reported better experiences in Japan than the men. This is often because most working Japanese men are married but the women are not. This means that the women have no family obligations and their Sundays and holidays are free. The foreign women scientists found that if they mentioned they were interested in kabuki, or shopping, or a trip to a shrine, one of the women in the lab would invariably say, "Let's go on Sunday."

The male scientists had different stories to report. Since their male colleagues generally spend Sunday with their families, and dating is serious business, they often found themselves at home watching videos or working in the lab on Sundays and holidays.

MOSTLY POSITIVE AND PRODUCTIVE

When asked to look over their time in Japan and predict its future value, most researchers felt that it would prove to be useful. Although there were a fair number of frustrations and irritations in the initial months, these tended to lessen as time went on. Many felt that, after you find out where the reagents are and get used to the system, it's really no different except that you are pampered and taken better care of in Japan than in your home country.

Most also felt that the experience would be beneficial because of the professional connections they were able to make. The American who had come so reluctantly said that his coming has certainly helped his boss politically and solidified the link between the two institutes. "And now I know that the work they do here is very good. But as far as productivity is concerned, I could have done it faster in the States. The unfamiliar surroundings slow you down."

The woman who had been working in Switzerland agreed that things would get done a lot faster there because everyone is more intense at work. "They just bend over the bench and work. You don't talk to anyone because you're too busy. You don't really have friends at work the way they seem to here. Here social life seems to be built into the work. I don't think one way is better than the other. It's a trade-off. I was more productive in Switzerland, but I was also tired by five o'clock. Here, if I want to stop and chat with someone they always have time. It's a lot more relaxed."

There are a host of Japanese government agencies initiating programs, many in conjunction with the U.S. National Science Foundation (NSF), to allow greater access to Japanese research.

In an effort to increase the number of U.S. investigators conducting research in Japan, the National Science Foundation began its "Japan Initiative Program" in 1988. The goals of the initiative are to increase the number of U.S. scientists and engineers who can operate in Japan's research community and follow developments in the Japanese literature, and to increase cooperative research with Japanese institutions, thus building relations between the U.S. and Japanese research communities. To accomplish these objectives, the NSF provides funds and fellowships and helps to secure opportunities for American researchers at Japanese laboratories.

Some private corporations are also seeking to close the information gap between Japan and the West. Fuji Xerox Company recently set up CIBER, Inc. to provide information on Japanese science, technology, business, and educational services to the U.S.

Fuji said they started the service because they recognized that although Japan "wanted to tell" and the U.S. "wanted to know" about Japanese science and technology, both sides were having trouble communicating effectively. Initially CIBER's services will consist of "The Japan Technology Series," a comprehensive English language bibliographic database on Japanese science and technology.

Japan's participation in international cooperative scientific ventures is growing as it realizes that it is good business and good politics for companies of different nationalities to enter into joint ventures. Since technology readily crosses national boundaries—through patent applications, licensing agreements, coproduction agreements, and so on, few companies or nations can hold a technological monopoly for very long. As nations realize that technology is one key to the world's stable economic and political future and that it is very difficult to have a monopoly on ideas and products, technological information will flow more freely around the world.

8. ARCHITECTURE

One of the nice things about Japan is that the cities are so unplanned—or they are so chaotically planned—that the little gems of architecture nestled in the general chaos sparkle through. When you stumble upon one, you feel like you've discovered buried treasure.

The young architect's voice grew more animated. "Have you ever seen the smallest house in Aoyama? It was built in the late sixties on a tiny triangular site. You might be able to park a Honda Civic along the longest side. It has three stories going up and one underground and there are no internal doors. It's totally modern but totally traditional in that sounds and smells go throughout the structure unhindered—like in any old Japanese house with paper *fusuma* (sliding doors) separating the rooms."

While the casual traveler or resident may never find this house—or any other structure of interest, let alone beauty—in the concrete jungles of urban Japan, the foreign architects do. This is just one of the reasons most of them find Japan a very stimulating environment in which to work. They say it is a good place to be not only because there are gems to be discovered, but also because Japan has gained prominence in certain areas of architectural design. In addition, Japan offers opportunity—to learn new styles and new techniques, to work on a wide variety of projects from dwellings to offices to overseas resort complexes, and to work with craftsmen who are devoted to their work and find joy in doing it. An additional consideration is that there is an enormous amount of construction going on in Japan and clients with plenty of money to finance it.

With all these reasons for foreign architects to work in Japan, it is somewhat surprising that there are only 100 or so in the country now. However, many of them predict a major increase during the 1990s. The increase will not be in the offices of the famous names like Isozaki or Tange or Ando, but in the offices of the big architecture and construction firms as well as in the small- and mid-size design companies.

The present paucity of architects in Japan belies a rather long tradition of Western design. In the mid-1800s Japanese government officials became enamored of the heavy, solid, German and British buildings which seemed like they would last forever, and invited a number of Western architects to Japan to design, among other things, the buildings of Tokyo University. In the early 1900s the Japanese courted Frank Lloyd Wright, who ended up coming to Tokyo to supervise the construction of his design for the Imperial Hotel. He was awarded the project because of his past accomplishments and because he had the right connections.

Even today, it often takes similar prerequisites for foreign architects to find work in Japan. In 1989 the well-known French architect Philippe Starck was asked to design a new beer hall for the giant Asahi Beer Corporation because of his relationship with the company's chairman and his prominence in the field.

Now, however, in addition to these high-profile cases, there are many Japanese firms ranging from design companies to construction companies to private offices, large and small, that are willing to hire foreign architects—even if they are not actively seeking them out. Some firms are hiring them for their specialized knowledge or experience in, say, office interiors, airport design, or facilities management. Many construction companies are hiring them to help with their overseas projects—both for their design input and simply to help with communication and planning. As with so many other jobs in Japan, the most important qualification may simply be having English as your mother tongue.

FINDING THE PERFECT MATCH

With ample reasons for foreigners to come and for Japanese firms to hire them, the next task would seem to be simply to find a good match—a firm that you feel comfortable and happy working for and that values your work. This is, however, not as simple as it may first appear. Fluency in Japanese is fast becoming a prerequisite to finding a rewarding job, and there is also the problem of revising your idea of "work" to fit the Japanese concept.

An American who can speak fluent Japanese said, "Unless you're only working on foreign commissions, you're hamstrung unless you speak and read Japanese. If you don't know any of the regulations and can't even read the plans, what good are you?" He feels that companies who hire non-Japanese-speaking foreigners are doing it mainly for window dressing. In a few years, when the novelty of having a foreigner with the firm wears off, he predicts that many Japanese firms will go back to having all Japanese staff or they may hire only foreigners who are fluent in Japanese.

The language advantage is clear in the case of an architect who first came to Japan on a one-year Ministry of Education scholarship and then went on to spend another three and a half years doing a Ph.D. at Tokyo University. He was fluent in Japanese by this time and ended up opening a firm with two Japanese partners. Soon, however, the partners left to continue their schooling and he found himself with his own business. Because of his language ability, the quality of his work, and his attitude toward work and toward working in another country, he has been extremely successful.

He contrasts the Japanese attitude with the typical attitude of Americans. "Americans look at a job as a tool to make the money to spend on things you like, as just a way to increase your bank account. This is not the attitude in Japan. Work is not a four-letter word here—not yet. Tolstoy said that you can feel your life is a success when you fulfill all the talent you believe you have, when you serve your community, and when your community recognizes and appreciates your service. This is pretty much what work means in Japan."

More concretely, this concept of work translates into very long working days and very few holidays.

CREATING AND DESTROYING

One reason for the non-stop work is the non-stop construction going on in Japan. Buildings have been going up at a furious pace since around the time of the Tokyo Olympics in 1964. No matter where you look—in the countryside, in the city, in the business or residential areas—there are buildings everywhere in various states of demolition and construction. The huge size of the construction industry is partly due to the Japanese tradition of not building structures to last more than a generation. Some say this tradition stems from the natural calamities that hit the Japanese islands with such regularity. What with typhoons, volcanoes, earthquakes, floods, and fires, it does not make sense to invest the time and money needed to try and make a building last 100 years or more. Others say the building up and tearing down are in part due to the Shinto religion which values the purity of new structures. The most important Shinto shrine at Ise, along with its surrounding buildings, is torn down every twenty years and replaced with an exact replica.

The architecture, construction, and design industries are closely linked in Japan. Unlike in the West, construction companies in Japan usually carry out both design and construction work. To integrate these two areas, large construction companies like Shimizu, Takenaka, and Kajima have their own design departments staffed by hundreds of architects. The *kensetsu gaisha* (construction companies) are involved in many "design and build" projects and their in-house design departments redraw architects' drawings into construction designs to be used on the site.

Many of the larger construction companies are hiring foreign engineers, designers, and architects to work in many capacities— from managing overseas projects to researching new projects to drafting designs to overseeing actual construction. Taisei Corporation, a major construction company, has perhaps the most ambitious plan. It is thinking about increasing the number of foreign employees from the current twenty-five to about one thousand (approximately 10 percent of its work force) by the year 2000. Company officials see this mass hiring of foreigners as a way to upgrade the firm's design division, increase overseas construction contracts, and reduce the potential for international friction as the company expands its overseas activities. They have already hired a personnel director fluent in six languages to begin the process.

In contrast to the *kensetsu gaisha*, the *sekkei jimusho* (design offices) are involved in the design phase only—from concept to finished drawings. In Japan there is a very close relationship between the client and the architect. Most foreign architects are pleasantly surprised to discover how cooperative and open-minded most clients are. An Australian said, "There is a feeling of mutuality. We both know we're in this together and we both want to make it succeed. So no one wants to make it rough on the other, no one wants to rock the boat. They are open to discussion, negotiation. We work together."

FINDING WORK

The quickest ticket to a job in architecture, as in most other fields in Japan, is a personal connection. If you can be introduced to someone working at a certain firm or if you know someone working there, your chances of being hired are greater. Job openings per se seldom exist, but most firms are on the lookout for new talent. A letter and follow-up phone call and interview sometimes work if you have a skill a firm needs or if it has been toying with the idea of hiring some foreigners.

One young architect came to Japan with only the most tenuous of connections and no language ability. After sending out resumes and going to interviews, he found that quite a few firms were interested in hiring him. Six weeks after arriving in Japan, he took a job in the design department of one of the nation's largest architectural firms.

Another man first worked for a large firm where his wife had done an internship, and then spent a summer apprenticing for a traditional plasterer to "learn more about the heart of Japan." He then researched and interviewed at a number of firms in Tokyo and joined a medium-sized company that had a philosophy he admired. He explained that, "They espouse 'creative humanism' and want to blend techniques and materials from around the world. Often they will use traditional Chinese building techniques with Japanese plaster work and European designs. We don't design office buildings or get involved in development projects, but do private residences, nursery schools, and community centers—both high and low budget."

Some firms emphasize the portfolio and are interested in what you've done before and what you can offer the company. But by and large, attitude counts more than any talent or connections you may have. A foreign architect who runs his own office observed that, "Some *gaijin* can operate in the Japanese environment and others can't—generally because they are too aggressive. You need sensitivity—you have to show your emotions, show you're human—to be able to work well with your colleagues and with the client."

After working for about five years in a small two-man office in New Zealand, one architect found work in a large Japanese architecture and construction company. Large firms like his often get government-funded work for overseas development projects. Japan is now the world leader in overseas development assistance and so the amount of this sort of work will undoubtedly continue to increase as Japan turns plans into reality in various underdeveloped countries around the world.

A few foreigners have complained of the impersonal nature of the largest firms. After working with one for a year, an American said he'd run a mile from "team architecture and design." He said that good work comes from a single mind with a particular vision and that team work tends to dilute strong ideas so that in the end every design is only lukewarm.

This is a very Western attitude and one that does not go down well at the smaller firms, which are generally very close-knit. Most small firms are run like family businesses and there are close personal relationships that involve both genuine respect and raw emotion.

The American who decided to work for the creative humanists found that he had signed up for a lot of teamwork. It began at about 9 A.M. and went on until about 9 P.M. six days a week. After the twelve-hour day, the eight people in his office, which was in a medium-sized apartment, would *janken* (the Japanese "paper, scissors, rock") to see who would cook supper that evening, who would clean up, and who would make and serve the tea. Only after the communal meal would they say good night and go to their respective homes. The togetherness at this firm even extended to vacations when all eight went off to Burma and Thailand for their communal holiday.

A number of other firms have found that their cohesiveness tends to break down when they hire foreigners. The problems usually stem from the differing attitudes toward work. Too often the foreign staff will want to pack up and go home at six o'clock and this makes the Japanese feel that he or she is being cheated because the foreigner makes the same amount of money but puts in less time, emotion, and physical and psychic energy.

The foreigner retorts that he's just more efficient and that efficiency shouldn't be penalized, and goes on his merry way. While it may well be true that the Japanese employee consumes more hours to get to the same point as the foreigner, that is not really the point. The point is that he is not showing solidarity with the Japanese staff and not willing to change his work habits to fit those of the people in his new environment. This kind of intransigence invariably leads to bad feelings, and often to an aborted stay in Japan.

ON YOUR OWN

A few foreigners have struck out on their own. A Scottish woman who had worked in England found the idea of setting up her own firm with a partner more attractive than working for someone else. After attending a Japanese university, she joined forces with a Japanese architect and they opened their own firm.

"Here I can work on my own as an individual. In England you have to work in a big office or in a partnership. And even then, it's usually only part-time. You have to support yourself by teaching or doing something else. And the work tends to be routine and boring—kitchen renovations and big office buildings. Here I do all sorts of work, from family dwellings to skyscrapers.''

While she feels that modern Japanese architecture is by and large nothing to write home about, she says that there are interesting things being built. In general, she finds it easier to convince Japanese people to try something different.

"The U.K. is so conservative that people can be hostile to new ideas. But people here are willing to accept a crazy building, willing to accept new ideas. There is a limited amount of Western architecture and few Western architects in Japan. So, as a foreign architect, I represent the whole Western tradition to them. This may be part of the reason the Japanese are very open-minded about my suggestions.''

A Hungarian who has run his own office for about eight years said the first few years were very tough, but that things have gotten better each year. He agrees that the openness of the clients, and the latitude they allow and even encourage the architect to take, are part of what have kept him happy. But the heart of the matter, he said, is simply, ''I like the people I work with and I like the work I do.''

Different architects identify different positive aspects of working in Japan. One Australian asserted that ''you have more artistic freedom, you're not confined to a classical language in architecture, so there is more dynamism here.'' An English architect said he liked Japan because, ''there isn't such a stifling old-boy network. Just by being a foreigner, you're in demand. You're a weird customer. You have a different perception and people want that input.''

A number of foreigners mentioned the high quality of work that Japanese contractors do. One said he loved ''working with craftsmen who still devote themselves, pour themselves, their strength and emotion, into their work. They work long hours not for overtime but to solve a problem, to do something right. It's a joy, an inspiration, to work with them.''

Most also mentioned the positive aspects of working with Japanese clients. The Hungarian said, ''If you play it honestly, this business is more honest here than anywhere in the world. Japanese clients are better than any others.''

On the negative side, the main complaint from the foreign architects was simply the long hours. A few also complained of low pay and others complained of not being able to function as ''insiders.''

Those who were happiest with their situations were generally those who were able to accept the Japanese work environment as different and not in need of reform. While Europeans tend to be more easygoing and understanding of cultural differences, many Americans seem to feel that there is one right path in any given circumstance and that the Japanese are generally not following it. They also get in trouble at times for promoting themselves—something the Japanese find very distasteful.

One long-time resident architect said, "It is important to be flexible and open-minded and do the appropriate thing for a given case. Of course as a foreigner you have a different education and a different way of looking at things and analyzing them. But in the end, if you're doing work in Japan, then you've got to realize that you're doing Japanese architecture—making something that will fit into the Japanese environment."

9. ADVERTISING

Americans sing about it, the British tell a joke, the French sell it with sex, and the Japanese—well, they do something unexpected.

International adman extraordinaire

The "something unexpected" has resulted in a new game for illiterate foreigners in Japan. It's called "Guess what the ad is for" and it's not as easy as you would think. If you see an ad with a good-looking man tipping up the chin of a beautiful girl to kiss her as Cupid aims his arrow in the corner, you might reasonably suppose it's an ad for a wedding hall or a dating service.

But if you've been in Japan long you'd know that it's an ad for an English school. You'd also know that that isn't far from a dating service in some cases.

Other ads are even trickier. Picture these: a leggy lady, shot from behind, walking down the street in a very tight, very mini skirt; a fashion plate photo of a coolly beautiful Western model wearing *haute couture*; a human hand holding a card out to a robot hand that is clenching a metallic fist full of wrenches, drills, and other tools.

Now which is the ad for a new model car? a steel company? an electronics company?

That's right. That's the order.

Not only is advertising in Japan creative to the point of obtuseness, it is also a booming industry that has risen to prominence in tandem with the meteoric rise in Japan's production and domestic consumption of consumer durables. In an attempt to compete more effectively for a larger share of the expanding

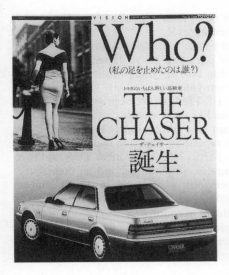

A typically eye-catching ad—one version showed only the model and copy, rendering the message cryptic for illiterate foreigners. Photo courtesy of Toyota.

domestic market, corporations have been increasing their expenditures on advertising. This means ad agencies in Japan are enjoying massive billings—so much so that the problem is not so much getting the account as getting the space in the advertising media.

In 1988, spending increases were across the board, covering every industry and every media. Japanese government policies designed to promote domestic consumption led to a 12 percent boost in gross advertising expenditures in 1988, leading to an astounding total of 4,417 billion yen or 35.2 billion U.S. dollars. Such a lucrative market is prompting many foreign advertising firms to link up with Japanese firms and inducing many foreigners to try and get a piece of the action in this expanding market.

GETTING INTO THE BUSINESS

As in many other job areas, it isn't as easy as it used to be for foreigners to get in and haul in the big money. The days when a university degree and an ability to speak English could get you into a top ten agency are pretty much gone. But if you want to give it a try, follow these "Do's and Don'ts" culled from those who are or have been there themselves.

Do use any connections you or your friends may have to help get you through the doors once you get to Japan. Connections are the surest way of getting into anything in this country. But don't expect too much from your connections. Chances are no one will greet you with, "Hi, Fred, we've been waiting for you. Now, how much would you like each month. . . ." The best way to use connections in Japan is to obsequiously seek their advice and direction. This is an especially effective tactic if you have some Japanese contacts—particularly older men. They will love playing mentor to your novice, so go ahead and let them.

Do emphasize any previous experience in the business. Remember, Uncle Bob's hardware store you wrote copy for back home is an international account here.

Do read the Monday classified section of *The Japan Times*. You will find many smaller agencies advertising for copywriters, account people for foreign accounts, and, less frequently, creative people.

Do learn some Japanese—at least how to introduce yourself and greet someone respectfully. For any position at any company, some Japanese is better than none. As more and more foreigners are becoming fluent in Japanese, the trend is to hire only those who are competent in Japanese, but . . .

Don't be too daunted by all the ads saying candidates must be bilingual—a surprising number of companies will put that in even though it may not be absolutely essential. You can make up for your lack of language ability by being respectable-looking, polite, and serious about doing your best for the company for at least a couple of years. A related point for your resume . . .

Don't ever have worked for less than a year at any job. While Japanese expect foreigners to change jobs and be feckless, less than a year at a job implies one of two equally bad problems: you can't *gambaru* (try your best) for that long, or you couldn't get along with your co-workers or superiors. Either of these is a major personality defect in Japan and will seriously affect your chances of being hired.

Don't go to interviews looking flash in your GQ gear thinking to dazzle the agency people with your creative, fashionable flair and dress sense. You'll probably bring out all their insecurities as they sit facing you in blue suits and red ties, or, if they are really avant garde, one of those cute old yellow ties with black dots.

Do forget everything you've heard about the fabulous salaries they pay in Japan. You may luck out, but most probably you'll start working like the Japanese do—ten- to twelve-hour days six or seven days a week. Even if you are offered a decent salary in comparison to back home, a few forays into the local supermarket or department stores will bring new meaning to those graphs showing that Tokyo is the most expensive city on the planet. Nevertheless . . .

Do take any reasonable job you get offered. As mentioned above, the way into the business and the way to move up in the business is through contacts, and the way to make contacts is by starting to work in the field. Also, you need to build up your "Japan experience." No matter how good you were at your last job in the real world, this is the important thing in Japan, so . . .

Do be prepared to commit yourself to working in Japan for at least three years. One or two years will probably not be enough to get you into the higher pay brackets. You may luck out and get a plum job straight away, but more probably the breaks will come only after a lot of hard work under lousy conditions.

Do join the FCC (Forum for Corporate Communications), ACCJ (the American Chamber of Commerce in Japan), ABA (the Australian Business Association), SWET (Society for Writers, Editors, and Translators), KAISHA (for foreign employees of Japanese companies), FEW (Foreign Executive Women) and other professional and social organizations (see appendix). Do this as soon as you come to Japan—the sooner you start meeting people and letting them know what sort of work you're looking for, the better. Attend meetings even if you are just teaching English while waiting for The Big Break to come.

THE WONDERFUL WACKY WORLD OF JAPANESE ADVERTISING

A long-time resident of Tokyo who has worked in advertising for a number of companies, including a major Japanese newspaper, commented that there are five taboo subjects in the Japanese press: 1) Korean-Japanese, 2) *Burakumin* (Japanese outcasts), 3) the emperor in any role but that of national grand-father, 4) the *yakuza*'s (Japanese mafia's) political connections, and 5) Dentsu.

Dentsu is Japan's largest advertising agency and makes the list of taboo subjects not because it is, like the others, a nasty little secret that no one wants brought to light, but because Dentsu has the sort of power that can break publications that probe its operations too closely.

Dentsu handles about one-fourth of all advertising budgets in Japan, including 60 percent of the prime time advertising for Tokyo Broadcasting System, Japan's largest commercial radio/ TV station. In addition, all of the media are riddled with Dentsu alumni who can see to it that news favorable to Dentsu clients is played up while unfavorable news is played down, or, more often, not played at all. Long-term foreign residents of Japan have noticed that it is very unusual to find an article in the newspaper or a program on television that is highly critical of a major advertiser. There is an antitrust law in Japan, and were Japan like any other country, it would have been invoked against Dentsu long ago. That no one has even tried is an indication of just how powerful Dentsu is.

In 1988, for the sixteenth consecutive year, Dentsu topped the list of advertising companies in volume, with an increase of 39.5 percent in billings over 1987. It also ranked number one in profits for the third consecutive year, up 38.9 percent from the previous year. Part of these profits are spent on 500-million-yen New Year's parties for up to 10,000 influential guests.

Because it is so big and so powerful, Dentsu is even able to handle competing accounts. It has no problem dealing with the advertising campaigns of all of the major car manufacturers, beer breweries, and electronics giants. To deal with this volume of business, Dentsu employed 852 copywriters, art directors, commercial planners, and creative directors, plus 164 creative administrative staff in 1986.

The monolithic Dentsu does hire foreigners, but it is not easy to get in. Almost all of their foreign staff are recruited from overseas. A woman with experience on Madison Avenue answered one of Dentsu's ads in a trade journal and was asked to come to an interview. The overseas division was looking for a copywriter who was about thirty years old with three to four years' experience. The interviewers took a few minutes to glance through her portfolio and then spent an hour and a half talking to her.

When she was chosen for the position, and before she actually began the job, she was under the impression that she had been hired for her experience and to help the Japanese staff learn how to do good Western-style advertising. But at her first client meeting she discovered her mistake. The client told her that the copy she had written was "not correct English." She began explaining that it was, and that it was just right for the ad. During her explanation she heard scraping noises from her colleagues' chairs as they pushed them back. Then she heard whispers of, *Gomen nasai, gomen nasai* ("We're terribly sorry"). Only some weeks later did she understand that her colleagues were apologizing to the client for her behavior, and that her duties in the company were mainly to help Dentsu do what Dentsu has always been doing, and not to rock the boat.

Whiz kids who are hot in advertising in the West are picked up by Dentsu and given enormous salaries, but they soon discover that being a big gun elsewhere doesn't mean you'll be a big gun in Japan. Another American said he felt his job description should have said "warm seats while imparting a sense of Dentsu being a big-time international agency." He pointed out that a quick look at any of the top ads that Dentsu produces shows that the creative director, copywriters, art director, director, and producer are all Japanese.

According to an Australian with five years of advertising experience in Japan, "Big guns get paid a lot and have no real power. Small local guns get paid much less, are expected to work like the Japanese, and also have no real power. All power stays with the Japanese."

Hakuhodo, Japan's second largest agency, has power similar to Dentsu's. Dentsu and Hakuhodo dominate the Japanese advertising industry because they are the two with the most clout with the media where advertising is placed. This means they can extort cheaper prices from the media for their clients.

Below the Big Two are the Other Eight. These ten virtually dominate all business done for Japan's leading industrial and service advertisers. Like the two big guys, most of the Other Eight are *sarariman* shops (blue-suited businessman-types sitting at their desks working steadily on routine tasks) rather than what Westerners understand as advertising agencies (swarms of hip, hot egotists clambering up the ladder of success past the corpses of burned-out fellows).

Surprisingly enough, there is life beyond the Top Ten. These agencies range in size from one man and an office lady to twenty or so people. They handle all the minor work for newspaper inserts, brochures, and manuals. Many of them have connections—direct or indirect—with the major agencies, which farm off work during peak periods. Some have small smoky offices, and others work out of small, smoky apartments; everyone works overtime, and foreigners are expected to as well.

Exhaustion may be part of the reason for the amusing copy to be found in Japan—particularly in English. One wonders just how much sleep deprivation it takes to produce gems like "My Life, My Gas" for Tokyo Gas and "Heats Up, Cools Down, Control Yourself" for an electric heater.

Copy like that does just fine in Japan, where it's a matter of mood over meaning, but for products to be sold in the West, appropriate copy in the target language is necessary.

WRITING COPY

Copywriting is considered a glamorous job in Japan, but most foreigners doing it find the glamour wears off very quickly. Agencies use foreigners mostly for writing copy for goods destined for overseas markets—North America, Europe, Africa, and Asia. A lot of the work is actually rewriting of Japanese translations of warnings and instructions. Creativity is actively discouraged in this kind of work, and you are expected to keep as close to the original Japanese as possible. This requirement sometimes leads to those nonsensical bits and pieces of English you see on goods in Japan: "Dish of Quickie," "I feel Coke," "For Your Joyful Life."

Foreign copywriters report a variety of experiences, but one constant is the client-ad agency relationship in which the client is God. While in the West the client and the agent have a reciprocal relationship with equal input coming from both and much back-

and-forth discussion, in Japan you do what the client wants you to do, whether you think it is a good idea or not, and whether it will be an effective ad or not. This master-servant relationship goes so far that the agent opens doors and carries bags for the client.

One American woman working in a Japanese agency asked her Japanese colleague if he wouldn't rather have a more equal relationship—actually advise the client and work together as partners, and certainly not have to carry his bag. He said no, he wouldn't want that kind of relationship, because if he suggested an idea that failed he would be held responsible.

While this relationship is basically the same no matter where you work in advertising in Japan, other aspects of the work situation vary widely. One man complained that the pressure to perform was very high and that he was bent over his desk in a "produce or die" sort of atmosphere for eight to ten hours a day. Others thrive in the frenetic, chaotic environment. An Australian with some experience back home found work with a small Japanese agency and loved it because the Japanese were far more productive and demanding. "They can do a lot in a short period of time. It made me realize how much time we waste in Australia."

Some wilt in the large companies, preferring a smaller, more human scale. A man recruited from a top American company by a large Japanese agency ended up leaving for a smaller agency because he felt like he was working in a factory. Unlike his U.S. office, which was comfortable and fairly plush with flashy ads covering the walls, the large Japanese company's office was all gray—gray lockers in gray halls, gray cubicles with steel desks painted gray.

It not only looked like a factory, he said, it was also run like one. He and all of his colleagues were required to sign in by 9:30 A.M. every morning. After 9:30 the sign-in paper disappeared and the naughty employee would have to fill out a slip explaining why he was late.

The attitude toward the work was also very different from what he was used to. The excitement and real joy of creativity were nonexistent. The copywriters and the creative staff all had the same production line mentality of "just get it done."

Many copywriters agree that copy cannot be translated and that a copywriter can only write good copy for his or her native land. A medium-sized Japanese agency brought over foreign copywriters and designers for domestic ads and ended up with conflict after conflict. In one case, the Japanese creative staff had put together an ad for a $40,000 piece of computer hardware with cute bunnies hopping all around it. They brought it to the foreign staff for their input and the foreigners said, "You must be joking. Get the bunnies out of there." The Japanese were equally shocked and said, "No, the bunnies are critical. They soften the ad." A long argument followed, the Japanese won out, and the ad went on to win an award—bunnies and all.

It has often been said that Japan is much more a visual than a verbal society. At first foreigners are surprised at the endless meetings where the client looks at the layout before he even looks at the copy, which tends to be vague with very little information content. Later they come to see that information is not so important, because Japan is, by and large, a homogeneous society. What evokes a good feeling in Tanaka will evoke a similar good feeling in Suzuki. This contrasts with the U.S. where ads are competitive and information-oriented. Because the U.S. is a melting pot, Americans have to talk with each other and they have to be explicit. Japanese ads, more than most, sell a feeling, not a product. Feelings are very tightly bound to the culture and what prompts X feeling in Japan may provoke quite another in a different country and vice versa.

THE BOTTOM LINE

It is hard to generalize about what kind of money to expect in any job area in Japan because there are so many variables: your experience, your personality, the company's financial situation and attitude toward foreigners, etc. Nevertheless, here is a rough guide to remuneration in the ad business in Japan:

¥3–4 million: If you get a job in a smaller agency, you'll probably start in this range. Your Japanese is poor to nonexistent, but you have a university degree and can write a decent phrase in English. U.S. $30–35,000 a year sounds fantastic, right? Wrong. In Tokyo, you'll live in a miserable little room miles from where you work and eat poor quality food. You may have to supplement your income with English teaching.

¥4.5–6.5 million: You can start in this range if you have some fairly decent previous experience and you find an agency that happens to want you at that time. You could pull in this kind of job with no Japanese ability, but a little will help.

¥7–9 million: You lucked out. This is good pay if you can get it. To earn this sort of money, your Japanese is OK to good, you have an interesting portfolio, and have been working in Japan for some time. You probably found this job via contacts because work like this isn't often advertised.

¥10 million and above: You were recruited from overseas or you've been working the traps in Tokyo for some time. You may be so good, or, more probably, so well recognized at what you do, that you don't even need Japanese at this level. You definitely have contacts in Tokyo—or you lied brilliantly on your resume and therefore fully deserve this job. The upper limits in salary are in the ¥30 million range with all expatriate benefits.

For some, a hefty salary will offset the frustrations of the ad scene in Japan. But for quite a few others this is not enough. One hot young American was paid handsomely to come work in Japan, but only lasted a year because he soon realized his career was on hold for as long as he stayed. Because he had to follow whatever his Japanese superiors told him to do, he knew he wouldn't be able to be involved in producing one ad that he would feel comfortable putting in his portfolio. And he felt that a one-year or longer gap in his portfolio would be deadly to his career, so he jumped ship and headed home.

One woman quit after four years in a plum job, partly because her colleagues gave her so little feedback and support. "Not once," she complained, "did anyone ever come over and say, 'Nice job.' "

AD INDUSTRY-RELATED JOBS

Research—You'll need fairly good Japanese unless you want to spend the rest of your life as an English-language report writer. Research jobs can be a good way to start in the ad business and a good way to meet people. Some special knowledge of an arcane research field may help. It would be best to send speculative resumes to the agencies and see if there are any bites before wasting a lot of time visiting them.

Art Directors—You really need to be good and recognized as such to get in the door. Sell your experience at home for all it's worth because you won't be doing any domestic work here. In Japan, domestic work is high status, international work is low status (although more interesting in many ways).

Media Buyers/Account Execs/Marketing Staff—Stay at home if you expect to find this kind of job right away. You will need lots of experience and knowledge of how the market works in Japan (it doesn't work in any way you would easily understand, according to veterans). If you're willing to spend a few years doing low-level jobs to build up your knowledge, experience, contacts, and Japanese, then go ahead. Remember, fluent Japanese is a must in this area.

Public Relations—PR activities are playing an increasingly important role in helping foreign companies skirt around the many cultural booby traps of the Japanese market. One common mistake in the past was to simply translate corporate brochures and other documents into Japanese. The message a Japanese receives from a direct translation is usually very different from what was originally intended and PR companies help restructure messages conceived in one language so that they communicate effectively in another.

Because of the many Japanese companies that are investing abroad and the continuing trade friction between Japan and other countries, the Japanese are also starting to appreciate what PR firms can do for them. Japanese companies, large and small, are now attempting to improve their corporate image by publishing PR periodicals, mostly English-language monthlies or quarterlies, for free delivery to their overseas dealers, clients, and workers at affiliated firms.

FOREIGN AGENCIES AND JOINT VENTURES

The Japanese advertising industry is not heavily legislated or restricted and looks, on paper, remarkably open to foreign participation. However, foreign firms who have come here say it is a cutthroat industry and Dentsu and Hakuhodo have a choke hold on most of it.

The only international agencies to have made it in Japan are those that have been willing to invest a large amount of money over a long period of time.

McCann-Erickson Hakuhodo Inc. was ninth in overall billings in 1987. J. Walter Thompson Co. Japan ranked sixteenth and HDM-DYR, a multinational combining the joint ventures of Havas-Dentsu Marsteller and Dentsu-Young and Rubicam, was listed seventeenth.

Initially most of these companies came to Japan because they wanted to offer international, Western clients in Japan the same type of full service they were used to getting back home. But as the domestic market has expanded and it is the Japanese companies who have money to burn, the foreign-based agencies are devoting more of their energy to Japanese clients and are trying to sell themselves as full-service agencies—not just the media-space buyers that many Japanese agencies are.

Some of the foreign forays into Japanese territory have succeeded while others have failed. Leo Burnett Kyodo doubled its billings in 1987 and added forty people. Although most of its clients are foreign companies, it expects to add more Japanese business. In contrast, Ogilvy & Mather Worldwide pulled out of Japan after four frustrating years of trying to crack the market. The dilemma facing foreign agencies is that the market is growing so rapidly that it can no longer be ignored, while the obstacles to doing business in Japan remain formidable. Foreign agencies often do not have the financial resources or the patience to stick with it long enough to succeed.

Working in a joint venture is usually an education in cross-cultural relations and international diplomacy. One woman who was born and spent the first twelve years of her life in Japan, and spent the next ten years in the U.S., found that she constantly had to serve as a mediator.

"The foreign managerial staff was obsessed with turning a profit every quarter and couldn't care less about the long-term consequences of any decision because they would be back home by then," she said. The Japanese staff, however, tended to always take the long view and wanted to court clients and maintain relationships even if there was no payoff in sight.

While the offices of these joint efforts tend to look more like

Western ad agencies, with nice office furniture and decor, they are often forced to adopt Japanese work habits to keep up with their Japanese competition. This means long hours, few holidays, and after-hours spent entertaining clients.

In a market where the top ten agencies account for 55 percent of the total market, you have a good chance of failing, so the savvy foreigner looking for a long-term position in Japanese advertising should look to the bigger firms with good track records.

10. PHOTOGRAPHY AND MODELING

■ PHOTOGRAPHY

There is not nearly as much pressure here as I used to feel as a fashion photographer in New York. You can relax and do a better job when no one is threatening to pull the rug out from under you if you screw up once.

English photographer

This is just one of the positive aspects of working as a photographer in Japan. There are many kinds of jobs available, some of which are very well-paid. If a picture is worth a thousand words in the West, a photo can be worth ten thousand yen—or much, much more—in Japan. Of particular worth (from the yen point of view) is fodder for the sensational photo-journals like *Friday* or *Focus*. These magazines wallow in the horrible, the illicit, and the bizarre—children stricken by disfiguring diseases, peeps into bedrooms, or scenes of bloodshed and cruelty.

Luckily, there is a wide range of options for photographers without these sorts of predilections. As Japan and the Pacific rim are more and more in the news worldwide, foreign magazines and newspapers are constantly in need of both news and feature photos of Japan. There is also a burgeoning need for non-news editorial and advertising photographs to meet the needs of business. These needs run from photos for PR material, advertisements, and brochures to annual reports. In addition, there are opportunities for photographers who want to specialize in a certain area such as fashion or portrait photography. Although it is not easy to find, there is very lucrative work available in these fields through agencies contracted by Dentsu or Hakuhodo.

135

All this adds up to a multitude of possibilities for photographers of just about any stripe. But lots of opportunity does not mean clear sailing from the moment you step off the plane. There are the usual impediments to starting a job in a foreign land—money, language, and a different way of doing business. And in Japan each of these is amplified.

In addition, the foreign photographer has to be a little creative in getting a visa. The easiest solution is to work on a spouse visa. But single people must find a sponsor—either a language school, a wire service, a newspaper or magazine, or a corporate client that you are doing a fair bit of work for.

When you first come to Japan, it is easiest to get sponsored through an English school. The problem is that you will have to guarantee the school a certain number of teaching hours in exchange. The immigration officials say that you must be working at least twelve hours a week to qualify for a working visa. However, some companies will give the teacher only four or five hours a week and still supply a visa.

The other option is to get a wire service or corporate client to be your sponsor in return for a certain amount of work. It will take a little longer to get this sort of sponsor unless you come to Japan with a lot of experience and a good portfolio.

MONEY MATTERS

After solving the visa problem, the next obstacle is money. It would be an insurmountable obstacle for most, were it not for the saving grace of Japan's need for English teachers. Depending on how much of a cash cushion you come with, you may have to spend six months or so supporting yourself by teaching English until you make the connections that will enable you to support yourself through your photos. Often, the first connections will come through your students and the companies they work for.

One photographer came to Japan after finishing her university degree because her husband had been transferred to Tokyo. Making the first contacts was difficult, she said—particularly because she was living out of the center of Tokyo. "No one would take me seriously. So I just set up a darkroom and buried myself there. I also took up *ikebana* (flower arrangement) and *yakimono* (pottery) to try and get some Japanese cultural input.''

When she moved to Tokyo, things picked up. ''I took whatever came my way—a lot of advertising photos—just quick cheap things for local shops—but as more and more people got to know me and my portfolio grew, I could pick and choose the more interesting, more lucrative jobs.''

She also found that one of the easiest ways to make contacts at first was through the foreign reporters and photographers at the Foreign Correspondents' Club. Other photographers join professional organizations such as the Forum for Corporate Communications or the Society of Writers, Editors, and Translators to make contact with writers and editors who may need photos for their stories.

But finding work does not necessarily signal the end of money problems. While most professional photographers in the U.S. and a number of other countries work under the standards of the American Society of Magazine Photographers, these standards are not recognized in Japan. The standards call for certain levels of payment, certain advances, and certain rights to the photos taken.

But in Japan all these items are negotiable and usually the client ''gets much more for much less money,'' according to a long time resident photographer. In most cases, he said, ''you have to fight tooth and nail to get an advance, and then your pay is minimal and the client wants all rights to all the photos you take.'' Since most photographers sell spare photos to stock companies (photo libraries), this last item can really hurt the pocketbook.

However, photographers who come to Japan with a long-term view and stick it out for a year or two usually manage to weed out the lower-paying jobs and piece together a base of clients who pay reasonable rates. The advice from one photographer who has been working in Japan for five years and recently set up her own business is to ''do all the jobs uncomplainingly and as well as you can and then, when you feel the relationship has progressed to a point of mutual respect and trust, begin to subtly hint that things are done differently in your home country.'' She found that the clients who valued her work took the hint and contract conditions improved. The intransigent few, she dropped.

THE DEVIL'S TONGUE—AGAIN

The second obstacle for most people is the Japanese language. Unless you work exclusively for foreign clients, you will need to have at least a working knowledge of the basics in Japanese. Most veteran foreign photographers recommend taking an intensive Japanese course before or just after coming to Japan. Those that started working with some knowledge of Japanese said they were glad they had it under their belt and those that didn't said they wish they had.

If you have no Japanese ability, you will need to prevail upon a bilingual friend to help you make your contacts and appointments, negotiate the pay, and communicate with the people on the set. Most photographers, however, soon realize that time invested in language study will soon more than make up for time wasted dealing through a translator. Also, although they don't show it openly, the Japanese tend to have little patience or respect for foreigners who are living and trying to work in Japan but who do not make the effort to learn the language.

An American photographer who has been working in Tokyo ten months a year during the past four years has built up a clientele of both editorial and corporate clients. She feels that a good deal of her success with corporate clients is thanks to the Japanese that she learned when she answered an ad for part-time work in her first days in Japan.

The ad promised good pay and said that no Japanese language ability or special experience were required. She thought this sounded like the job for her, so she went along for the training sessions and discovered the idea was that they would train her in the speech and manners necessary to get into the doors of companies, past the secretaries, and into the president's office. There she would turn on the charm and give a sales pitch in the most elegant, most polite Japanese imaginable.

Although she quit before actually doing any work, she did learn very polite ways of saying things and has found that it always tickles the vanity of her clients to be spoken to in such deferential phrases.

She had been a news photographer in the U.S., but was disappointed with that side of the business in Japan. "There is so little impromptu news here. The stories are all business stories, so you end up taking photos of the Tokyo Stock Exchange or the Bank of Tokyo or politicians or bureaucrats."

Because she found that aspect of the trade unsatisfying, she turned to more work with corporations and soon developed a reputation as someone who could make people look natural and at ease in a set-up, contrived situation. When she is assigned to take photos of a president or chairman of the board, the publicity people "count on me to get them in a good mood so they look good in the photo." Her polite Japanese, as well as her personality, seem to always do the trick.

Another American photographer also became bored with news photography in Japan after three years as a staff photographer for a wire service. But instead of going the corporate photography route, he decided to see if he could make a living from his long-time love—travel photography. His Japanese is very good and when he brought his portfolio around to Japanese magazines and book publishers he had little trouble finding takers. He attributes this to a combination of luck, personality, the quality of his work, and the fact that he plans to live in Japan for the long-term. He generally divides his time between assignments in Japan and throughout Asia for various Japanese publications. The pay can be very good, depending on his sponsor, but it is not regular and he must often deal with a feast or famine kind of existence.

Photographers are not immune to the cross-cultural misunderstandings that plague most other fields. One photographer got a job to shoot photos of a board of directors for their annual report. With the client, she worked out exactly when and where and how to do the photographs. Then she notified the company that she would be arriving two and a half hours early to set up the shoot.

They said fine, but when she arrived, she found all the doors locked and the security men told her there was a stockholders' meeting and no one was allowed inside. She protested, but they said it was *chotto muri* (literally, "a little impossible"—the Japanese way of saying absolutely impossible).

So she sat down with her crew and equipment and fumed and

made phone calls to her contact people at the company for nearly two hours. Finally she reached someone who could help and he rushed to let her in with deepest apologies. She raced around to set up the shot and, miraculously, had everything in order by the time all the bigwigs came in for the photograph. She arranged them as she and the client had decided and made all the preliminary polaroid shots. When she was about to start the real shots, the company's PR person walked in and said, "No, no, no, this is all wrong."

At this point, the photographer said, any American would have stalked out with a few choice epithets. In fact, she said, had it happened a few years earlier, when she was greener to the ways of the Japanese, she would have. But she knew that temper tantrums don't do any good here so she just laughed and sat down and let him set it up.

ADVICE TO BEGINNERS

While a sense of humor generally helps you out no matter where you are or what you're doing, it is almost a prerequisite to working in Japan. In addition, as you start to get work from Japanese clients, it is important to remember how important relationships are here. In fact, a relationship can be more important than the actual quality of work. Once a relationship is established, it takes a major screwup on the part of the photographer, or a major change in management, to change it.

An English photographer was able to get started in fashion photography when a big-name designer wanted an image change and asked her to shoot their fall catalog. Once she was "in," she was asked to do the spring catalog and then next fall's and so on, indefinitely into the future. Even once when she made a basic mistake and ruined an afternoon's shooting, the relationship held. She apologized; they redid the session, and continued to use her. As many other foreigners have noted, a business relationship in Japan is more like a family relationship in the West—you forgive and forget and keep the relationship through thick and thin. Depending on how you feel about family relationships, this can be a pleasant or difficult situation. Some complain that it is unprofessional while others find it makes life easier and jobs more enjoyable.

Being a foreign photographer has its pros and cons. As a foreigner, you are noticed and there is initial interest in your work because it is a foreigner's work. At first, this can open doors, but ultimately, many foreign photographers find that they are kept forever in the *genkan*, the entryway to the house.

For all the opportunities and experiences open to foreign photographers in Japan, this is probably the major frustration.

One man said, "You are really the isolated artist and that can be good and bad. It keeps you working concentratedly, but you can reach dead ends when there's no one else to provide input."

Another photographer complained of the lack of information. "If I have questions about paper or chemicals, I can't just run to the library and research it."

Putting all these pros and cons together, most photographers end up recommending that only those foreigners with a real desire to be in Japan come here to work. Without that desire, the petty annoyances soon reach critical mass and explosions of various kinds can occur.

Some recommend coming, getting a fat portfolio, and then going home. But others say you have to be willing to make a long-term commitment to really make it in Japan. One photographer says, "Clients will always ask, 'How long will you stay in Japan?' If you say only a year or two they aren't really interested."

The common sense answer is to stay as long as you feel happy and productive. With a desire to be in Japan, plus preparation and perseverance, most problems can be dealt with.

■ MODELING

Naff means uncool. For a model, naff is being successful in Japan.

This definition, provided by an English friend, reveals two prevailing attitudes held by many of the foreigners in Japan who are not in the modelling business: first, that any amateur can be a model in the land known for its white-hot worship of Caucasians, and second, an ill-disguised resentment of the huge sums which reward the felicitous arrangement of genetic material that produces long-limbed, fair-skinned beauties.

It is true that Western faces can be seen in print and television ads all over Japan. Many are not models, but internationally prominent sports, rock, and film stars. Sylvester Stallone urges you to eat Ito sausages, lovebirds John McEnroe and Tatum O'Neal want you to try Assess toothpaste and Paul Newman pushes Fuji Bank.

Why the Japanese are so fond of Westerners in their ads is a topic of endless speculation. A German model said he thought it was the Japanese inferiority complex. "They seem to believe they have ugly faces, bad proportions." A Japanese owner of a modeling agency says it is simply because foreign is considered "interesting," and felt the bottom line was sex appeal. "Western women are seen as erotic and that's how they're used in advertising here. It's more blatant than in the West. When Japanese women are used in ads, it's because they're cute, not sexy."

Whatever the reason, there seem to be more and more foreign models coming to Japan—both professionals who are sent over by top international modeling agencies, and amateurs. The work that they do ranges from highly paid fashion show work to TV and print ads to posters to "event" work like trade shows and department store promotion extravaganzas.

The "events" are shows where product manufacturers or distributors want a foreign model to enhance the image of their products. Most models would be reluctant to call this modeling, but there are quite a few of these kinds of jobs available. An American girl will hand out orange juice samples in a department store, or a French girl will hand out cheese samples, or a British girl will lean against the latest model Jaguar at a trade show.

Until about ten years ago, most agencies recruited foreign models from the streets and anything with light skin would do. People traveling through Asia would stop by Tokyo, get a few modeling jobs to replenish their pockets, and continue traveling. Blond hair and blue eyes would make up for a multitude of sins as far as complexion and weight were concerned.

But times have changed. Now the Japanese have the money to attract top professional models and they have become more sophisticated in their tastes. Most of the top agencies go to Europe and North America to recruit their models.

These top-of-the-line pros come to Japan on fixed-term contracts of two or three months. They enter the country on an "entertainer" visa and must work exclusively for the agent that hired them. Top models can make up to a million yen a week—making Tokyo the world's most lucrative market for models.

Most top models agree that Japan is now as professional as Paris, London, or Milan. "There are a lot of fashion shows in Tokyo now to show the work of famous Japanese designers and so there is a lot of runway work," said one young Danish male model, brought over by an agent to work for two months.

But not all professionals can find work. A dark-skinned Jamaican woman who was a former beauty queen with training and experience modeling in Jamaica and London was only able to find three modeling jobs in six months. She registered at all of the agencies and called up regularly to let them know she was still around, but ended up supporting herself by teaching modeling to young Japanese girls rather than doing it herself.

"A few times I asked them why I didn't get a job at an audition and they'd look nervous and say, 'Uh, you're too short.' And I look around me at the other girls and 75 percent of them are shorter than me. It's just an excuse.

"One of the jobs I got was because they specifically wanted a black person in the ad to make it look international. But when I got to where they were shooting, all the makeup people freaked out. They had no idea how to do my hair or face."

JOBS FOR NOT-SO-BEAUTIFUL PEOPLE

While you do have to be white, you do not have to be beautiful to model in Japan. There are quite a few agencies who also work with "character models." This is a nice way to say odd-looking people—fat people, short people, people with bug-eyes or huge noses.

One such "character" confessed, "Inspired by megalomaniac dreams of fame and fortune, I registered at two or three agencies. There followed six months of silence. So I sat down and reviewed my thespian qualifications: A short, squat body; a morose, gloomy manner; a total absence of any vestige of physical grace; in the good looks department, I could easily pass for the Hunchback of Notre Dame on a dark night—or even a cloudy afternoon.''

Then one day an agent called him up and asked him to go to Roppongi to audition for the part of a marionette in a thirty-second TV ad for a pasta company. He posed for innumerable stills and was asked to turn around. "Employing all my dramatic talents, I moved stiffly, as I presumed a marionette would. Somehow or other I passed the test."

For a day of alternately waiting and prancing about with a tuba strapped to his shoulder, he was rewarded with 60,000 yen.

A veteran of this circuit says, "It's pure nonsense, but they pay you, so I do it. I'm on the list of a bunch of agencies and they call me up and say, 'We've got a job on Saturday from nine to six and it pays 100,000 yen. Do you want it?''

He accepts about two jobs a month. The pay varies widely according to the sponsor, with the talent agency taking a 40 percent cut. On the high end of the scale are TV commercials for major corporations that can pay about a million yen for a day's work. On the low end are jobs as extras that pay about 10,000 yen.

THE AMATEURS

While the pros jet in and out of Tokyo between shows in Paris and New York, and the characters do the odd job for the money and a laugh, there is another class of models who can make a living modeling in Tokyo even though they have had little or no professional training or experience.

Lured by rumors of big money and a glamorous lifestyle, these men and women come to Japan, make the rounds of the agencies, and after they become known, can make anywhere from ¥60,000 to ¥200,000 a day.

In general, qualifications for this kind of model are:

For men: the Top-Gun look—clean-cut, square jaw. Blond hair and blue eyes are always a plus. To gauge your chances, put on a blazer and an old school tie and look in the mirror. Do you see a young pre-war WASP looking back? If not, think about English teaching and the occasional character model job.

For women: long legs and a devastating pout will get you in quicker than you can say "*gaijin* model." To make sure, try on the most romantic dinner gown you can find. Could you mistaken for Michelle Pfeiffer, or the Nastassia Kinsky of *Tess of the d'Urbervilles*? If so, then by all means come over and give it a try.

Be warned though, that it's not all money and glamour. The glossy amalgam of legs, fingernails, and teeth is the created illusion. The real life of a *gaijin* model in Japan involves a lot of pavement pounding and a lot of rejections.

A young American woman first came to Japan to visit a friend and found everyone encouraging her to be a model. Slim, tall, and blond, she fit the bill. So she went back to New York and had some professional photos taken, and then moved to Tokyo.

She began by going around to all the professional agencies. But they wanted to see tear sheets (pages from actual magazines)— proof that she had worked before for big agencies abroad. When she said she didn't have any, she was often dismissed after a brief flip through her portfolio, sometimes without even a glance at her face.

Discouraged and frustrated, she then turned to the agencies that dealt more with amateurs and part-timers. She found them more than willing to put her on their lists. Her lucky break was getting a job as an extra for a television drama. The client chose her without even meeting her because he liked the photos and because she was a New Yorker. So with no acting experience and no modeling experience, she was flown to New York to play the part of a foreign newscaster.

All this happened while she was still on a three-month tourist visa. The Immigration Bureau clearly states that this is a big no-no, but in her two years of experience, only one agency has ever asked to see her visa. "They always ask, 'Do you have a proper visa?' and I always say, 'yes,' " she explained.

Her age (twenty-four) is also seldom a problem. If the agent says the client wants someone under twenty-one, she is nineteen; if they want someone over twenty-five, she is twenty-six. Again, she says, "No one is ever so rude as to ask for proof." Generally, though, there is no life for models over twenty-five, as the Japanese are particularly partial to the dewy look.

After coming back from New York, she got a job doing an English conversation program on the educational television sta-

still on a tourist visa, so all the money was under
...s job gave her a lot of exposure and started the ball

...er tourist visa expired, she enrolled in a Japanese
...course and switched to a cultural visa. It is rarely
...y for a model to speak Japanese since most of the agents
...ak English, but, unlike others who sign on for Japanese
courses just to get the visa, she actually goes to her classes and
studies and hopes to use her language skills later when she
finishes modeling.

Most amateur models who start working in Japan take
whatever work comes their way: TV and print ads, promotional videos, posters, and "events." Event work is the easiest
to come by but pays fairly mediocre wages—¥30,000 to ¥50,000
for a day's work. Depending on the sponsor, promotional
videos and magazine advertisements are some of the highest paying jobs.

The standard procedure is to go around to agent after agent
and sign on with the ones who think they could use you. Then
you buy a telephone answering machine and wait for the agents
to contact you. In effect, you are running your own business.

When an agent calls, he will describe the job, and, if you are interested, will tell you where and when to go for the audition. He
will meet you there, show your portfolio to the client, and tell
them about you. A few days later they may call and say you got
the job.

A model who had done a little work in the U.S. before she
came to Japan said the auditioning scene here is much easier and
low-key. "At home they put you up on the stage and make you
walk and talk and ask you to sing or dance. Here you just sit and
smile while the agent does all the talking."

Some models complain about the hassle of traipsing all over
town—of not being able to read signs on buses or subway maps,
and of getting hot and sweaty in the summer, wet in the winter.

And you never know just what the competition might be at a
particular audition. "Sometimes they'll choose two out of eight
girls or one out of seventy. I'd guess that if I go to twenty-five
auditions, I'll get about two jobs," said one New Zealander.

KEYS TO SUCCESS

Most models agree that the main factor for a successful modeling career is simply to be able to live in Japan. Some advise reading up on Japan before you come to get an idea of what cultural differences you can expect.

Most also advise that you invest in a series of professional photographs before you come. If you come with at least six or eight fashion plates taken by a professional, you will get work much more quickly. In addition, look at some Japanese fashion magazines before you come to see what the latest "look" is and have a few photographs in that style. One model told of her friend who came with a set of incredibly sexy-looking photos that just about burned the emulsion off. But the look in Japan was cute and virginal, not sexy, and her friend had difficulty finding work until she got some new photos.

Another long-time model says, "Get organized. Get an answer phone. Return every call. Call agents who haven't called you recently and tell them you're really interested in working for them. Promote yourself. Go out and meet people. Be dependable. Always show up on time for auditions and jobs and always smile and be polite. If you're someone they like to work with, they'll call you again, even if you're not the best looking model around."

11. ART AND MUSIC

■ **ART**

There is a Japanese proverb that says, "When you have enough food and clothing, then learn gentility." With more than enough money for food, clothing, and shelter, many Japanese seem to be going after gentility—in the form of acquiring works of art—with a vengeance.

The price of art, like most everything else in Japan, is out of scale with the West. A young artist will want 800 dollars for a print, while in New York 800 dollars would buy you an indifferent Hockney. For the foreign artist, there are two sides to this coin. On one side is the opportunity to actually make a living from art. But if the works are not sold, the other side is the risk of having to live off the kindness of strangers or sleep on the floor in Shinjuku Station.

The accommodations at the station can easily be avoided, however, if you are a native speaker of English and are willing to teach at least part-time until that fine day when someone will recognize your artistic genius and commission a few million-yen works to set you on the way to fame and fortune (or at least financial security).

THE WESTERN ART BOOM

A quick glance at the art in Tokyo's museums and galleries would lead one to believe that the Japanese have an extraordinary avidity for Western art. When the *Mona Lisa* was exhibited, millions lined up to see it, even though it was behind thick bullet-proof glass. At art auctions around the world, the most expensive, most famous Western masterpieces are routinely bought by Japanese. One stumbles upon small galleries with Western-style paintings on the ground floor of many office and apartment buildings. Many of the 500 new museums that have opened in Japan since 1978 host major exhibitions of the works of such artists as Manet, Degas, and Rubens, and it is not difficult to see exhibitions of Modigliani, Van Gogh, or Picasso at any of the department stores, where the top floor is generally devoted to large-scale exhibitions.

However, this avidity for Western art does not necessarily translate into sackfuls of yen for any contemporary foreign artist who comes to Japan. Making a living as an artist is never easy, and trying to do it in the land with the highest rents and food costs in the world is quite a challenge. Most foreign artists in Japan say they would not recommend that one of their countrymen try it.

The reason is that the Japanese are not so much fond of Western art as they are of famous names. And they do not value a work of art so much for what it is in itself as for its status-giving and investment potential. In fact, art and commerce are as fiercely entangled in Japan as the lovers in Rodin's *Kiss*.

The two main sponsors of art in Japan are department stores and newspapers. This may seem a rather odd way to do things, but in Japan it makes perfect sense. The department store or newspaper is given favorable tax breaks and both have been in the business of importing exhibitions of Western art since before the war, when there were very few museums in the country.

There are as many reasons for artists to come to Japan as there are artists in Japan. Most of them, however, did not come primarily to practice their art. They came because of an interest in Eastern philosophy or Zen or martial arts or because a friend or lover got a good job in Japan. Or they came to be exposed to new surroundings and new ideas, in order to produce new work. Some came simply because they didn't know what else to do.

A Canadian sculptor said she likes living and working in Japan because of the "fabulous wealth of visuals." A painter says it's easy to function as a professional artist in Tokyo, easy to show your work. Others agree that this is so because as a foreigner you're exotic, but point out that this has its negative side because you're never really taken seriously.

Other negative aspects of working in Japan are the isolation and the lack of serious feedback about your art. Often artists say they feel very cut off. In addition, there is the lack of studio space and the outrageous expense of any space, living or other.

A foreign owner of a gallery in Tokyo says he sees no reason for a foreign artist to come to Japan. "Before they come, a lot of people think there's such an input of culture here, a long tradition and appreciation of beauty. Look around you. Do you see it any place? I don't. You really have dig for it and digging takes time. I think a young artist could get a lot out of traveling around Japan—not just Mt. Fuji and Kyoto, but the slums of Sanya and the wonderful Japan Alps. But the art?"

He shrugs his shoulders and makes a gesture of emptiness. "There are no pros to being an artist in Japan. There are the usual hardships of trying to be an artist plus the liabilities of being an outsider."

While many artists share his point of view, there is a fair number who would agree with another foreign gallery owner who said, "Who wants to be Japanese? We shouldn't complain about not being admitted into their claustrophobic, hierarchical system. We should just sit back and enjoy our special position."

GETTING INTO A GALLERY

The gallery system in Tokyo is different from most other places. Ninety percent of the gallery space is rental space—anyone who puts up the money can exhibit his work. This means that any artist has an equal shot at getting exposure. In New York or London, there is much more competition and the galleries are only available to a certain "in" crowd and those with links to the "in" crowd.

There is a catch, though, and that is money. The popular galleries in Ginza cost at least 100,000 yen for a six-day run. In addition, the artist has to pay transportation fees and mailing and publicity fees. Most end up doing all their own publicity, from mailing out notices to contacting the newspapers and even setting up interviews. Getting into the other 10 percent of galleries is more like the New York scene—you have to know the right people.

Most foreign artists can only afford to pay for their own show once. If their work is received at all well, they will then be invited to show at other spaces, usually free of charge, with 40 percent of any sales going to the gallery. Even at these galleries, though, the artist is expected to do all the coolie work of addressing, sealing, and stamping the invitations and dealing with all the publicity.

SUCCESS FOR THE STALWART

To succeed as a foreign artist in Japan requires the same perseverance and long-term commitment as any business endeavor in Japan. You cannot expect to stay for only one or two years and go home rich and famous.

After a number of years, most foreign artists develop some kind of following and begin doing commissioned works. A foreign securities analyst asked one young artist to paint his yacht for a cool one million yen. "I had never painted anything larger than poster size, so it blew me away at first," the artist said. "But it was a great experience and size doesn't intimidate me anymore."

Artists who stay in Japan longer build up contacts and eventually can support themselves almost solely through their art. A French woman who has been in Japan for seven years said that she could probably be more commercially successful in Europe, but that Japan somehow meets her other needs. With a Japanese husband and a young daughter, she has put down roots and has become well-known and respected both in the foreign and Japanese art communities.

One American artist's advice to other young artists thinking of coming to Japan is to "do everything slowly, in stages. Be patient. Don't try to rush anything—especially relationships."

The relationships he was referring to are those with Japanese gallery owners. They are always a little reluctant to show a foreign artist's work because there is a general feeling among Japanese that foreigners are transients—just stopping by Japan for a quick buck. If you show them that you are serious about art and about staying in Japan for the long term, then they begin to trust you and want to show your work.

It is the beginning that is difficult. Many artists start out by living with friends, teaching English, and making the rounds of galleries. One young artist found it rough going for about six months until he got to show his work at an exhibition at a department store. After that, he found Japanese gallery owners much more receptive to his work.

"It's a status thing," he explained. "They're not willing to gamble on an unknown. But if someone else, like a big department store, thinks your work is good, then the rest of them feel like it's not so much of a risk.

"The Japanese don't like to step out on a limb. They don't care so much about the picture itself; they want to know where your work has been shown. Now that I can drop some names, things go a lot more smoothly."

Two years after coming to Japan, most of his income is from his art. He continues to teach some English classes because his work visa is sponsored by an English teaching company. His works are mostly watercolor on Japanese paper (*washi*) and most are sold at one gallery for prices ranging from ¥80,000 to ¥150,000 with the gallery receiving a 40 percent commission.

Some artists say it's easy to get into the mediocre galleries because the gallery owners feel that having a *gaijin* show draws more people. But after awhile, they say, your self-esteem suffers if you are only a curiosity item.

But another artist found that gallery owners do not treat him differently from Japanese artists. "They are primarily interested in the work I produce. They want to show work that their clients will like, work that will sell. And they want someone who is productive."

Some artists do make a profit. While the common wisdom is that you should get famous in your own country first and then come to Japan to sell your work, a number of foreign artists are trying to do the opposite. One young American hopes to do a lot of work in Japan, make a lot of money from it, and then take a fat portfolio and bank account back to the U.S. and carry on painting and selling his work there.

He sees Japan as a place to speed up his career and feels that what he has accomplished in two years in Japan would have taken ten in the U.S. He states unequivocally that "Japan is the best place to be an artist."

There is also a handful of resident foreign artists who have taken up traditional Japanese art forms such as woodblock prints and pottery and have become very successful.

FOREIGN GALLERY OWNERS

In addition there are a few foreigners who own galleries and others who import and export art works. The galleries are divided into two basic camps—those that cater to the average expat who doesn't know anything about art but wants to bring something Japanese back home, and those that are seriously interested in exhibiting quality modern art. The members of each camp regularly disparage the other side, but Japan seems big enough for both, as both have been quite successful.

Since there are far more Japanese in Japan than foreigners, one would suppose that gallery owners would aim to attract the Japanese. This is not the case, however, because the Japanese generally buy very famous works or nothing at all.

One gallery owner who does not cater to the foreign expat community says a lot of his time is spent educating his clients. "The Japanese don't know what good art is because they don't really trust their own feelings about things. They have to be told. Things have to have a pedigree. It's hard to convince someone to buy an unknown artist's work. They don't look at the work, they just look at the name.

"Foreigners are easier to convince, but since the fall of the dollar, they have disappeared as major buyers."

Another gallery still sells over 99 percent of its art to foreign customers. The owner attributes his success to his talents of "being seen" and "getting my name around." He now supplies sixty galleries and dealers around the world with work by Japanese artists. Of his regular twenty to thirty artists, only three are foreign and they do work that is more "Japanese" than that of the Japanese—idyllic country scenes of thatched roof farmhouses tucked in the mountains or of geisha clambering up Mr. Fuji.

The proprietor of the other type of gallery clearly holds this sort in low esteem. "The best in contemporary shit," he sneers, "I mean it's really just grotesque. It sells because most people don't know good modern art from a Cheerios box. His clients are all from Podunk or West Podunk. I have to find those few people who are really interested in learning about the contemporary art market in Japan, and have enough money to buy.''

He admits that business would be better in New York. ''In New York there are a lot of really moneyed people. There's lots of money in Japan too, but the Japanese are not going to spend it on good contemporary art pieces. Most Japanese just buy ceramics, crafts. So I kind of balance heavy duty avant-garde shows with ceramics.''

Finally, one artist advises, ''If you're going to come to Japan, come for the experiences. If you get money or recognition, consider that a bonus, but don't count on it.''

■ MUSIC

The Japanese love Western pop, rock, and jazz.
True.
You are a Western pop, rock, or jazz musician.
True.
In Japan everyone will love you, sign you on to make records as fast as they can, and you will be rich and famous before you can say ''Jumping Jack Flash.''
True? Not quite.

The first premise is valid. The Japanese recording industry is one of the few which does not have a trade surplus with the West. Each year millions of tapes and CDs from well-known and lesser-known Western groups are sold, and superstars like Madonna, Michael Jackson, and the Rolling Stones routinely play to packed stadiums. Even groups like Iron Maiden and Twisted Sister have a large, vociferous, and dedicated following.

But you don't have to go to a big concert to see the influence of Western music and musicians in Japan. Turn on the television or radio and you are bound to hear jingles written in English and sung by foreign artists. When Japanese pop stars go on tour around the country, they invariably have a backup band with at least a few foreigners. And you can find a number of clubs in any largish city that feature foreign bands or Japanese groups that reproduce the greatest hits of the Beatles, the Kinks, the Cars, and even John Denver. If imitation is the sincerest form of flattery, then Western pop musicians should be more than flattered.

But this does not mean that Japan is the promised land for any Westerner who can carry a tune. The conclusion to the opening syllogism is false because loving Western music doesn't necessarily equal loving you, the Western musician. A singer and songwriter from the U.S. who has been living in Japan for eight years said, "If you're already an established star, sure, the Japanese will go for it. But if you're not already internationally acclaimed, people in the music business here figure you came over because you're second rate and couldn't make it at home. Never mind that you may be more talented than any Japanese star that prances around on TV. When I first came and saw those so-called singers on the variety shows, I cringed—not one of them could sing in tune and not one could move naturally on stage. I thought, 'These people are so bad, I'll be a shoo-in.' But the fact of the matter is that they don't want you upstaging them and that talent has nothing to do with being successful here."

A music reviewer for one of the English-language dailies has spent nearly ten years watching foreign talent come and go. He concludes, "Really, the Japanese only want famous foreigners for window dressing—a foreigner that looks groovy on stage—moves cool, dances well, looks sexy—but they're not supposed to be the main attraction."

An American woman who composes music and lyrics for commercials agreed, "For eighteen years I've been saying the system's gotta change. But it hasn't. They don't care whether you've got talent. They don't care about good music. You're locked out. It's not that different than any other business that tries to make it in Japan. There are very subtle, very strong barriers to foreign participation in a lot of fields, and this is just one of them."

This is not to say there are no foreign musicians working in Japan. There are and they work as studio artists, backup musicians, lyricists, jinglewriters, singers, and performers. Music is probably the only field where blacks have it easier than whites. The music reviewer says, "The Japanese have totally bought into the idea that blacks are cool, funky, and have rhythm. There are lots of black drummers and bass players working here." Virtually nobody of any color, however, manages to make a living off their music.

An American bassist who has been playing with groups in Tokyo for four years and supporting himself by teaching English says, "The people in all those *gaijin* bands do English teaching or translating or hostessing or modeling or some combination of the above to sustain themselves. The take-home pay from a good night at a live house gig is ¥8,000-¥9,000 each— ¥15,000 if you're really hot."

Those who are committed to staying and working in Japan can usually manage to piece together enough different kinds of music-related work over the years to support themselves. This limited "success" comes through cultivating contacts and being very patient.

"It's not like the U.S. where you bring around a portfolio or a tape and introduce yourself," said one singer who first came to Japan in the 1960s with a pop group. "Everything is word of mouth and personal connections. Speaking Japanese puts you miles ahead of the competition because it immediately puts people at ease. The music business here is a very small world and there are very strong loyalties. I'd love to think people choose me for jobs because they love my lyrics and my voice—but I know it's because I speak Japanese and I've been here for fifteen years. If Billy Joel came along tomorrow and said, 'I'll write your next song,' they'd say, 'no thanks.'"

Since there is really no systematic way to go about finding work, the best thing to do is find the musicians who are doing the kind of work you want to do and get to know them and their network. You can find them by going to the clubs where they play. (See appendix or pick up a copy of *International Rockers Infozine* at Tower Records or at the clubs listed in the appendix.)

ALL THAT JAZZ

Jazz musicians seem to be able to find work more quickly than other musicians since there are quite a few Japanese jazz trios that would love to have a foreigner on stage with them. As mentioned before, this is not so much because of the talent the foreigner might have, but because he or she is excellent window dressing and gives the group a "classy" look.

One avant-garde jazz musician said that he prefers living and playing in Japan because, while there are fewer clubs in Tokyo than in New York, they are much easier to break into. Unlike the New York or London jazz scenes, he feels that in Japan, "the more avant-garde, the less lyrical your music is, the better your chances.

"This scene is perfect for me. I play weird avant-garde stuff and have a following at the clubs I play. It's not commercial— I'd never make it big anywhere, but here I teach English a few days a week and have all the rest of my time for my own stuff. It's the people who want to be commercially successful who run into trouble here. Me, I'm happy to hang out and play my own thing. Japan gives me the time and space to do that."

A jazz/funk/fusion musician who had played for Kenny Loggins, Al Jarreau and other big names in Los Angeles was overwhelmed by his initial reception in Japan. "I got all kinds of studio work and did lots of arranging, writing, and playing. I did quite a bit of studio work for Japanese groups and for TV and radio commercials. There's lots of work here for studio musicians—technically good guitarists and keyboardists. Of course, it helps a lot to have a name—to be able to say I backed up Al Jarreau or whoever."

His honeymoon with Japan was short-lived though. "After a while I realized I was only seeing 5 to 10 percent of the money I thought I was making. They treated me like an idiot. They'd lead you on and then a day before the gig, they'd back out. They figured I was some dumb starstruck kid. I know you have to pay your dues in any business, but here that translates as 'you have to get burned—and keep getting burned.' "

Most of his venom is reserved for JASRAC, the Japan Association for the Rights of Artists and Composers, an organization that administers royalties and sets rates for different kinds of work. It is something like the U.S. organizations BMI or ASCAP. According to a U.S. attorney who was working with this musician, the JASRAC bureacracy is not very well structured and can be abused since it does not require documentation to, say, register a song. Combined with the fact that record companies tend to be negligent in handling contracts, it is easy for foreigners to get frustrated and feel that they are being cheated.

He points out, however, that Japan is not that different from any other country. "Getting work in the industry and getting the compensation you want is a matter of agreement between you and your employers." He admits, though, that the Japanese still haven't caught onto the idea of contract law or copyright law. "They often just assume a person will sign a contract and don't ever bother to check that they really have. Sometimes contracts are not even handed out until the recording has been made and is already out in the stores. Even asking to see a contract can be interpreted as being mistrustful and will result in bad feelings. Also, there doesn't seem to be much awareness of the fact that you have to get permission to use copyrighted material. This often leads to problems when foreign musicians come to work here."

The jazz musician soon learned what happens if you make waves and don't play by the rules. "The JASRAC bureaucrats control the record companies, who control the production companies, who control the managers, who control the artists, who control the studio musicians. JASRAC has an iron hand on the whole thing and dishes out all the rules. If you don't play by their rules, you're out.

"When I started talking to my lawyer, he said I had a case, but he also said, 'you've got to go along with the system or you'll never play in this town again.' So I held back, but still no record company will sign me now. It's been two and a half years and I've put together my own group, and we play the clubs and I work for some small producers."

There are quite a few versions of this story in circulation. Another American was brought to Japan in the early seventies by a large recording company which signed him on a two-year contract as a studio musician. Upon arriving in Japan he learned the project had been cancelled and he was left high and dry. He too thought about bringing legal action against the company, but decided just to get back on his horse and see what he could do. By keeping quiet and swallowing his pride, he has gone on to do a lot of studio work for movie soundtracks and pop idols.

His advice to neophytes is to "be wary of all promises. Especially watch out for the vague promise that is so easy for the Japanese to make. They want to say what you want to hear so they say, 'We might make a record. We might go on tour.' Just remember, those mights are mighty big."

THE ENGLISH CONNECTION: LYRICS, JINGLES, TRANSCRIPTIONS

Straight pop musicans, particularly those who want to perform, find the going fairly rough. A member of a popular R & B group says, "Sure, there are clubs that have their *gaijin* bands, but you'll be lucky if you get over 10,000 yen when the night is done. That's just vanity stuff—you do it 'cause you like it—not to get famous or make a lot of money. It can be fun, but it's not real challenging. You have to play standards and cover tunes—whatever's hot at the moment. It's a little bit mercenary—playing the tired old clichés."

"Anything that deals with English lyrics is tough because no matter how great you are, it's wasted on the Japanese," according to a writer and performer of "adult-oriented pop."

"I turn out English lyrics for Japanese groups. It's a craft, not an art. They pay between ¥30,000 and ¥40,000 for one song so it's not really worth putting your heart and soul into. If you want to say something from your heart in your own language, don't come here to do it."

A woman who has been associated with the Japanese music scene for eighteen years writes lyrics for commercials and finds it lucrative but frustrating. "There's almost always at least one word or phrase they object to. I was doing lyrics for a commercial for a chain of ersatz Denny's restaurants and had a line, 'You'll feel like a king . . .' and they said we couldn't use 'king' because the emperor was ill at the time and it would be disrespectful toward him.

"They only have one meaning for each word—it's very strict and they can't understand slang or the connotations of certain words. You can always spot lyrics written by a Japanese because they are so straight: The sun is shining. The water is clear. I am happy with my chocolate—that kind of stuff."

Although she has been successful and had some of her lyrics sung by stars like George Benson, she knows that it is not a transferable experience. "Working as a musician in Japan is not valuable if you want to make music your career elsewhere. The Japanese music scene is too narrow—and it certainly won't impress any music companies in the U.S. or U.K. if you say you worked in Japan. You can't really learn anything here, except how the Japanese system works—and that doesn't transfer back.''

She spends about one-third of her time writing music and lyrics for commercials and for Japanese stars, one-third performing, and one-third transcribing English lyrics. When a recording made overseas by a foreign group is released in Japan, copies of the lyrics, in English and Japanese, are included as a service to the customer. She gets paid about 2,000 yen per song to write down the English lyrics, and can do the ten songs on an album in a couple of hours. Since she has been doing this for nearly twenty years, she has now built up files of over 1,000 songs on her computer, and so when she is given an album with some old standards, she can just access her files and finish the job much more quickly.

Another woman who does part-time singing says, ''If you've got the right kind of voice, you can get jobs doing background singing and jingles for TV and radio commercials. It's schlock but it pays.''

FOR THE RECORD

Many foreigners have been suprised to find that it is not too difficult to get a Japanese record company to put you on disc. One woman made an album and got it released, but then found that her record company was not at all interested in trying to promote it. It ended up selling about 2,000 copies. A year later she made another recording and the same thing happened. Her advice to others is to be aware that ''you can make as many albums as you want in Japan, but there will be no promotion and you won't make any money and you certainly won't become a household word.''

While recordings by foreign artists made and produced in Japan are not promoted, the Japanese stars are promoted furiously. Some foreigners cash in on this by playing or singing with the ''idol'' of the month. Even then, the foreigner doesn't end up with any name recognition because the marketing push is all focused on the Japanese star.

Japanese record companies hire few foreigners, but one musician who had been working in Japan for five years and spoke good Japanese convinced a major company that it needed him. Now he is involved in A & R (artists and repertoire). His job is to discover new talent and sign the act to his record label. He is also responsible for finding songs for recording artists to perform.

PRODUCING

There may very well be only one *gaijin* producer in all of Japan. His story, though, shows that nothing is impossible here if you do your homework and work hard. He had never imagined that he would end up making recordings, designing CD jackets, engineering, composing, and producing music—even getting his own label from a Japanese record company. But he came to Tokyo with some Japanese language ability and continued studying diligently while working as an English teacher and meeting Japanese musicians, engineers, and producers. Then "things just started happening."

He believes that the acoustics of a good hall are better than any studio and he makes all of his recording in concert halls—usually with only two microphones. He puts the whole thing together, from contacting the musicians he wants to record to reserving the hall to composing and arranging some of the pieces to borrowing state-of-the-art recording equipment from music stores and studios to producing the master to getting it pressed and designing the CD cover. He even packages the discs in his house—placing the disc into each jacket, slipping the notes in, and putting it in its plastic cover.

He's just about breaking even—selling 1,000 to 3,000 copies of the discs he's made so far. Considering he's only been in Japan five years and only had his label for two years, he may end up doing very well given a few more years. But he is clearly not in the business for the money. His satisfaction comes from making recordings of music he likes and having complete control over how it is done.

Even with his success in the music business, he continues to teach English about ten hours a week at a high school for visa reasons.

It is very difficult to get a working visa as a musician. Most people get a cultural visa and study Japanese or aikido, or get a work visa by teaching English. Because it takes at least a few years to make connections and get rolling, it is best to have some other work to fall back on. Just about every musician, Japanese or foreign, supplements his income with teaching or something else.

Because the name of the game is personal connections, you have to be willing to stay long enough so that your name is passed around and you have to be willing to settle for significantly less than stardom. "The best money comes from doing your music as a business—just farming yourself and your skills out—not investing too much, but playing by their rules, giving the Japanese what they want," according to one studio musician.

The reviewer who has seen so many come and go says, "A lot of people come here with rose-colored glasses on. They say 'I know it's hard, but I'll make it.' Wrong. There's no reason for the Japanese pop world to want *gaijin*—they've got plenty of stars, 'idols,' of their own."

The lyricist says, "As an artist you'll get little or no gratification here and you certainly won't get rich. The studio costs are phenomenal. It's cheaper to fly a band over to L.A. and put them up in a hotel for a week and record in an L.A. studio than it is to work here."

An eight-year veteran of the Japan music scene admits that "There's no rational reason to be a musician here. It's precisely the opposite of a strategic career move. If you can make it in L.A. or New York or London, you wouldn't be here. I know that. I didn't come here as a career move. I came as a life move. I'm here for other reasons. I'm here because I can work for a few hours and have a lot of time for myself and my music."

The woman who writes music for commercials is even blunter in her advice. "If you're really interested in making it in music, don't come to Japan. As a musician, you want to impress your peers. Are your peers in Japan? There's no one here that I really want to knock the socks off of. On the other hand, if you just want to do it as a recreational thing, fine. There are some good points to the music business in Japan—it's cleaner—there isn't really a drug problem. It's a pretty good place to come and do your own thing. You just need perserverance and patience. And you need something else going for you because you're not going to live off your music and you're certainly not going to get famous."

12. HOSTESSING

The sexuality in hostess clubs is discursive. Nothing happens.

Anne Allison, anthropologist

The hostess bar is an astonishingly successful institution throughout Asia, and there are an estimated 3,000 such establishments in the Ginza area of Tokyo alone. What makes a hostess bar are the hostesses—women who run from classy to crass, sophisticated to sassy. Their job is to offer alcohol, conversation and titillation to adolescent men of all ages at prices that make cocaine addiction look positively cost-effective.

Depending on the level of the establishment, a few hours of drinking and chatting can set the customer back from 10,000 to 100,000 yen. At most bars, a plethora of charges come upon the patron as soon as he steps in the door. First there is a cover charge or "charm fee," then there is a table charge, a drink charge, and a hostess charge—per hostess per hour. The drinks are usually whiskey or brandy and the hostess helps the customer drink. Of course, water and ice are charged extra.

The bar owner gets the lion's share of the returns, but a full-time hostess can make from 300,000 to 600,000 yen a month, depending on the club.

"A-ha!" you say, "I wasn't born yesterday. Clearly the 10,000 yen notes are a fig leaf to cover a certain transaction that has been going on between men and women for a long time."

Guess again.

"This business is just dangling the carrot," says Leslie, a British woman who has worked off and on for six years at some of the top hostess bars in Ginza. "There's a lot of talk, a lot of sexual innuendo. They ask me if I like Japanese men and I say, 'Oh, yes. Very hard,' and they love it."

But, in 99 percent of the cases, all the men are paying for is a girl to light their cigarettes, mix their drinks, give them hot towels to wipe their hands after each visit to the toilet, sing duets with, dance with, chat with, and sit with.

It is all quite innocent. "It's like my first date in junior high," said Debbie, an American. "The most the guys ever do is put their hand on my knee or dance close to me on a slow song. Mostly it's talking—getting them to relax and laugh a little."

BECOMING A HOSTESS

As with most jobs in the *mizu shobai* (water-trade), the floating world of quasi-legal entertainment, hostess positions are usually not openly advertised. Leslie first came to Japan as a model and was working at a lot of "events," such as demonstrations of accessories at department stores. A friend told her she could make a lot more money hostessing, so she stopped by a club that the friend recommended and was hired.

There are some bars that do advertise in the English language press and these are usually on the up and up, although the pay is generally not as good as the ones you hear about from women in the business.

Qualifications for the job are reasonably good looks and a talent for light conversation. Some Japanese comes in handy, but many women say they started working with absolutely no language ability. Some women who become proficient in Japanese don't let on because the men enjoy the feeling of superiority in being able to joke with each other in Japanese, usually at the expense of the foreign hostess.

An Australian girl who had studied Japanese often overheard the men joking about the size of her nose and commenting that she looked like a witch. "I wanted to turn around and ask them if they'd all had childhood accidents with a steam roller, but I bit my tongue."

For the average Western male, talk and relaxation can be had for free and a dangling carrot that never gets close enough for a nibble results in frustration, anger, or boredom. After the initial thrill of being surrounded by admiring women, most find they are marooned in the meaninglessness of the phenomenon.

"What's the point?" an Englishman complained. "It's all a

bit silly. You can't get laid, you can't even ask her out for a date.''

But for the Japanese, talking is usually enough. Anne Allison, an anthropologist who studied the hostess bar scene during the early 1980s, suggested that talking about sex may actually be a form of sex in Japan, and that all talk and no play doesn't make Tanaka a dull boy because the men ''are really more interested in relating to men. The woman is the vehicle by which the men become comfortable with each other.''

This is generally the case in the higher class establishments—the ones that hire Western hostesses. But the vast majority of foreign hostesses are Southeast Asian women who come to Japan because of the oppressive poverty in their own countries and the promise of some quick money. The Filipino, Thai, Korean, and Taiwanese women usually come on six-month entertainer visas arranged by questionable ''agents'' who often have underworld connections.

The women are told they will be waitresses or dancers, but are then threatened and abused and forced into prostitution once they come to Japan. In many cases the boss takes their passport and keeps them virtually locked up except for their working hours. There are agencies in Tokyo such as HELP that provide assistance for these women.

Western hostesses sometimes get into trouble, but generally they find work at the relatively respectable clubs in Ginza or Akasaka where typical hours are from 6:00 P.M. to midnight at about 5,000 yen an hour. Other clubs pay the hostess a percentage of the bills that her customers rack up.

While Western women are seldom treated as badly as the Southeast Asian women, they are at risk if they have any latent tendencies toward alcoholism. The hostesses are encouraged to drink because that encourages the men to drink and that's how the bar makes its money.

The altered state that alcohol produces also helps to make the time go more quickly and pleasantly. In a moment of lucidity, one hostess said she looked around her at the men, ''drunk, infantile, helpless, being fed, pampered, flattered—and I thought, 'they're running this country.' It was incredibly depressing.''

Many hostesses feel that hostessing is one of the best ways to get inside modern Japanese culture and begin to see what goes on during those important after hours, when business relationships are cemented. One German woman said, "The expressionless mask they wear all day slips off as soon as they sit down, and they turn into real people—not always likeable, but real."

13. SERVICE INDUSTRIES

Like the United States, Western Europe, and other first world nations, Japan is moving from an industrial/manufacturing economy to one based in the service, information, and high-tech industries. This shift will affect the employment picture for Japanese and foreigners alike as the service-oriented economy creates a variety of new positions to be filled.

One of Japan's traditional strengths in all of her business dealings has been service. The politeness of the Japanese shopkeeper is legendary. But there are also the late-twentieth-century renditions of this politeness to be found in the gas station attendants who dash into the street to stop traffic as you leave and the beauticians who massage your scalp, neck, and shoulders and serve you green tea when you go for a haircut. Service permeates many fields but is concentrated in the service sector jobs found in the hotels, department stores, and travel agencies of Japan. The coming decades will undoubtedly see the creation of more jobs in these fields and elsewhere—especially for those with a flair for creativity and the inclination to be innovative.

The hiring of foreigners for jobs in the service industries is still in its first stages, and now is the time to get in on the ground floor. While nearly all of the major hotels and department stores in the major cities of Japan do have foreigners on their staff, the numbers are still very low. In many cases, there is only one foreigner and his or her primary duty is to deal with foreign customers.

DEPARTMENT STORES

The Seibu-Saison group of department stores, restaurants, hotels, travel agencies and other services was the first to start hiring foreigners for a variety of jobs. There are presently around one hundred foreign employees of the group working in Japan. They work on the floors of the department stores, in the hotels and travel agencies, and behind the scenes in the international planning, buying, merchandising, licensing, trade, and legal divisions. They are also being trained as management staff to be assigned to Seibu's hotels and department stores overseas.

Although Seibu-Saison used to have regular hiring drives for foreign employees, they now hire only sporadically on a "case by case" basis. The only hard and fast qualification for applicants is that they speak Japanese. Other than that, an educational background at a well-known university or work experience in a related field is helpful but not necessary. Whether a person with a given background or experience will be hired is largely a matter of timing.

A Chinese-American said she called Seibu's foreign personnel section to ask a few general questions about employment and was asked to come in right away. After a brief interview they asked her to work on the team planning a hotel to open in Beijing. She said she is sure she was hired because they just happened to need trilingual (Japanese, English, Chinese) people on the project. Her educational background was East Asian history and she had no experience working in the service sector.

Another man just out of a one-year intensive language program at Tokyo's International Christian University said he was hired within a week after sending in a resume. After being assigned to the merchandising section he found out it was because his predecessor had suddenly quit and they were in desperate need of someone to take over his duties of handling the English paperwork involved in the joint ventures the company was involved in.

While some job hopefuls like these two begin their search by contacting Seibu's foreign personnel section, others work backwards to that point. An American woman married to a Japanese had met some of the staff of a particular section that dealt with importing food and they asked her if she would be interested in working with them. She decided to give it a try even though she had no experience in the area. Her interview with the personnel division was perfunctory.

CONTRACTS

After the company decides to hire you, then you have to decide what contract basis you would like to be hired under. Seibu-Saison was the first Japanese corporation to offer *gaijin* the same contract conditions as Japanese. Although the company was rightfully proud of taking this step to treat its foreign employees equally, it turned out not to be what most foreigners wanted.

The classic Japanese "lifetime employment," with its low beginning salary and incremental raises throughout the thirty-odd years of employment, does not generally suit the needs of foreigners—most of whom have no intention of spending a lifetime in Japan. Seibu caught on quickly and now offers its foreign employees the choice of a yearly, renewable *shokutaku* contract or the lifetime *seisha-in* contract. Seibu has gone on to be even more flexible and offers, in addition, a variety of part-time and temporary contracts as well. In this the company has again shown itself to be at the forefront of change.

Many foreigners note that this is what first attracted them to Seibu-Saison. One five-year veteran of the international planning section said, "Seibu is very progressive in terms of a Japanese company. The high-level management is very forward-looking and sophisticated in their thinking and the younger staff in their twenties are also very modern and good to work with."

She and others comment that any problems usually lie with the middle management, many of whom are the conservative, straitjacketed bluesuits that people stereotype as the Japanese "salaryman." A man in the merchandising section said that many of the forty- to fifty-year-old middle managers are the reason a fair number of foreign staff don't stick with the company for more than two or three years. "Many of them are way behind the times and don't like to have foreigners in their section giving the young employees funny ideas about leaving before 9:00 P.M. I've even heard them use derogatory terms when speaking about foreigners."

A number of foreign Seibu employees point out that while foreigners get the same pay as the Japanese, they never serve in the same capacity as a Japanese employee. The woman who dealt with food imports explained, "The workload for foreigners tends to be heavier because it invariably includes proofreading, translating, interpreting, and writing and correcting letters in English for the management.''

Another man complained about the interpreting that he was regularly asked to do. ''It's a joke. I can speak pretty good Japanese, but I'm not a professional interpreter and I usually make a fool of myself. But they keep asking me to interpret for the groups of foreigners who come through making presentations and whatnot and I can't really say no.''

The stories that Seibu employees tell vary widely according to the section they work in and the people they work with. Some get along with the boss and have fun, but others say they feel that while they're getting some good experience, it's not really worth the aggravation.

Working conditions also vary with the section. Some expect the foreigners to work late every night and others don't. The man in merchandising said he made it clear when he began working that as long as there was work to do he would stay, but that he had no intention of staying late just to cement the section's team spirit. Although he said there have been a few occasions where he stayed all night to complete a paper or presentation, he generally leaves at six-thirty.

Many ex-Seibu employees are still in Tokyo working at a variety of jobs. Some have moved into a job that uses their particular skill—computer systems design or legal matters—while others have gone on to change fields or open their own businesses. Nearly all say the Seibu experience was valuable, especially in improving their Japanese language skills. Most cited the pay, reasonable but not spectacular, as their reason for leaving.

One man who worked in three sections over his two years with Seibu said, ''In terms of knowledge of Japanese business practices, I've gotten a lot of valuable experience. I know their line. I know when they're telling a lie just to be polite. Now I have the ability to discern and judge a lot of things that would have had me totally confused before I began working here. It's this knowledge that'll help me in any future job that has anything to do with international business dealing with the Japanese.''

A number of other department stores have followed Seibu's lead and begun hiring foreigners to a greater or lesser extent. The most visible foreigners are those working in the store's information centers. Seibu has its Foreign Customer Liaison Office and Isetan has its I-Club, which help foreign customers with just about anything from buying opera tickets to sending gifts back home. The main qualification for the job seems to be a pleasant personality. Backgrounds vary from the spouses of expatriates to ex-English teachers to those with previous experience in the service industries. The job includes dealing with foreign customers' inquiries over the phone and helping those in the store find what they want and get it delivered in Japan or overseas.

HOTELS

Many hotels in Japan are expanding their foreign staff and hiring people to work in room sales, banquet sales, reception, staff training, and other positions. Japanese language ability and previous experience in the field are of course helpful, but usually not critical factors in getting hired.

One woman who is working at a large hotel in the center of Tokyo outlined the four characteristics that she felt were most important in a job applicant. "The person must be hospitality-minded and willing to bend over backwards to please the guests; they can't be afraid to get their hands dirty, since you can expect to lug the odd suitcase, type letters, and stuff envelopes; and you must have a pleasant appearance, and a willingness to work hard and uncomplainingly."

She said that with these qualities, experience in the hotel or other service industies is not so important to most Japanese. In fact, "previous experience is sometimes considered a negative point because the management prefers working with a blank slate and creating a person to match the hotel's image."

Jobs in hotels are seldom advertised. Notice of an opening sometimes circulates through the foreign community's grapevine, and intensive networking with others in the field or related fields generally pays off. More often, it seems that positions do not even exist until a foreigner comes along and suggests it and expresses his or her desire to do it.

One woman had a friend working in room sales at a large hotel in Tokyo, and started to visit other hotels that had no foreigners on staff. She met the managers and explained to them that she could help bring in foreign guests, and within a month she had her choice of three jobs. She, like most others working in hotels, was a local hire. She had been teaching English and studying Japanese and wanted to work somewhere where she could improve the Japanese she had learned.

At first, she said, there were a lot of problems that came from the uncertainties involved in trying to create a position. "It took a while to create a meaningful job. They probably would have been happy to just have me around as a *kazari* (ornament), but I wanted to do more."

Now that she is in the system and has made connections with others in the industry, she has had a number of job offers. Although she finds her present position interesting and lucrative, she says she will leave soon because "there is just nowhere to go, no career advancement, no matter how good a job you do. I increased room sales to foreigners over 100 percent, so I'm probably in line for some kind of promotion in about five years. But that time frame doesn't match mine. I don't want to wait that long. And besides, I'll never get into any position of real authority here."

After about five years of teaching and doing other assorted jobs in Japan, another woman was hired by a five-star hotel as a sort of international liaison. Her job was to work with the hotel's VIP foreign guests and make sure that they were happy and that everything went smoothly. In addition, she was involved in the hotel's public relations, promotions, and advertising activities.

She feels the job has been valuable because of the wide variety of experiences it has provided and the opportunity to improve her Japanese language ability. In addition, she has learned about the organization and running of a Japanese company. She hopes to use this knowledge to find a job back home that deals with international relations.

One woman working at a Japanese branch of an American hotel had a lot of experience in hotels before coming to Japan with her husband. She ended up being very disappointed and frustrated with the job. "My career is at a dead standstill because the upper management have no intention of promoting me. The Japanese management feel threatened by me because I'm just about the only foreigner here who can understand what they are saying, and then the expats don't trust me for the same reason. Each side thinks my loyalties lie with the other side and the whole situation is intolerable.''

CREATE YOUR OWN SERVICE

For those who have had enough of working for a boss, there is always the option of setting up a service industry business of your own. Many of the foreigners who set up their own businesses in Japan are setting up service companies—and often the company is providing a service largely to the foreign community. Many times, though, the service jumps over to the Japanese community as well.

An American woman who opened a color consultancy had thought that her color and image service would be primarily for the foreign community, but found that the Japanese also jumped in and her business took off.

Another foreigner left his job at an English-language daily newspaper to open a bakery. He then expanded into a lunch time sandwich delivery service, targeting ex-East Coast expatriates who were missing their New York ham-on-ryes. He was surprised and pleased when the Japanese began to order his sandwiches as well.

Other services started by foreigners range from a host of consulting companies (management, computer, financial, writing, public relations), to corporate communications, producing newsletters, doing interior design, providing housing services to foreigners, and setting up health and fitness centers.

14. ENTREPRENEURS

I go zooming up to the top one day. Then I get batted around; I bounce from here to there, go through chutes, hear bells ringing, spin around, and fall toward the abyss. Then at the last minute I get whacked up to the top again.

The owner of a food importing company

Starting up and running your own business in Japan presents more challenges, frustrations, and potential rewards than doing so just about anywhere else, according to most foreign entrepreneurs here.

The challenge is in trying to make it in the world's second largest market. The rewards lie in succeeding.

The frustrations are a function of the market itself—an extremely responsive, competitive, almost paranoid one that has often been characterized as closed because of the different business practices, language and culture of Japan, not to mention its labyrinthine distribution system.

To many, the rewards are worth the struggle. The Japanese economy is booming and the government is doing its best to boost domestic spending. With this official blessing, cash-rich, enthusiastic Japanese are poised to buy just about anything that meets a need, real or imagined. An American working as a market analyst said, "The Japanese are forever on the lookout for a new product or service to make business better or life more comfortable—and they are prepared to pay for it—sometimes the more, the better."

Over 2,000 foreign enterprises are operating in Japan today. They offer an enormous variety of products and services including graphic art and design, editing, translating, photography, food, cosmetics, imported furniture, software design, computer consulting, financial and tax advice, architecture, headhunting services, and relaxation and fitness centers.

Naturally, each of these endeavors has its own peculiarities and pitfalls. Yet there are certain common hurdles that everyone must leap in setting up a small business in Japan. The major ones include forming your company, getting a visa, and paying taxes.

SETTING UP SHOP

Most small business owners say that the red tape involved in setting up a company in Japan is minimal. Naturally, it helps to talk to as many people as you can who have trodden the path before you. You can find these people through organizations like the American Chamber of Commerce in Japan and the Australian Business Association (see appendix).

When it comes time to set up your business as a legal entity, you have three choices: you can have a sole proprietorship, a limited liability corporation (*yugen kaisha*) or a standard corporation (*kabushiki kaisha* or K.K.).

The sole proprietorship is a bit risky since the proprietor must assume complete responsibility for all debts and all tax obligations. Some foreigners who wanted to become sole owners of their businesses have had trouble with the immigration office when it came time to get or renew their visas. For these reasons, entrepreneurs generally choose to incorporate.

The *kabushiki kaisha* (K.K.) is the most popular route—mainly because of the status it confers. It is a standard corporation with shareholders and stock. To the Japanese, a K.K. is a stable, dependable, permanent, and prestigious entity that they can trust. Of course the letters ''K.K.'' do not conjure up these connotations in the minds of foreigners and so for companies that will be dealing with an exclusively foreign clientele, there is little difference between becoming a K.K. or a *yugen kaisha*. In fact, a number of foreign entrepreneurs have gone the latter route because the paperwork is simpler and cheaper and takes less time.

A *yugen kaisha* is very similar to a *kabushiki kaisha* except that the shareholders are called *yugen sha-in* or ''partners'' and the number of partners is limited to fifty. (There is no limit for the K.K.) The K.K. must have authorized capital, while the *yugen kaisha* needs only a fixed amount of contribution— 100,000 yen paid in by the contributors. The K.K. must have a minimum capitalization of 350,000 yen and each share of stock must be worth at least 50,000 yen. The Japanese government has been talking about increasing the minimum capitalization to twenty million yen and the minimum share price to 400,000 yen, but this does not appear likely to happen soon. Paper processing costs (for notary public, attorney's fees, registration fees, etc.) run to about 500,000 yen for a K.K. and 300,000 yen for a *yugen kaisha*. The K.K. must undergo a full audit every six months, while the *yugen kaisha* does not. Other slight differences between the two are outlined in Helene Thian's book, *Setting Up and Operating a Business in Japan*.

The decision is not terribly critical since it is possible to change from one to the other after the fact. However, some entrepreneurs have pointed out that the share capital (*shihonkin*) influences your standing at the bank. If you have low capitalization it is hard to get a loan from orthodox sources. Also, the letters K.K. on your business card (*meishi*) will impress any Japanese you have to deal with, from immigration officials to loan officers.

VISAS

While incorporation is fairly straightforward, getting a visa is another story. There are two main obstacles. The first is that there is no category of visa that specifically allows an entrepreneur to enter Japan to set up a business. Second, there is very little published information from the immigration people to let a prospective business owner know precisely what are the necessary papers and amount of capitalization that will qualify him or her to receive the appropriate visa.

The 4-1-5 visa is the object of desire—it officially allows one to be involved in business management, foreign trade, or capital investment. However, the Immigration Bureau seems to hand out this visa sporadically and inconsistently. While one immigration official was quoted as saying that a company must have a 30 million yen capitalization and 100 million yen in revenues to qualify, some entrepreneurs have found that this is not necessarily true—sometimes a visa will be given with amounts less than this and other times a visa will not be given even if these amounts are exceeded.

When you do manage to get the visa, it is still hard to breathe freely because the visa is generally given for only one year. When the time comes for renewal, you will again be up against the vagaries of the Immigration Bureau. This can make long-term planning very difficult.

A few people have mentioned that the catchall visa classification, 4-1-16-3, could be used for the beginning business person. The category was specially created to cover any situation not covered by the other classifications, and could, in theory, be given to any freelancer or small business owner. However, it seldom is.

Most people thinking of beginning their own business have already been in Japan a few years and are sponsored by another firm. Usually these people research their market and gradually begin their business before trying to change their visa classification. This is, of course, illegal, as the immigration laws specifically forbid one from engaging in any activity other that that specified by the visa classification. Nevertheless, it is often done because of the difficulty in getting a 4-1-5 visa in the early stages of running a business.

The difficulties often stem from the specification that the business be "viable and stable." Because there are no exact figures to go by, this is open to interpretation, and what is viable to one immigration officer may not be to another. The problem is that it may take five years before profit/loss statements and other documentation are persuasive enough. A number of entrepreneurs have warned that it will take you almost twice as long to turn a profit in Japan than in any other country because of the high start up costs. Most caution that it will take five years, rather than two or three.

More than a few small business owners are married to Japanese nationals. This obviates the visa problem, as they can get a spouse visa (4-1-16-1), and work virtually without restrictions.

The visa considerations for those few who come to Japan

specifically to open a business are slightly different. They will generally enter the country either on a reciprocal visa (a temporary tourist visa) or a regular tourist visa. At first glance, it would seem easiest to just come and get the temporary visa stamped in your passport when you enter Japan if you come from one of the countries permitted temporary visas. (Check with the Japanese embassy in your country.) However, current immigration laws will not allow that classification to be changed into any other inside Japan. It is easier in the long run, therefore, to get a regular tourist visa from a Japanese Embassy or consulate before you leave your home country. Then when the time comes to try and get a 4-1-5 visa, you can do it in Japan. The tourist visa can be used to research your business, go to meetings, or engage in any other nonremunerative activity.

MONEY MATTERS

A large part of running a business anywhere has to do with money. You will need to get financing and find office space and employees. Detailed information and advice on these matters can best be obtained from the publications and businessmen's organizations listed in the appendix.

I should, however, mention that foreign business people must pay both corporate tax and inhabitant's tax. The corporate income tax must be paid on any income after deducting your salary. Tax rates for a company capitalized at less than 100 million yen run from 30 percent for income of less than 8 million yen to 42 percent on income over 8 million yen. When dividends are paid, the figures are 24 and 32 percent, respectively.

Specific information for the tax liabilities of various foreign nationals can be obtained from the embassies of the countries concerned.

CASE STUDIES

The topics of incorporating, visas, and taxes can be illustrated by examining a few entrepreneurs and their businesses. These examples will illustrate the basic requirements for operating a successful business in Japan and will provide some insight into the possibilities and problems.

Some businesses spring, fully formed, into the world while

others go through various stages. Often English teachers or translators will do some other sort of language brokering on the side and then gradually cut down on the official job until most of their income is from the side job. Some stay at this stage while others want to hire staff and expand and so incorporate as a *kabushiki kaisha* (K.K.) or a *yugen kaisha*.

GETTING INTO IMPORTS

Bob had been working for an English teaching company in curriculum development when he simply got tired of paying 600 yen for a tiny jar of molasses that you could buy for the equivalent of 100 yen in the U.S.

But when he started talking about importing food, people said it was a nice idea but impossible. After all, it took a lot of threats and man-hours just to get beef and oranges into Japan. The feeling was, "if the U.S. government can't do it, how will you?"

Not being one to give up so easily, he did some research and found that it wasn't the import duty that was putting the price of the molasses at 600 yen; it was the tremendous markups that happen as the product is distributed. Since he had some business experience in the U.S., this seemed to him like a classic business opportunity: bypass the middlemen and offer cheap goods to your customers and still make a good profit. This, however, proved impossible for a person of his limited means. But since he was more interested in providing reasonably priced food than in turning a profit, he decided to go ahead and start importing food anyway, registering his business as a nonprofit organization.

He kept his job as a curriculum developer to maintain his visa and a reliable source of income, but his import business is flourishing. He now imports some 2,000 different products for 1,000 different customers, but it took a lot of time and a lot of fighting through layers of bureaucracy.

"At first, the customs people didn't want to deal with me at all. It was like pulling teeth to get them to lift a finger for me. I think I looked like a college student and the feeling seemed to be, 'Who the heck are you and why do we have to spend time with you?' I think they figured I'd give up and go away.

"But I persisted and now everyone knows me and they're all really super."

With his minimal Japanese, he finally jumped all the hurdles and filled out all the forms and started importing. Now he gets containers shipped in every other week and goes down to the dock in Kobe with some friends to unpack them and then repack each customer's order.

His business is successful, he says, because "we are the only company doing this—the only company that imports on a personal import basis. The main satisfaction in this is seeing and hearing how happy people are to get the stuff."

Even so, he said that if he had known the hassles before he started, he would have never begun. "But now, after this much time and energy, I won't give up. But I think, at the end of it, I'll write a book: 'How Not To Do Business In Japan.'"

The main problems he encountered were with the different business customs in Japan and the language barrier. "There is nothing mystical about Japanese ways of doing business," he says, "they're just different than what I was used to."

Also although he could usually understand the words spoken to him, he said he often misses the nuance. One time a trucking company that delivers to his customers throughout Japan told him it was having a little trouble with the time frame, and he let it slide with a joke, "I'm having a little trouble too, we all have trouble sometimes." What the company official was trying to say was that if he didn't change his delivery dates, the trucking company could no longer do business with him.

But through all the misunderstandings and setbacks, he feels now, "We're actually winning. Before, none of the Japanese people we dealt with had a good word to say. Now everyone says, 'Hey, how's it going. We're with you.'"

He feels the key to his success is providing goods and services that no one else does, and, most importantly, believing that it can be done. His advice to any would-be entrepreneur is, "be like Joshua and believe that the city is yours while you're still standing outside the walls."

IF THERAPY'S YOUR NICHE

While the Japanese reluctance to seek help for psychological and emotional problems means the market for psychologists is very limited, it is at the same time wide open because there are no restrictions or certification procedures for foreign psychologists. Therefore, with a little enterprise and innovative thinking, it is possible to use your talents and training to create your own niche in Japan. One person who did this was John, a clinical psychologist and management consultant.

About 10 years ago he began coming to Japan two or three times a year to do business consulting, psychological counseling and some touring. Four years ago he decided to take a step into the unknown and try living in Japan year round. It was a real gamble, he says, because he wasn't sure what he would be doing. But through a series of connections he began getting work, and before long he had more than he could handle.

The first obstacle, that of getting a valid work visa, he managed to get around by getting hired at a university as a visiting researcher. This means he gives a few lectures a year and publishes a few articles. Such jobs are not very easy to come by and he landed this one through (what else?) personal connections.

With that taken care of he was free to pursue his other interests—business and personal counseling.

A few years ago a major American corporation sent 300 families to Japan for three years. For many of them, the experience turned out to be a disaster. And considering that the company was putting up about one million dollars for each person for the three year period, it was a disaster for them as well.

John found himself dealing with the crises of a successful businessman suddenly failing, his career on the rocks, his wife on the booze and his kids coming home stoned at 4:00 A.M.. What had happened was that the company had sent successful Western managers—aggressive, confident, forceful types— without having a clue that this was exactly the wrong kind of person for Japan.

After helping the families through their crises and sending quite a few back home, he approached the managers who had decided who would be sent to Japan. He was amazed at the lack of awareness of the cultural differences between America and Japan, and, pointing out the recent failures to adjust to life and business in Japan, persuaded the managers that the crises could have been averted with a little pre-planning.

They agreed and now he talks with all potential candidates for postings in Japan before the final decision is made. When they come to Japan to look around, he talks with them, does some psychological testing and gives the company recommendations on the advisability of sending a particular person.

He has also begun doing similar work for some Japanese companies—advising them on who to send overseas. In addition, he has introduced the employee assistance program concept to some companies and they are now offering their employees help with alcohol and stress-related problems. What really sold them on the idea was the realization that such programs are cost effective because an unstressed, un-hungover employee is a more productive employee.

On top of his business-related consulting, he has a private practice to which he devotes about twenty-five hours per week. Most of his clients are foreigners, but some are Japanese who have returned from extended stays overseas and are now finding it very difficult to fit back into the rigid Japanese environment.

John is very happy with his situation here and calls it the "ultimate existential experience" because no two days are ever the same. He says his four years here have been "totally unpredictable in a positive sense."

On the negative side, he says that he finds Japan incredibly nationalistic and insular. "Scratch the thin Heisei veneer," he says, "and you find yourself back in Tokugawa Japan. The feudal mentality is out there—all around us. Basically they don't like foreigners and they treat us like puppies. Puppies are cute and everyone should have one, but you don't take them too seriously."

For these reasons he says it's easy to work in Japan, but not so easy to live here. He advises therapists thinking of coming to Japan to be patient and to build up a network of personal connections. Also he says it helps immensely if you are a licensed psychologist because then you can bill your services on your clients' health insurance.

LANGUAGE BROKERING ON YOUR OWN

Many foreigners involved in teaching end up doing part-time writing, rewriting, editing, and/or translating, and, after a few years of work at a Japanese or foreign company, will use their contacts to start their own business.

Many more people would go this route except for the visa problems. Unless you are married to a Japanese, it is extremely difficult to get a visa for these activities. What most people do is have one of their previous employers serve as their visa sponsor and guarantee that person a certain amount of time or work each month.

Susan taught English at Japanese universities for nine years and gradually began doing more and more copy writing on the side. When she felt she had a pretty good client base, she quit teaching and opened her own copywriting and advertising business.

At first she worked out of her home to save money, but soon was able to rent office space with a friend doing similar work. Most of her work comes from the big Japanese ad agencies like Dentsu and Hakuhodo. She prepares print advertisements, sales promotion material, catalogs, product brochures, and annual reports.

Usually, she will receive a translation in bad English—"a horrid flood of garbage in English." She then takes on the role of sanitation engineer and cleans it up. She also has a network of translators, rewriters, and designers that she can call on if she lands a job that requires extra expertise.

Richard began a similar business after about ten years in Japan "drinking too much and squandering my youth." He married a Japanese woman, gave up drinking, and got serious about doing business. He says the work is cyclical, with very busy times followed by no business. "Some days, I think I'm going to be a millionaire, and some days I think I'll go bankrupt. At one point we were losing a lot of money, so we raised our prices. This had the unforeseen and fortuitous effect of making people think we must really be good, and we ended up with more business than we had ever had before."

FREELANCE VS. OFFICIAL BUSINESS

Some people move from regular employment to freelancing rather than actually incorporating as a business. There are various pros and cons to doing it one way or the other, but if you are an American and freelance, you have to pay U.S. Social Security. Being a company, a foreign entity, shields you. In addition, you get the perks of the Japanese tax system, which allow for nearly unlimited business and entertainment expenses to be written off on your Japanese taxes, if you are incorporated.

COMPUTER CONSULTANTS, SOFTWARE DESIGN

This field is wide open for entrepreneurial-minded foreigners and quite a few have jumped in already.

Andrew, an Australian, went into business two and a half years ago with a friend. Their main products are accounting and multicurrency software and their services are custom software design and installation.

Their business began after the company they had been working for went out of business. "We had seen a lot of people with very little computer experience running around getting a lot of work even though they did a bad job. We knew we could do better, so we registered as a *yugen kaisha* and started up."

Registering was easier in Japan than Australia. "All you have to do is get a Japanese accountant and he does everything. It costs about 300,000 yen and takes about two weeks." This blithe attitude notwithstanding, it helps to have someone recommend an accountant used to dealing with foreigners, and probably a lawyer as well.

Since their clients are large international companies, Japanese language ability is usually not necessary. Andrew admits, though, "There are certain doors that won't open to us because we are not fluent. But this is not a problem since we have a product no one else has and it's of very high quality."

He also attributes his success to his willingness to invest however much time and money a project requires. "You've got to remember that rewards are proportional to investment. Most people are too impatient. A lot of people don't want to pay their staff salaries three times higher than what they would pay a person back home, forgetting that their customers here are paying five times as much as customers back home. Here I charge 100,000 yen a day for a consulting fee. Back home no one would ever ask for half that, let alone get paid it."

He advises others to come to Japan and live and work here for two to five years to learn about the culture and the business opportunities. "Then if you have a high quality product, go for it. Don't listen too much to other people. Every anecdote can be countered by another and often things are sensationalized. You tend to hear about the 5 percent of people's experiences that are great and the other 5 percent that are horrible. In fact, 90 percent of your time is just business as usual. There isn't much of that Japanese mystique that people want to dwell on."

Joe set up his computer consultancy five years ago. The consultancy provides both hardware and software to individual and corporate clients. After five years of fourteen-hour days, he is finally getting on top of things.

"The biggest hassle is getting financing," he says. Even though he has paid off three loans on time with no problems, the bank refuses to give him another without the signature of a Japanese guarantor.

However, the bank has absolutely no qualms about giving loans four to five times the size of the one he needs to a Japanese woman who owns a company with the same annual sales. They have worked out a scheme so that when he needs a loan she gets it for him. "It's getting embarrasing," he said. "The bank has said straight out, 'It's because you're a *gaijin*.' "

WINNING QUALITIES

Every entrepreneur named the same basic keys to success: perserverance, flexibility, optimism, and a competitive spirit. Language abilities also come in handy but are not critical.

In general, problems occur when the ways of doing business in Japan and in the person's home country are at odds. The most common complaint is the vagueness and mutability of agreements, and the web of relationships that must be maintained. But in a fairly short time, most foreigners adapt and see that there is nothing terribly mysterious about doing business in Japan: it is just a lot of hard work.

Some entrepreneurs complain about the fact that a foreigner can never enter the inner circles of Japanese business, but many others revel in their exclusion—one consequence of which is not having to ruin your liver on the entertainment circuit—and the gentle notoriety they achieve merely by being strangers here.

A few entrepreneurs say they have experienced "nontariff barriers." For example, a client will buy an inferior, more expensive product from a Japanese just because he's Japanese or because there is a long relationship to maintain.

However, most foreign entrepreneurs agree that the pros outweigh the cons in doing business in Japan. The tax laws are favorable, the economic climate is more than favorable, and the special treatment that foreigners get is by and large positive.

Perhaps the biggest plus is the tremendous challenge and stimulation of living and working in Japan. Because the market is so competitive, you know that you've got a good product when you can succeed in Japan. It's like New York—if you can make it here, you can make it anywhere.

Corporate Tax Burden in 5 Countries

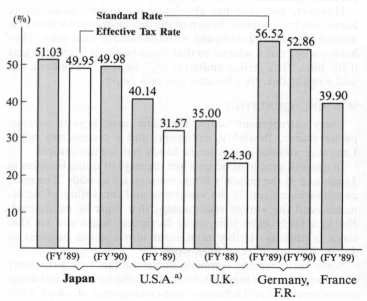

a) New York

Source: Keidanren (Japan Federation of Economic Organizations).

15. CORPORATE CULTURE

In the Japanese kaisha *(company), corporate conservatism dovetails with cultural conservatism and this can lead to a lot of frustrations for a liberal foreigner. But my two years in a* kaisha *have given me wonderful opportunities to use my Japanese and unparalleled insights into Japanese society.*

American woman working at one of the top ten Japanese trading companies

Many books have been written on the glories of the Japanese corporate system and these have induced many foreigners to come to Japan in recent years thinking they would flit from work to the bank gathering the pollen of "Japan Experience" and stashing away the sweet flowing money.

It is not so simple.

Even when foreign professionals are welcomed with open arms, they soon discover that they cannot function in Japan as they would at home. For behind the Western dress, the Western handshake, the Western tables and chairs and the Western food is the Japanese mind.

This means a different way of dealing with people, a different way of doing business, and a different mental starting point for every daily activity—from managing office staff to paying phone bills. In order to practice their professions successfully in Japan, foreigners find they must be sensitive to cultural differences and flexible enough to adapt to Japanese ways.

The differences between Western appearance and Japanese reality and the need to adapt are nowhere so apparent as in the immensely popular Japanese sport of baseball.

It looks like American baseball, but it's not. As Robert

Whiting explains in the foreword to his book, *The Chrysanthe-mum and the Bat*, "The Japanese view of life, stressing group identity, cooperation, hard work, respect for age and seniority, and 'face' has permeated nearly every aspect of the sport, giving it a distinct character of its own. American players who come to Japan quickly realize they have entered a different world. For some, it is fascinating and exciting; for others, exasper-ating and occasionally devastating."

The same could be said for any profession: when practiced in Japan, it takes on a different hue and the foreigner must adapt or face frustration, exasperation, or even devastation.

THE BASEBALL WINDOW

Initially, most foreigners in Japan are pleasantly surprised by the warm welcome they receive. This feeling is amplified for the new foreign baseball players who arrive in Japan each spring. They are overwhelmed by the banquets and the media blitz. "It's like we're astronauts," said one player, "Or the Beatles," added his teammate, as the pair were accosted by pen-wielding fans on a trip to a local department store.

These two had come to play pro ball in Japan for the Hiroshima Carp, a team that had prided itself over the preced-ing years for playing "pure baseball." The odd meaning of this phrase—playing the all-American game with no foreign players—demonstrates the kleptomaniacal way the Japanese sometimes appropriate foreign culture, as well as the am-bivalence of their attitude toward foreign players.

The experiences of these two and the lessons they learned about practicing their profession in Japan, as recounted in Whiting's book, apply generally to most other foreigners. The first thing they learned was that the game they were to play in Japan bore little resemblance to what they had been playing all their lives. Left-fielder Rick Lancellotti said, "When reporters ask me if Japanese baseball is different, I've learned to say, 'No, it's the same; you hit the ball; you run around the bases.' I don't bother to tell them that everything else is different. Everything that matters is different. Here, it's all done by the books with no creativity or risk-taking. Everything is form and formula."

They also found that, although they were expected to perform, teamwork was more important than winning. Their function was to *help* the Japanese players, not to excel.

In Whiting's book, Jim LeFebvre, an American who played baseball in Japan for three years, said that any player thinking of coming to Japan should: "Leave your major-league pride in the States. Pretend you're a rookie at a minor-league camp. Try to learn the Japanese way. Don't try to change it. Do that and you might make it. If you don't think you can make the adjustment, stay home."

This "When in Rome. . ." advice should be followed by anyone going to live in another country, but it is particularly valuable for Westerners to keep in mind while in Japan. Drop any ethnocentric arrogance you might be tempted to adopt and be open to another way of functioning in another cultural setting.

THE INSIDE STORY

The misinformation in many descriptions of Japanese companies generally comes from those who have spent little or no time actually working in a *kaisha*. A quick glimpse of the *kaisha* yields little. But even a brief three- or six-month internship usually results in a lifting of the veil. Upon peeling away this thin transparent curtain and reaching something hard and unyielding, the foreigner is certain that he has penetrated through the enigma and inscrutability of the Japanese, and rushes to his word processor to write confidently of the hidden mechanisms in the Japanese corporation.

What appears so smooth and solid, though, is usually only the first of many levels of illusion. The *kaisha* is like an onion and the first layer that is peeled back only leads to another and another. The analogy is hackneyed, but useful nonetheless. For when peeling an onion, whether or not there are tears is due in large part to your methodology and your own body chemistry. Even if there are tears, they do not necessarily lessen one's appetite for the finished product. In fact, it can be quite the opposite, as the hardships and pain are preludes to the sensual indulgences to follow.

To begin with, though, it is up to you to determine whether the onion is worth peeling at all. Before applying for jobs at *kaisha*, you should weigh your motivations for wanting to do so, and you should be prepared for:

Long hours. Forget about eight-hour days and five-day weeks. In most *kaisha*, working Saturdays and late into the night is still almost obligatory.

Low pay. Most *kaisha* have pay scales that they use for all employees and which are often half of what a foreigner would make doing a similar job at a foreign company. It is possible to negotiate better salaries, but even then they aren't significantly higher than what an English teacher would make after a few years.

Conservative environment. You won't hear any irreverent banter about the boss or the latest LDP scandal or the imperial family in most *kaisha*, and you'd be wise not to indulge in any yourself.

Togetherness. Your office will be a large room with a lot of desks and no partitions. This is to facilitate communication and teamwork. Privacy and a quiet space to think are not considered important—if they are considered at all. Expect to work elbow to elbow with people on either side of you and eye to eye with those across from you. Ears are everywhere and you can be sure that any private calls you may make from your desk will be hot gossip around the office.

Alienation. You will always be an outsider—outside the culture, the system. In addition to the psychological problems this can lead to, it means your advancement opportunities are virtually nonexistent, although this may change in coming years.

Conformity. Although you are an outsider, you are expected to try and fit in as much as possible. If your Japanese colleagues work until 10:00 P.M., you should too. If there are plans to socialize afterward, you should join in.

If you are willing to put up with the above conditions, you will probably find that you are able to gain valuable knowledge and experience working at a *kaisha* and that this experience will serve as a stepping stone to a good position back home. If you don't want to put up with these working conditions, you should look elsewhere for a job.

As is always the case in Japan, it is hard to identify a "typical" experience. There can be major differences between working for a large *kaisha* or a small one—or even between working in two sections of the same *kaisha*. The first thing to do in your job search, whether you are new to Japan or just new to the corporate job hunt, is to make as many contacts as you can with people already working at corporations. Personal contacts are the best, sometimes the only, way to learn about what working at a particular company or in a particular section is really like. It is also the best way to meet the people who will hire you.

Many of the foreigners working for Japanese corporations are working at the *sogo shosha*—giant trading companies that have offices around the globe and deal in over 25,000 products, from clothing to steel and from natural gas to chocolate. They are also involved in financial ventures such as bond issues and M & A. The *sogo shosha* confer a good deal of status and prestige on their employees and therefore do not have to offer high salaries or perks. Presenting a *meishi* (business card) with the name of one of the top ten *shosha* will result in deep bows and terms of respect.

Smaller companies will often be more flexible in contract negotiations and often end up being more generous than their big brothers. For this reason, you shouldn't restrict your search to only the large corporations.

QUALIFICATIONS

An academic background and actual job experience in a field related to your prospective job are preferred but not always vital. In some cases, companies prefer those with little or no background or experience since *kaisha* are geared toward hiring and training nothing but recent university graduates.

An American with a strong liberal arts education and no business experience said, "I came to Japan two and a half years ago with no Japanese ability, two suitcases, and my laptop computer. Working out of a small business hotel room, without contacts or connections, I had several job offers within ten days."

She had been awarded several international graduate fellowships and had studied at Cambridge and Johns Hopkins University's School for Advanced International Studies. These qualifications notwithstanding, she felt lucky to be hired with no Japanese ability.

"I think I caught the tail end of the wave. The job market a few years ago was more immature, and corporations were anxious to hire anyone arriving off the plane who could survive the interview process. If you could boast brand name schools and were pleasant and pale and could muster a 'hajimemashite' ('how do you do') you would have been in the door in a flash."

In the 1990s, the market is still eclectic, but *kaisha* are apt to require a certain level of Japanese proficiency or an area of expertise or both. With more multi-skilled people around, competition is keen, making timing and personal connections critical. Those who will find jobs most easily, according to an Englishman working in the personnel section of a *kaisha*, will be engineers, lawyers, and financial and computer wizards. Fluency in a language other than English can also be a boost because of the increasing amount of business between Japan and the unified EC market.

INTERVIEWING

Interviews at *kaisha* generally extend over several weeks. The five or six rounds can easily total twenty to thirty hours in a ritual that seems something like a courtship as both you and the *kaisha* try to determine if the link-up will be successful or not.

If you find yourself made unhappy, impatient, irritated, bored, or irate during the interview process, it is a sign that you should look elsewhere for employment.

One woman said that after some pleasant preliminaries, one of her interviewers asked if she was married. She answered yes, thinking that would end the line of questioning—but it went on:

"When will you start a family?"

"In three or four years."

"I don't think so."

"What?"

"I don't think so."

"Well, I'm sorry, but I do."

When the next question was, "What birth control do you use?" she got up and walked out.

This is an extreme case, but it points out both that no questions are "out of bounds" and that the interview provides a good time for you to feel out the company and whether you will enjoy working there. Part of the interview process is building the relationship with your future manager and team, and part is hammering out a mutual vision of what you can do for them and vice versa—generally in connection with the *kaisha*'s desire to "internationalize." When both you and the *kaisha* have decided it will be a match, you should begin talking about the concrete issues of salary and benefits.

One woman who had kept her cool over jokes about serving green tea to the men in her section decided not to smile when the salary they offered was half what she expected.

"I told them there had been a serious miscalculation on their side. I pulled out my calculator and showed them that I would be paid less than half what they had paid me as a consultant. Then I left, allowing them room to return and renegotiate."

She says she is still not sure if that first salary figure was a bargaining ploy or a real blunder or if they were completely serious about it. Later, one of her colleagues explained that they just looked at their salary tables under "female, twenty-seven" and read off the salary. Japan is still very much a seniority-based and patriarchal society and most companies decide what to pay an employee according to age, sex, and marital status.

While one would like to think that academic excellence, work experience, language skills, and professional background are more important than what school you graduated from, this is not the case in Japan—especially in large corporations, which have always hired only from the top universities.

Talking to foreign *kaisha* employees, one finds a disproportionate number of "brand name" schools—names like Harvard, Yale, Oxford, and Cambridge that the Japanese know and love. One woman who graduated from Yale and works with a top Japanese insurance company said, "I know that's probably the main reason they hired me. It was like having 'Christian Dior' stamped on my forehead."

CONTRACTS

If the interviews go well, it will soon be time to talk about the details of your contract. Contracts for foreigners working in Japan typically are signed for twelve months, largely due to immigration laws. However, the understanding between *kaisha* and employee is generally that the partnership will run from two to five years. Anything less than two years is generally not worth your time or the *kaisha*'s investment in you. It will also look highly questionable on a resume, especially should you plan to continue in a corporate field related to Japan.

SALARIES

The most important item on the contract will probably be your salary. *Kaisha* salaries are not even remotely comparable to expatriate packages. Housing allowances are rare, and while dormitories are often available for a very low cost, they are usually only for men and include a lengthy commute and curfews. Although the dormitory experience can lead to greater fluency in Japanese, and closer personal relationships, you shouldn't be persuaded to take a lower salary just because your housing will be subsidized. In fact, you should be wary of dormitories from the word go, since many are old barracks-like facilities with few modern conveniences.

A salary of between ¥5 million and ¥7 million is what you should shoot for. Foreign women must be especially careful in salary negotiations. As noted above, they are sometimes put on the same table as Japanese women and expected to acquiesce to a grossly lower salary than that for men doing the same job.

BONUS

Most *kaisha* tie up a large percentage of one's income in a "bonus" paid twice yearly. As a foreigner, you may be able to convince your company to pay your salary, or at least your overtime allowance, in twelve equal monthly installments.

After two months and seven interviews, one man got down to salary negotiations and was asked whether he would prefer the "bonus" or a straight salary. He said to himself, "Hey, I did an M.B.A. I know the time value of money," and told them he'd take the straight salary. This worked out to 375,000 yen a month for someone with an M.A. and M.B.A. and two years of experience.

OVERTIME

Overtime is a key question in negotiating. Most companies

have an overtime allowance, and you should be sure to find out how much it is.

One American had borrowed about 35,000 dollars during his graduate schooling and "felt like a lesser developed country" by the time he found work in Japan. His *kaisha* had a time sheet system, and at first he hated it.

"It was so petty and juvenile. Because I didn't like it and because I was new and wanted to make a good impression, I only filled in my regular hours for the first few months. Then I realized, 'Hey, they're delegating to me the ability to give myself a raise,' and I started putting down my overtime. First I kept it at about twenty hours a month, then I gradually raised it until I was getting almost 600,000 yen a month. But then my boss took me aside and said I should cool it or my colleagues would think I was *fu-majime* (not serious), so I brought it down to forty hours a month and now take home about 500,000 yen each month."

This honor system is the exception. The usual routine is the—to many foreigners humiliating—punch in and punch out system, whereby extra hours worked are automatically recorded on your time card.

VACATIONS

Vacations in *kaisha* are notoriously short—ten to twelve days for the first year—and are seldom taken. Foreigners often find that if they try to take them in a block or pair them with national holidays, the boss will object. The fact is that Japanese employees seldom leave the office for more than a week at a time. Younger employees take more of their allotted time off, but the older salaried workers work year in and year out with no holidays, and would like to see everyone in their section do the same.

In most Japanese companies there are no distinctions between vacation days, personal days, and sick leave, so if you come down with a bad case of the flu you may end up with no vacation days that year.

BENEFITS

Japanese companies provide certain benefits such as paid transportation to and from work, health insurance, and pension funds, but little else. The government pension fund, *nenkin*, is collectible only if you continue to live in Japan after having paid your monthly contributions for at least twenty-five years. As a foreign employee there are certain benefits that can make your time in Japan much more enjoyable and interesting, though. Some companies are accommodating and some are not, but it shouldn't hurt to ask for:

Japanese lessons—some companies will pay for them and some won't, some will provide you with time off to study and others won't. Some even bring a Japanese teacher in two or three times a week to teach the foreign employees.

Paid home leave—preferably with the air ticket thrown in.

Memberships to professional organizations such as the American Chamber of Commerce in Japan or the KAISHA Society—places where you can perfect your networking talents and perhaps help your company's business. Smaller companies are often more flexible on these matters than larger ones.

Many foreign *kaisha* employees reach a low point after three to six months on the job when the salary, which seemed large when negotiated and translated into dollars, now suddenly seems like nothing. The thrill of being in a foreign country is dulled by the drag of having to stay at the office until nine or ten every night. What seemed like refreshing candor from your colleagues is beginning to seem like rudeness, and you are just getting tired of everything.

This is when it is important to have struck a good match, to remember why you got yourself into this situation. After about a year, the investment that you made in your *kaisha* and that the *kaisha* made in you will begin to pay off. This is also about the time you get deeper into the layers of the onion. If you have been sensitive and observant and adaptable, you should know by now how to avoid the tears and get the most out of the experience. You will also begin to realize that you have many more layers to peel away before you can begin to understand how the *kaisha* really works.

Personal career development is seldom a concern to *kaisha* management. It is therefore up to you to always have a clear view of what it is that you want to get out of your experience with the company and work toward that goal.

An Australian man advises, "In the interview process make

sure that, at some point, there is discussion of work responsibilities. If the reason for hiring you is just some nebulous desire on the part of the *kaisha* to "internationalize," you should be prepared to present your own idea of what you would like to do in the company."

He was speaking from experience. After six months he was so frustrated with having nothing to do that he sat down with his superior and asked, "What do you want me to do?" The boss replied, "What do you want to do?" He wasn't prepared to answer and left the meeting as cloudy about his responsibilities as before he went. A week later, however, he returned to his boss with an outline of what he wanted to do, and the company began working on making a real job for him.

Life in corporate Japan can be especially difficult for foreign women. A Canadian woman who had worked in a large corporation for nearly a year in Canada was dismayed to find herself surrounded by chauvinistic men in her company's Tokyo headquarters. The problem was not only that the Japanese men were unused to taking a woman seriously, but that the foreign men fell into the same chauvinistic attitudes. After a few months she noticed that nearly every foreign man had reverted to treating women as the Japanese did. "It's almost as if they feel their actions are sanctioned by the fact that they are in a male-oriented society," she said.

Perhaps the most telling incident was when one of the Japanese managers came to her desk to tell her that they would have to have a meeting on Saturday and could she please ask her husband for permission to attend.

On the other hand, some women report greater flexibility in a *kaisha* than that given their male *gaijin* counterparts. The women feel they are not expected to conform to the norms of the *sarariman*—the salaried male staff who are devoted to the company, cut their hair short, shave at least once a day, wear dark suits, white shirts, dark ties, and dark shiny shoes.

Despite all the gripes, some foreigners decide to work with a *kaisha* just to have that experience under their belt. It is undoubtedly a great opportunity to experience Japanese company life intimately, and it can provide valuable insight in any future job with Japan connections. Also, the Japanese *kaisha*'s ability to adapt to changing international conditions will determine Japan's place in an increasingly competitive global economy. Many companies are aware of the need for change and will take seriously constructive criticism from foreign employees.

One last piece of advice from a three-year *kaisha* veteran preparing to move to greener pastures in the U.S:

"If you do not have some understanding of the broader cultural context of Japanese society, you will not pick up on a lot of the codes and innuendos and prescribed and proscribed actions in the *kaisha*. The cultural differences can be appreciated and enjoyed or they can be frustrating and fatiguing. The more you know of Japan the more you'll understand.

"This is why I tell anyone who is new to Japan to read as much as you can about Japanese society, history, and culture. Pick up books on contemporary Japanese society and on doing business in Japan; read some Japanese literature. If it doesn't interest you to learn more about Japanese society, you should seriously reconsider your motivations for hiring with a *kaisha*. The Japanese corporate world is not divorced from society— quite the opposite, in fact. It is often more Japanese than regular Japanese society in its hierarchies and unspoken rules. The more you know, the more you'll understand, and the richer your experience will be."

16. CONCLUSION

A successful and enjoyable stay in Japan depends on much more than getting a high-paying job and living in a big apartment (though such things certainly help). While there are quite a few foreigners who have come, seen, and conquered, there is a significant minority who have come, seen, and been conquered. Not everyone leaves Japan with a light heart and a massive bank account—some leave broken or broke; others never leave.

As one long-timer put it, "Every time I wanted to leave I didn't have the money and every time I had the money, I didn't want to leave."

Like the unhappy families in *Anna Karenina*, the unhappy foreigners in Japan are all unhappy in different ways. But there is a common denominator: the unhappy state usually stems from an inability to adapt to the differences of life and work in Japan. Instead of taking some initiative and changing either their thinking or their situations, the unhappy people tend to fall like stones where they are dropped and do nothing but complain.

CAUTIONARY TALES

Following are a few stories as words to the wise. Any resemblance to persons living or dead is, of course, purely coincidental.

Like many foreigners, Tom came to Japan immediately after graduating from university with a bachelor's degree in liberal arts. He intended to stay only a year—to pay off debts, make a little money, and see a little of the world.

But after a year of teaching English he had just broken even and was starting to feel like he knew his way around. So he signed ed on for another year—and then was offered a better job and so stayed longer. Before he knew it five years had passed and he was afraid he might end up an English teacher for life.

But when he looked at his 45,000-dollar-a-year income he knew that he wouldn't be able to come even close to matching it if he went home. So instead of trying to move back home or find work in another field in Japan, he stuck with the teaching, feeling trapped in a dead end position.

Carol came to Japan to get some experience in international law after completing her degree in Australia. After the initial thrill of being in a strange land wore off, she began to feel frustrated. At work her colleagues did not take her abilities seriously and gave her only the most routine tasks or those that used her typing or English skills.

On the social side, she found Japanese men hopelessly boring and unattractive, and soon discovered that nearly all of the foreign men were either married or going out with Japanese women. After a while she joked wryly that her only physical contact with other human beings was in the packed trains.

To fill in the emptiness, she began pouring herself into her work. Although she was eventually given more interesting and important work, she was never given any recognition or advancement. Never once in three years did she hear a colleague say, "Good job, Carol."

Many foreign men here find themselves in complicated situations because of a weakness vis-à-vis alcohol and/or the fairer sex. While these are hazards in most countries, it seems that many men succumb more readily in Japan where carousing of most kinds is condoned.

Bob came to Japan when his company sent him over on a two-year expatriate contract. He brought his wife and thought that it would be a second honeymoon. He was working in the sales division of a large company and part of his duties included going out for drinks after work with clients and colleagues. Since there was none of the stigma attached to getting drunk (quite the opposite in fact—alcohol is seen as the glue that cements human relationships), he found himself doing it just about every night.

His wife began complaining about his late nights and the little time they spent together. After a year, she decided to go back home. Bob stayed on, but when he was about to go home a year later, his wife told him not to bother. He figured he no longer had a life in America and found work with a Japanese company and continued to drink heavily. If it wasn't business, he would go to bars and look for female companionship. He often thought of going back home but deep down, he knew that his drinking habits would get him fired from any job in the U.S. and so he stayed.

Perhaps the saddest thing about these tales is that the difficulties and frustrations and unhappiness could have been avoided. Loneliness and alienation, irritation and aggravation can be countered by keeping an open mind and getting involved in various activities.

There are also quite a few organizations, professional and social, to help foreigners adjust (see appendix). More serious problems with alcohol and other destructive behavior can be dealt with by health and mental health professionals (see appendix).

While common pitfalls of the various types of jobs are outlined in each chapter, the overall advice given by foreigners is that you must throw away all assumptions and preconceptions, and be adaptable and flexible, open and patient. As in any endeavor, at home or abroad, you will get out of it what you put in. If you put in the time required to learn at least a little Japanese and to make a few friends, foreign and Japanese, the experience will be rewarding both personally and professionally.

LIFE AFTER JAPAN

There is yet another point that must be considered: Is there life after Japan? And if so, what is it like?

As contracts draw to a close or as the thrill of living abroad fades, many foreigners begin wondering and worrying about the future. Will the "Japan experience" be useful? Will there be a lot of Japan-related jobs waiting back home? Or will I find I'm out of circulation, with no marketable skills?

There are many variables, but those who have returned are nearly unanimous on two points. First, that living in Japan is an enriching experience—as living abroad nearly always is. In terms of personal development it is always very positive. However, in terms of career development, it may or may not be valuable. This is the second point—to have a valuable career experience you will need to gain some real and transferable experience or knowledge in your field, whether it is banking or import/export, teaching or photography. Whether you get this kind of experience is largely up to you, and you should consider what a job in Japan will give you to take back home (other than money) before you take it.

There is a number of people who have come to Japan, had an enriching and enjoyable time, and then returned home to find themselves unemployable. One man taught English and did freelance photography and design work and played in a rock and blues band. He had a wonderful time and made a lot of friends, but when he got back to London, he didn't find people knocking his door down to hire him. In fact, he found himself drifting, and two years later was still living on the dole.

Another man got back to the East Coast of the U.S. after two years teaching English in Osaka and took a look at the "talent for hire" section of *The Wall Street Journal*. "There were people with experience and accomplishments longer than my arm. I thought, 'What chance do I have against people like this?' "

His fears were confirmed when he went to job interviews and found that "Americans don't give a hoot about Japan. They wanted to know what my skills were. All I had done in Japan was teach English and rewrite a little and these were nontransferable skills. My advice is don't spend your time in Japan doing things you can't do in the U.S. Get some kind of skill that will be valuable back home."

Of course, for professional language teachers, teaching in Japan is a transferable skill. One man spent two years teaching in Hiroshima and then was given a position as a head teacher in a language school in Barcelona, Spain.

Journalism and photography experience in Japan can also be transferable since it can provide you with a good portfolio to take around to newspapers and magazines in your home country.

Any specific industry experience is also transferable. If you spent your time as a stock analyst in Tokyo, you will have a marketable skill just about anywhere. If you were involved in the plastics or biotech industries, you will also have gained valuable experience.

A man who had spent about two years with a Japanese electronics company was transferred to its office in California. Since he stayed with the company he did not have to look for a job, but he has found himself advising other returnees. In his area, the key qualifications are a degree in electronic engineering and a few years of experience. Without this, no amount of Japan experience will get you a job. On the other hand, if you do have the letters "E.E." after your name and have spent some time in Japan, he said you can just about write your own contract anywhere in Silicon Valley.

He warned that on the West Coast of the U.S. there is a lot of people with some Japan background—either second generation Japanese or people who have lived in Japan or Japanese who come to attend school or work and then end up staying. This means that when a job requiring some Japan-related experience comes up, there will be a lot of competition for it. He advises that those with Japan experience but without specific skills would have a much better chance finding work in the Midwest where such experience is rarer.

One man who had spent ten years in Japan working for English-language publishers in Tokyo went back to the U.S. and set up his own small publishing company. For him, the Japan experience was critical in determining his eventual career because he had been able to get intimately involved with all aspects of publishing while in Japan—from line editing to layout to publicity. In most publishing houses in the U.S., editorial functions are very compartmentalized, and he said he would never have been able to learn all of the things that he did in Japan had he stayed in the U.S. He also felt that the time in Japan was valuable because he was exposed to a high degree of craftsmanship through the Japanese printers and designers.

As Japanese companies continue to set up branches around the globe, people with experience working in Japan and those who have some Japanese language ability will certainly be at an advantage if they want to work for a Japanese company. Even there, though, the primary consideration for hiring employees is likely to be a specific skill or area of knowledge, and you should bear this in mind when choosing your job in Japan.

APPENDIX

TEN FACTS ABOUT VISAS

FACT ONE: Inconsistency reigns.

While this appendix is meant to give you a general outline of the variety of visas and how to go about getting them, it can only be a general indication because the Immigration Bureau treats everyone on a "case by case" basis.

Because of their fickleness, the best way to deal with immigration officials is be properly obsequious. If they don't give you the visa you want, ask what you need to do or have in order to get it, and then get cracking. Don't be fazed by the bureaucracy. If the immigration officials say you need X, Y, and Z papers and you produce them, then they will probably give you the visa.

Any questions can be addressed to The Visa Section of the Ministry of Foreign Affairs, Tel: (03) 580-3311.

FACT TWO: To enter Japan, you must have a valid passport and visa.

There is no getting around this one. But if you are from one of about fifty countries that have agreements with Japan, you can get a temporary tourist visa as you enter the country. As the list is constantly changing, with new countries entering reciprocal arrangements and others revoking them, you should check with your local Japanese Embassy to see what the current situation is in reference to your country.

If your country is not on the list, you can get a visa from the nearest Japanese Embassy or Consulate in your home country by submitting the proper forms and a few photographs. Even if your country is on the list, it might be a good idea to go to a consulate and get the regular tourist visa because this can be changed to a work visa in Japan if you find a job. If you do not get a regular tourist visa, a temporary visa will be stamped into your passport if you are from one of the countries on the list. This visa, however, cannot be changed and you will have to leave the country in order to apply for your work visa and then again to pick it up when it is approved. If you want to leave Japan only once, you can get the regular tourist visa in Korea or Hong Kong and then get that changed to a work visa back in Japan.

Until mid-1990, there were eighteen visa classifications, and most working foreigners fell under the catchall 4-1-16-3 category. In December of 1989, the government passed a bill to create ten new categories so that the lawyers, accountants, teachers, etc. that used to all be lumped together would have separate visa classifications. The new categories were to go into effect sometime in 1990 and the latest information can be obtained from the visa section of the Ministry of Foreign Affairs (see Fact One).

FACT THREE: Having a valid passport and visa does not necessarily mean you will be admitted into Japan (see Fact One).

The Immigration Bureau can bar entry to anyone it considers a hazard to the interests or security of Japan. This loose definition of undesirables gives individual officers a great deal of leeway. It seems that one of the main criteria for determining who is undesirable is the amount of money the person is carrying and the condition of their clothes and suitcase.

Long-haired, backpacker types might consider a hair cut and new set of clothes before leaving for Japan. Also, be warned that there is absolutely no forgiveness or second chance for anyone caught bringing even the tiniest amount of recreational drugs into the country. In their paranoia, immigration officials have been known to confiscate even vitamins and prescription drugs. Also, if you bring in any pornographic magazines, or even art that shows pubic hair, it will be confiscated. Never mind that once you get on a city train you will see respectable businessmen perusing the most lurid, violent, perverted, sadistic pornography—all, however, minus pubic hair.

If you look halfway respectable, though, and have a healthy supply of cash (around 1,000 dollars), chances are you will be admitted.

FACT FOUR: Some people who come to Japan to work do not enter on a work visa; they come on a tourist visa and then find work once they are here, leave the country if necessary, and reenter on a proper work visa. It is, of course, possible to enter on a work visa the first time around, but this means you must get a job while still in your home country.

The tourist visa is usually good for ninety days. You should be aware that activities related to money-making—and that includes research for a book, performing in the streets, teaching English—are strictly against the rules for a 4-1-4 tourist visa.

FACT FIVE: Cultural and student visas have been widely used as a way to stay in Japan by those with absolutely no interest in studying anything except Machiavellian principles of money making.

The immigration folks have become wise to this, and the chances of being able to work under cover of a student or cultural visa are getting slimmer by the day. To get these visas you have to show documents about the institution you are studying at, documents showing you can pay for tuition, living expenses, etc., and a certificate to show that you are actually attending the classes at said institution.

With a student or cultural visa you are legally entitled to work a maximum of twenty hours a week. If you get carried away with the money-making and don't attend classes, however, it may be difficult to extend your period of stay, because the school will be keeping track of your attendance for the benefit of the immigration office.

FACT SIX: Spouse visas make life a lot easier because you can work as much or as little as you like.

If you are married to a person with a visa from 4-1-5 to 4-1-13 or to a Japanese national, you can do as you please as far as work is concerned—as long as you're not involved in anything illegal.

FACT SEVEN: Working holiday visas are an easy way to get to Japan and work legally for up to one year.

The arrangement known as "working holiday" is intended to promote youth exchange and deepen mutual understanding between nations. Young people aged eighteen to thirty from Australia, New Zealand, and Canada can get a working holiday visa if they have a valid passport and the purpose of entry is not solely to work in Japan. Engaging in remunerative activities is only to cover the travel expenses of sightseeing. The job must be "appropriate for the purpose and spirit of promotion of exchange of youth and mutual understanding."

The holder of a working holiday visa will be given a 4-1-16-3 status of residence with a six-month period of stay, extendable for another six months.

FACT EIGHT: Entertainer visas are more strictly controlled than others because nearly all of the "entertainers" are from the poorer countries of Asia, and are therefore, in the eyes of the Japanese government, undesirables. Many of them end up going into the *mizu shobai* (water trade)—prostitution and other quasi-legal "entertainments."

Most women interested in this sort of work do it without the blessing of the Immigration Bureau, since their clients' expenditures are generally not recorded. Young men also have a few options in this business. Recently, host bars have opened where the young men flatter the ladies, and, if asked, will spend the night, or at least an hour or two with them in private.

FACT NINE: If you have not entered on a work visa, you will have to change your "status of residence," which is much easier said than done.

The tourist visa plays a significant role in many foreigners' early days in Japan. But the time comes when you find a job and must change to a work visa.

The official word from the immigration people is that you may only engage in activities allowed under your residence status. This means that a tourist cannot teach and a student can only work a maximum of twenty hours a week. It is no secret that many people violate these rules with impunity, but to do so is to risk deportation.

To change your visa status, you must get permission and authorization from the immigration officials. If you are teaching at X English school and want to join Y, you'll have to go through the same procedure as you did when you got hired in the first place. Or if you want to change from teaching to running your own business, you'll have to again go to the immigration office with the right papers.

When you find someone who is willing to hire you and sponsor your work visa, they will put together a package of materials to bring to the immigration office. These documents include: passport, visa application form, two photos, resume, diploma, personal statement, statement of reason of employment, contract, and proof of your company's capitalization.

To change from one employer to another, you will need to submit a certificate of resignation, a statement of reasons for resigning, a new employment contract, a statement of reasons for employment, a letter of guarantee, documents of the enterprise, and a list of foreign employees.

Required documentation changes from year to year, so you should get a check list from the immigration office.

FACT TEN: The latest detailed information on visas can be obtained from the Visa Section of the Ministry of Foreign Affairs (*Gaimusho*), 2-2-1 Kasumigaseki, Chiyoda-ku, Tokyo 100. Tel: (03) 580-3311.

The status of residence and period of stay provided for in the Immigration Control Act are as follows:

Status of Residence	Qualifying Persons	Period of stay
4-1-1	Diplomats and consular officials accredited to Japan and their families	During mission
4-1-2	Officials of foreign governments or international organizations recognized by the Japanese government and their families	During mission
4-1-4	Temporary visitors with the following plans: sightseeing, sports activities, visit relatives, inspection tours, participate in meetings or short courses, attend business meetings	90 days, 60 days, 30 days, or 15 days

4-1-5	Persons engaging in management of business, foreign trade, or capital investment activites	3 years, 1 year, 6 or 3 months
4-1-6	Students engaging in study or research at the junior college level or above	1 year, 6 or 3 months
4-1-6-2	Persons accepted by a public or private organization in Japan to acquire industrial techniques or skills	1 year, 6 or 3 months
4-1-7	Lecturers and professors engaging in full-time teaching at educational or research institutions	3 years, 1 year, 6 or 3 months
4-1-8	Persons engaging in activities of a high level in the arts and sciences (music, fine arts, literature, science, etc.)	1 year, 6 or 3 months
4-1-9	Paid entertainers such as singers, actors, professional athletes, their managers and entourage	60 days, 30 days, or 15 days
4-1-10	Persons dispatched to Japan by foreign religious organizations to conduct religious activities (including non-paid educational or medical activities)	3 years, 1 year, 6 or 3 months
4-1-11	Persons dispatched to Japan for news gathering purposes by foreign newspapers, radio and TV broadcasters and other journalistic organizations (excluding freelancers, etc.)	3 years, 1 year, 6 or 3 months
4-1-12	Persons invited by public or private organizations in Japan for the purpose of furnishing high-level or specialized skills and know-how	3 years, 1 year, 6 or 3 months
4-1-13	Persons engaging in skilled labor (e.g. cooks in Chinese or French restaurants, Western-style confectioners, etc.)	1 year, 6 or 3 months

4-1-14	Persons seeking to reside permanently in Japan	Permanent
4-1-15	Spouses and unmarried minor children of any person coming under status 4-1-5 through 4-1-13 above (excluding minor children who are college students, employed, or otherwise engaged in any activity which falls under another status of residence category)	Same as supporting spouse or parent
4-1-16-1	Spouses or children of Japanese nationals (if residing in Japan as family members of Japanese nationals)	3 years, 1 year, 6 or 3 months
4-1-16-2	Children whose Korean or Taiwanese parent has been living in Japan since before the end of World War II or since birth if born between the end of war and April 28, 1952, and who were born after April 28, 1952	3 years
4-1-16-3	Persons who do not fall under any other status but are permitted to reside at the discretion of the Minister of Justice (under this status medical doctors, teachers at foreign language schools, students at Japanese language schools, dependents of Japanese nationals, etc. are permitted to enter and stay)	Up to 3 years, the precise period determined on a case-by-case basis

Note: The numbers in the Status of Residence column indicate the article, paragraph and item of the Immigration Control and Refugee Recognition Act under which the status falls. Thus, 4-1-4 (temporary visitors) indicates Article 4, Paragraph 1, Item 4.

PROFESSIONAL ORGANIZATIONS

These organizations (most based in Tokyo) are an excellent place to begin if you are interested in finding out about jobs in a particular field. They are a good way to meet people, gather information, and spread the word that you are looking for work. Often a person who is leaving Japan will announce the vacancy to be created via the organization's newsletter or at a meeting. Since Japanese companies often prefer hiring someone the departing person recommends rather than going through an open application process, the insider information available through these organizations can be invaluable.

Most of these organizations have both Japanese and foreign members and conduct activities in English. The contact names and numbers below were accurate as the book went to press, but, given the transient nature of most foreigners in Tokyo, some organizations disappear and reappear at irregular intervals. If a phone number is no longer correct, contact someone working in the field you are interested in to find out if the organization is still intact, and if so, how to get more information.

TEACHING

Japan Association of Language Teachers (JALT)

6-27 Hirakata Motomachi, Hirakata-shi, Osaka 573
- Tokyo Chapter (03) 444-8474
- Kyoto Chapter (075) 392-2291 or (075) 361-5428

This is the largest association for language teachers. Monthly meetings and an annual conference are held. Branch chapters are found in most large- and medium-sized cities throughout Japan. Contact a fellow teacher in your area to find out more.

Association of English Teachers of Children

2-7-11 Takaido Higashi, Suginami-ku, Tokyo 168. (0422) 53-0024
Monthly meetings on Sundays from one to four.

Association of Foreign Teachers in Japan

Meets third Sunday of every month at International House in Roppongi. (03) 238-3909

ADVERTISING, JOURNALISM, PUBLIC RELATIONS, PUBLISHING, WRITING

Forum for Corporate Communications

Meets third or fourth Tuesday of the month at 6:15 P.M. on the twentieth floor of the Yurakucho Denki Building. (03) 433-3874

Society of Writers, Editors, and Translators (SWET)

Meets irregularly, has guest speakers, parties, sponsors tours, writes manuals. 450 members. Write 2-19-15-808 Shibuya, Shibuya-ku, Tokyo 150.

Japan Association of Translators

Meets on third Saturday of the month. 2-31-20-607 Shimo-toda, Toda, Saitama 335. (0484) 44-8567

Society for Technical Communication

Monthly evening meetings. (03) 455-8711

COMPUTERS

International Computer Association

Users, professionals, manufacturers, and sales people meet monthly at 6:00 P.M. on the twentieth floor of the Yurakucho Denki Building. Or write to Akasaka P.O. Box 67, Minato-ku, Tokyo 107-91. (03) 823-4394

Tokyo PC Club

Monthly meetings offer training, expertise, and camaraderie.
P.O. Box 1145, Tokyo 100-91, Woody Hodgson, Public Relations Chairman.

MacTokyo Macintosh Users Group

Meets on the fourth Thursday of the month at 7:30 P.M. at Tokyo Union Church. Contact Frank Onda, Focal Point Computer, (03) 417-2294.

FOREIGN LAWYERS

The Roppongi Bar Association

Meets the third Wednesday of every month at Beer Bar 25 in Roppongi. Call the newsletter editor, M. Barrett, for more information. (03) 280-2847.

There are also informal associations of lawyers from various countries. Contact a lawyer from your country who is working in Japan for more information.

SCIENTIFIC RESEARCH

U.S. National Science Foundation Office

Provides a wealth of information on research opportunities in Japan. American Embassy, (03) 224-5505.

ARCHITECTS AND ENGINEERS

Far East Society of Architects and Engineers

Meets monthly at 6:15 P.M. on the twentieth floor of the Yurakucho Denki Building. Works to promote the fields of architecture, engineering, and construction. Contact Mr. Yasuda, Dai Nippon Construction, 2-35 Ichigaya Tamachi, Shinjuku-ku, Tokyo 162. (03) 267-7086.

SERVICE INDUSTRIES

Foreigners in Travel

An informal group that meets monthly. Contact Michel Mertens at Bel Top Travel, (03) 454-6339, for more information.

ENTREPRENEURS

Business Owner's Club in Japan

Formed to aid European entrepreneurs. Monthly meetings. 201 Shibuya Homes, 2-1 Udagawa-cho, Shibuya-ku, Tokyo 150. (03) 477-7488

The Australian Business Association

Meets six or more times a year and publishes a newsletter. 3-14-6 Ginza, Chuo-ku, Tokyo 104. (03) 5565-1361, Fax (03) 545-8949

The American Chamber of Commerce In Japan's Independent Business Committee

Meets monthly and provides a forum for information exchange and support. Contact the ACCJ at seventh floor, Fukide No. 2 Building, 4-1-21 Toranomon, Minato-ku, Tokyo 105. (03) 433-5381

The Canadian Chamber of Commerce

May be contacted through the Canadian Embassy, 8-8 Azabu Juban 2-chome, Minato-ku, Tokyo 106. (03) 453-2640

The British Chamber of Commerce

Kowa 16 Bldg. Annex, 9-20 Akasaka 1-chome, Minato-ku, Tokyo 107. (03) 505-1734

JETRO (Japan External Trade Organization)

Provides advice to foreign firms seeking to enter the Japanese market and has published a number of detailed guides to the Japanese market. 2-5 Toranomon 2-chome, Minato-ku, Tokyo 105. (03) 582-5511

GENERAL NETWORKING AND SUPPORT ORGANIZATIONS

KAISHA Society

Meets on the third Wednesday each month on the twentieth floor of the Yurakucho Denki building at 6:15 P.M. A support, education, and social group for the non-Japanese employees of Japanese corporations and institutions. Contact the current officers or write The KAISHA Society, c/o The Press Club, Yurakucho Denki Bldg., 20th floor, 1-7-1 Yurakucho, Tokyo 100.

Foreign Executive Women (FEW)

Meets the second Thursday of each month on the twentieth floor of the Yurakucho Denki Building at 6:15 P.M.. Same as above but only for women and not necessarily working for Japanese companies.

Toastmasters International

Meets twice monthly to develop members' public speaking abilities. American Chamber of Commerce club meets at noon in the Tokyo American Club. Contact Mr Murai at (03) 274-2961. Tokyo club meets the first and third Thursdays from 7:00 to 9:00 P.M.. Call Nobuyuki Moriwaka at (0429) 65-1284.

SOCIAL AND LEISURE ORGANIZATIONS

International Adventure Club

Meets monthly at 7:30 P.M. at Tokyo British Club to plot upcoming adventures (hiking, hot springs, etc.). (03) 27-2905, 333-0419

Tokyo Leisure Club

Hosts classes, parties, excursions, etc. (03) 466-3925

Tokyo Motorcyle Touring Workshop for Foreigners

GPO Box 2064, Tokyo 100-91. (03) 402-5385

International Community Circle

Promotes cultural exchange via discussion, parties, classes. Lounge open daily after 5:30 P.M.. Shuwa Roppongi Bldg. 5F, 3-14-12, Roppongi, Minato-ku, Tokyo 106. (03) 423-0660 after 3:00 P.M.

OTHER HELPFUL ORGANIZATIONS

Newcomers often experience some sort of culture shock, depression, or loneliness. The major churches provide orientation programs and support services and are a good place to start making friends:

Franciscan Chapel Center (03) 401-2141

Jewish Community Center (03) 400-2559

St. Alban's Church (03) 431-8534

St. Paul International Lutheran Church (03) 261-3740

Tokyo Baptist Church (03) 461-8425

Tokyo Union Church (03) 400-0047

Welcome Furoshiki

Newly arrived foreigners can call (03) 352-0765 and a representative will visit your home with a bundle of information about living in Tokyo or Yokohama.

Tokyo English Life Line (TELL)

Trained volunteers listen to callers and, when appropriate, provide referrals to doctors, therapists, support groups, crisis centers, women's shelters, and AIDS information. (03) 264-4347 9:00 A.M. to 4:00 P.M. and 7:00 to 11:00 P.M., seven days a week.

Tokyo Community Counselling Services

TCCS provides a wide range of individual and group counseling as well as seminars, workshops, and discussions. Fees are on a sliding scale and no one in need of help is turned away. (03) 780-0336

Oak Associates

Career counseling. Misawa Bldg, 504, 5-21-5 Sendagaya, Shibuya-ku, Tokyo 151. (03) 354-9502, Fax (03) 350-5216

Counseling International 03-408-0496

International Social Service of Japan (03)12-6661

Association of Foreign Wives of Japanese (044) 366-2760 or (03) 263-6786

International Feminists Of Japan (03) 792-4110

COMPANIES THAT HIRE FOREIGNERS

This list is by no means exhaustive, but it covers the major firms in each of the fields mentioned in this book. There are countless smaller firms wanting to hire foreigners, but the only way to find these jobs is to live in Japan for a year or so and keep your ears open.

Because most foreign firms bring their foreign employees from overseas, the bulk of the firms listed here are Japanese or joint ventures. Even some of these do most of their hiring overseas, but hiring policies are constantly in flux and employment in Japan is always "case by case." If a firm thinks you may contribute in some way to its operation, it will often hire you, regardless of its "official" hiring policy and whether or not there is a position open.

If you are already in Japan, the best way to approach a company is through a personal introduction from someone already working there. A little networking (using the Professional Organizations appendix) should produce these connections. If not, don't despair. There are quite a few foreigners who called a company cold, went for an interview, and found themselves hired.

Sending a resume and cover letter to one of these companies from overseas has been known to produce results—but very rarely. If you are really serious about working in Japan, you should indicate in your letter that you are definitely coming to Japan by a certain time. The letter should then be followed by a phone call and a meeting once you are in Japan.

ENGLISH TEACHING

There are literally tens of thousands of companies and schools that need English teachers on a regular basis. Because of the concentration of population in urban areas, this is where most of the English schools are and this is where most foreigners go when they look for jobs. There are, however, many small schools in rural areas desperately seeking foreign teachers. These jobs are difficult to hear about unless you are in Japan.

This list includes only the larger schools (those with about fifty to 100 foreign teachers). The high turnover rate means that these schools are almost always looking for new teachers. Their head offices are generally in Tokyo, but they often have dozens of branches throughout Japan. For a more detailed list of over 100 private schools in the Tokyo, Osaka, Kyoto, and Fukuoka areas, see *Jobs In Japan* by John Wharton.

Nichibei Kaiwa Gakko, Yotsuya 1-21, Shinjuku-ku, Tokyo 160. (03) 359-9621

Interac, 2-10-28 Fujimi-cho, Chiyoda-ku, Tokyo 102. (03) 234-7717 (head office) or Munemura Bldg. 3F, 1-12-5 Iidabashi, Chiyoda-ku, Tokyo 102. (03) 234-7814 (Recruiting Department)

Time T. I. Communications Co., Ltd., Time & Life Bldg, 3-6 Otemachi, 2-chome, Chiyoda-ku, Tokyo 100. (03) 270-4711

ASA Community Salon, Shinjuku Building, 1-19-6 Yamate, Nishi-Shinjuku, Shinjuku-ku, Tokyo 160. (03) 348-6225

ECC, Dairuoku Arai Bldg, 1-5-4 Kabukicho, Shinjuku-ku, Tokyo 160. (03) 209-3733

Kanda Institute of Foreign Languages, 2-13-13 Uchikanda, Chiyoda-ku, Tokyo 101. (03) 254-2731

International Language Center (ILC), Iwanami Jimbocho Bldg., Jinden, 2-1 Jimbocho, Chiyoda-ku, Tokyo. (03) 954-5173

ELEC, 3-8 Jimbocho, Kanda, Chiyoda-ku, Tokyo 101. (03) 265-8911

SONY Eigo Kyoshitsu, 1-6-12 Nishi-Shimbashi, Kurihara Bldg., Shimbashi, Minato-ku, Tokyo. 160 (03) 232-0290

Tokyo Foreign Language College, 7-3-8 Nishi-Shinjuku, Shinjuku-ku, Tokyo 160. (03) 367-1101

Tokyo Business Gaigo Senmon Gakko, 1-14-6 Jiyugaoka, Meguro-ku, Tokyo 152. (03) 724-0551

Gregg Gaigo Gakko, 1-14-16 Jiyugaoka, Meguro-ku, Tokyo 152. (03) 724-0552

Stanton School of English, Rokubancho·7, Chiyoda-ku, Tokyo 102. (03) 262-3300

Berlitz School of Languages, Yurakucho Bldg., 7th floor, 10-1-1 Yurakucho, Chiyoda-ku, Tokyo 100. (03) 214-2611

Excellence, Kawaguchi Bldg., 1-8-11 Iidabashi, Chiyoda-ku, Tokyo 102. (03) 234-4025

There are also YMCA English schools scattered throughout the archipelago. You can apply to a specific one or send your curriculum vitae to YMCA Overseas Service, International Div., YMCA, 291 Broadway, NYC, N.Y. and ask to be notified of any openings.

You can also apply from overseas for the Japan Education and Training (JET) Program, a government project that places about 2,000 foreign teachers in Japanese junior high and high schools each year. Citizens of the United States, Canada, Britain, Australia, New Zealand, and Ireland can get information and application materials from Japanese Embassies and Consulates in their own countries.

The address of the largest U.S. association for Teachers of English to Speakers of Other Languages (TESOL) is: TESOL, Transit Building, Georgetown University, Washington, D.C., 20057. They publish a monthly newsletter that lists job openings.

TRANSLATING, WRITING, AND EDITING

Many language brokers work independently from their homes and there are many foreigners who have set up their own companies to do translation, copywriting, rewriting, editing, and general production work for advertisements, pamphlets, and brochures. A good way to get your feet wet in this field would be to get involved with the Society for Writers, Editors, and Translators (see Professional Organizations appendix). Many people begin by doing part-time freelance work and then move on to start their own company or work for another. Some of the main companies that hire language brokers are listed below.

TRANSLATORS

Investor Relations Japan, 1-15-13 Yotsuya, Shinjuku-ku, Tokyo 160. (03) 351-1120

Japan Convention Services, Nippon Press Center Bldg., 2-2-1 Uchisaiwaicho, Chiyoda-ku, Tokyo 100. (03) 508-1211

Japan Interpreters Association, Chiyoda Seimei Bldg., 1-5-20 Takadanobaba, Shinjuku-ku, Tokyo. (03) 209-4741

Japan Translation Center, 1-21 Kanda, Nishikicho, Chiyoda-ku, Tokyo 101. (03) 291-0655, Fax (03) 294-0657.

Kokusai Enterprises, 1-2-1 Minami Naruse, Machida-shi, Tokyo 194. (0427) 23-8221

Obun Printing Co., 17-2, Hongo 1-chome, Bunkyo-ku, Tokyo 113. (03) 817-5930, Fax (03) 818-4382

Simul International, Inc, Kowa Bldg. No. 9, 8-10 Akasaka, 1-Chome, Minato-ku, Tokyo 107. (03) 586-5641, Fax (03) 505-4794.

THE ENGLISH MEDIA—NEWSPAPERS, MAGAZINES, TV & RADIO

The English-language newspapers are nearly always looking for rewriters, translators, proofreaders, and editors. Some also need columnists and writers. Freelance writers, photographers, and illustrators often find the English-language magazines a good outlet for their work. There are also translating, rewriting, editing, and narration jobs available in radio and TV.

NEWSPAPERS & WIRE SERVICES

Asahi Evening News, 8-5 Tsukiji 7-chome, Chuo-ku, Tokyo 104. (03) 546-7132, Fax (03) 543-1660

The Daily Yomiuri, 1-7-1 Otemachi, Chiyoda-ku, Tokyo 100-55. (03) 242-1111, Fax (03) 279-6324

The Japan Times, 4-5-4 Shibaura, Minato-ku, Tokyo 108. (03) 452-1799, Fax (03) 453-7085

Mainichi Daily News, Hitotsubashi 1-1-1, Chiyoda-ku, Tokyo 100-51. (03) 212-0321, Fax (03) 212-0635

Agence France Presse, Asahi Shinbun Bldg., 5-3-2 Tsukiji, Chuo-ku, Tokyo 104. (03) 545-3061, Fax (03) 546-2594

Associated Press, Asahi Shinbun Bldg., 11F, 5-3-2 Tsukiji, Chuo-ku, Tokyo 104. (03) 545-5901 Fax (03) 545-0895

Knight-Ridder Financial News, Ichibancho F.S. Bldg., 8 Ichibancho, Chiyoda-ku, Tokyo 102. (03) 230-1155, Fax (03) 230-4828

Kyodo News Service, 2-2-5 Toranomon, Minato-ku, Tokyo 105. (03) 584-4111, Fax (03) 505-6630

Reuters Japan, Shuwa Kamiyacho Bldg., 4-3-13 Toranomon, Minato-ku, Tokyo 105. (03) 432-8479, Fax (03) 432-5392

United Press International, Palaceside Bldg., 1-1-1 Hitotsubashi, Chiyoda-ku, Tokyo 100. (03) 212-7911, Fax (03) 213-5053

The Wall Street Journal and **The Asian Wall Street Journal**, Nihon Keizai Shinbun Bldg., 1-9-5 Otemachi, Chiyoda-ku, Tokyo 100. (03) 241-1671, Fax (03) 246-1098

MAGAZINES

Business Tokyo, Keizaikai Bldg., 2-13-18 Minami Aoyama, Minato-ku, Tokyo 107. (03) 423-8500, Fax (03) 423-8505

Far East Traveler, 1-4-28 Moto-Azabu, Minato-ku, Tokyo 106. (03) 452-0705, Fax (03) 452-0474

Journal of the American Chamber of Commerce In Japan, Fukide Bldg. No. 2, 4-1-21 Toranomon, Minato-ku, Tokyo 105. (03) 433-5381, Fax (03) 436-1446

Look Japan, 2-2 Kanda Ogawa-machi, Chiyoda-ku, Tokyo 101. (03) 291-8951, Fax (03) 291-8955

PHP Intersect, 3-10 Sanbancho, Chiyoda-ku, Tokyo 102. (03) 239-6238, Fax (03) 222-0424

The Tokyo Journal, Cross-Cultural Communications Bldg., 12-2-1 Minami Motomachi, Shinjuku-ku, Tokyo 160. (03) 5379-6214, Fax (03) 5379-6219

Winds, inflight magazine of Japan Airlines, Emphasis, Inc., Central Roppongi Bldg., 1-4-27 Roppongi, Minato-ku, Tokyo 106. (03) 585-8857, Fax (03) 585-1596

TELEVISION & RADIO

British Broadcasting Corp, Nihon Terebi, 4-Bancho, 5-6, Chiyoda-ku, Tokyo. (03) 288-0011 Fax (03) 288-0010

NHK (Japanese Public TV & radio), NHK Hoso Center, 2-2-1 Jin-nan, Shibuya-ku, Tokyo (03) 465-1111

Visnews, Aoki Bldg., 4-1-10 Toranomon, Minato-ku, Tokyo 105. (03) 433-2280, Fax (03) 433-8351

PUBLISHING COMPANIES (English language)

Addison-Wesley Publishers Japan Ltd., Nichibo Bldg., 1-2-2 Sarugakucho, Chiyoda-ku, Tokyo. (03) 291-4581, Fax (03) 291-4592

Charles E. Tuttle Co., Inc. Suido 1-chome, 2-6, Bunkyo-ku, Tokyo 112. (03) 811-7106, Fax (03) 811-6953

Harcourt Brace Jovanovich Japan Inc. Ichibancho Central Bldg., 22-1 Ichibancho, Chiyoda-ku, Tokyo 102. (03) 234-3913, Fax (03) 285-7186

Kodansha International Ltd, 17-14 Otowa 1-chome, Bunkyo-ku, Tokyo 112. (03) 944-6493, Fax (03) 944-6394

Longman Penguin Japan Co., Ltd., Yamaguchi Bldg, 2-12-9, Kanda Jimbocho, Chiyoda-ku, Tokyo 101. (03) 265-7627, Fax (03) 239-8748

McGraw-Hill, Inc., Kasumigaseki Bldg., Room 1528, 3-2-5 Kasumigaseki, Chiyoda-ku, Tokyo 100. (03) 581-9816, Fax (03) 581-4018

Weatherhill, 7-6-13 Roppongi, Minato-ku, Tokyo 106. (03) 263-4391, Fax (03) 263-4392

FINANCE

These institutions hire foreigners in a wide variety of jobs, from foreign customer liaison work to foreign exchange to translation to research.

First, the Big Four:

Nomura Securities, Personnel Department, Overseas Personnel Section, P.O. Box 33 Nihombashi, Chuo-ku, Tokyo 103-91. (03) 271-8069, Fax (03) 281-4597

Daiwa Securities, 2-6-4 Otemachi, Chiyoda-ku, Tokyo 100. (03) 243-2111 Fax (03) 245-0797

Nikko Securities, 3-3-1 Marunouchi, Chiyoda-ku, Tokyo 100. (03) 283-2211 Fax (03) 283-2470

Yamaichi Securities Co., Personnel Department, 4-1 Yaesu 2-chome, Chuo-ku, Tokyo 104. (03) 276-2656, Fax (03) 276-3086

And lesser, but still mighty:

The Bank of Tokyo, 1-3-2 Honishi-cho, Nihombashi, Chuo-ku, Tokyo 103-91. (03) 245-1111, Fax (03) 246-2132

The Mitsubishi Trust and Banking Corporation, 4-5 Marunouchi 1-chome, Chiyoda-ku, Tokyo 100. (03) 212-1211, Fax (03) 214-8699

Mitsui Bank, 1-2 Yurakucho 1-chome, Chiyoda-ku, Tokyo 100. (03) 501-1111, Fax (03) 501-8531

Dai-ichi Kangyo Bank, 1-1-5 Uchisaiwaicho, Chiyoda-ku, Tokyo 100. (03) 596-2415, Fax (03) 596-2539

Fuji Bank, 1-5-5 Otemachi, Chiyoda-ku, Tokyo 100. (03) 216-2211, Fax (03) 216-6055

Industrial Bank of Japan, 3-3 Marunouchi 1-chome, Chiyoda-ku, Tokyo 100. (03) 214-1111, Fax (03) 285-0368

Kokusai Securities Co. Ltd., Shinjuku Nomura Bldg., 1-26-2 Nishi-Shinjuku, Shinjuku-ku, Tokyo 163. (03) 297-2111, Fax (03) 297-9538

Nippon Kangyo Kakumaru Securities, 1-6-1 Marunouchi, Chiyoda-ku, Tokyo 100. (03) 286-7111 (03) 216-4965

Sanwa Bank, 1-1 Otemachi, Chiyoda-ku, Tokyo 100. (03) 216-3111, Fax (03) 214-8090

Sumitomo Bank, 3-2 Marunouchi, 1-chome, Chiyoda-ku, Tokyo 100. (03) 282-8980, Fax (03) 282-5111

Tokyo Forex Co. (Foreign Exchange), General Affairs Dept., 2-15 Nihombashi, Muromachi 3-chome, Chuo-ku, Tokyo 102. (03) 270-8801, Fax (03) 245-1225

Wako Securities, 6-1 Nihonbashi-koamicho, Chuo-ku, Tokyo 103. (03) 667-8111, Fax (03) 669-8749

Yasuda Trust and Banking Co., Mr. Wada, Human Resources Development Dept., 2-1 Yaesu 1-chome, Chuo-ku, Tokyo 103. (03) 278-8111 or 274-9033 (direct line), Fax (03) 272-8067

LAW FIRMS

There are many Japanese firms hiring foreign lawyers as "trainees." Here are a few:

Mori Sogo Law Offices, Dowa Bldg 5 Fl, 2-22 Ginza 7-chome, Chuo-ku, Tokyo 104. (03) 572-6641 Fax (03) 574-8664

Nakagawa & Godo, 3-11-3 Akasaka, Minato-ku, Tokyo 107. (03) 589-2921, Fax (03) 589-2926

Tsuchiya, Sakuragi, Sogi & Ito, Hibiya Park Bldg No. 925, 1-8-1 Yurakucho, Chiyoda-ku, Tokyo 100. (03) 201-0401 Fax (03) 201-0403

ARCHITECTURE FIRMS

Kume Architects and Engineers Co., 1-13-11 Nishi Azabu, Minato-ku, Tokyo 106. (03) 403-0251

Matsui Construction, 1-17-22 Shinkawa, Chuo-ku, Tokyo 104. (03) 553-1151 Fax (03) 553-1152

Mitsubishi Estate Co., (Design Dept.) 2-4-1 Marunouchi, Chiyoda-ku Tokyo 100. (03) 287-5100 Fax (03) 214-7036

NIKKEN (Kenchiku Shiryo Kenkyusha Co), 2-1041-21 Ikebukuro, Toshima-ku, Tokyo 171. (03) 5992-3091, Fax (03) 5992-3564

Nikken Sekkei, 1-4-27 Koraku, Bunkyo-ku, Tokyo 112. (03) 813-3361

Sekkei Design, Yamatane Bldg., 1-11-22 Minami Ikebukuro, Toshima-ku, Tokyo 171. (03) 989-9511

CONSTRUCTION COMPANIES

Kajima Corp, 1-2-7 Moto-Akasaka, Minato-ku, Tokyo 107. (03) 404-3311 Fax (03) 470-1444

Kumagai-gumi Co. Ltd., 17-1, Tsukuto-cho, Shinjuku-ku, Tokyo 162. (03) 260-2111, Fax (03) 235-5389

Komatsu Construction, 3-5-4 Shiba Koen, Minato-ku, Tokyo 105. (03) 434-5131, Fax (03) 434-5309

Obayashi Corporation (in Tokyo), 3-2 chome, Kanda, Tsukasa-cho, Chiyoda-ku, Tokyo 101. (03) 292-1111

Shimizu Corp., No. 16-1, Kyobashi 2-chome, Chuo-ku, Tokyo 104. (03) 535-4111, Fax (03) 564-0467

Taisei Corporation, Shinjuku Center Bldg., 1-25-1, Nishi-Shinjuku, Shinjuku-ku, Tokyo 163. (03) 348-1111, Fax (03) 343-4046

Takenaka Co., 2-5-14 Minami-suna, Koto-ku, Tokyo 136. (03) 647-3161

SCIENTIFIC RESEARCH

The Tokyo Office of the U.S. National Science Foundation has put out a "Directory of Japanese Company Laboratories Willing To Receive American Researchers."

The Japan Society for the Promotion of Science offers fifty postdoctoral fellowships annually for work at public or private Japanese universities or other research facilities affiliated with the Japanese Ministries of Education, Science and Culture.

The Japanese Science and Technology Agency offers a parallel program for researchers wanting to work at certain institutions.

The National Science Foundation and the Agency of Industrial Science and Technology of the Ministry of International Trade and Industry supports thirty young scientists and engineers per year at any of the AIST facilities.

For further information, write to the National Science Foundation, Japan Initiative, Room 1208, Division of International programs, Washington, D.C., 20550, or contact the NSF Tokyo Office in the American Embassy.

R & D IN HI-TECH COMPANIES

Many of these firms hire foreigners in both technical and administrative positions.

Control Data Japan, Sunshine 60 Bldg., 27F, 3-1-1 Higashi-Ikebukuro, Toshima-ku, Tokyo 170. (03) 982-9084, Fax (03) 988-0989

Fujitsu, 1-6-1 Marunouchi, Chiyoda-ku, Tokyo 100. (03) 216-3211, Fax (03) 213-7174

Fuji-Xerox Company, 3-3-5 Akasaka, Minato-ku, Tokyo 107. (03) 585-3211

Hitachi, Ltd., 4-6 Kanda-Surugadai, Chiyoda-ku, Tokyo 101. (03) 258-1111, Fax (03) 253-2186

Matsushita Electric Co., Ozawa Kadoma 1006, Kadoma-shi, Osaka-fu 571. (06) 908-1121, Fax (06) 906-1762

Minolta, Osaka Kokusai Bldg., 2-30 Azuchi-machi, Higashi-ku, Osaka 541. (06) 271-2251, Fax (06) 266-1010

NEC, Shiba 5-33-1, Minato-ku, Tokyo 108. (03) 454-1111, Fax (03) 798-1510

Ricoh, 1-15-5 Minami-Aoyama, Minato-ku, Tokyo 167. (03) 479-3111, Fax (03) 479-2900

Sony Corp, Kita Shinagawa 6-7-35, Shinagawa-ku, Tokyo 141. (03) 448-2111, Fax (03) 447-4378

MANUFACTURING

The larger companies need foreign employees in many fields, from legal assistants to language teachers to sales representatives to public relations to computer systems and mechanical engineering. Many foreigners find work in overseas business administration, public relations, education, research and development, and engineering.

Brother, Horita-dori 9-35, Mizuho, Nagoya-shi, Aichi-ken 467. (052) 824-2511, Fax (052) 821-8204

Hitachi Chemical Co., 2-1-1 Nishi Shinjuku, Shinjuku-ku, Tokyo 163. (03) 346-3111, Fax (03) 343-8488

Isuzu Motors Ltd., 6-22-10 Minami Oi, Shinagawa-ku, Tokyo 140. (03) 762-1111, Fax (03) 761-4236

Japan Steel, (NKK) Marunouchi 1-1-2, Chiyoda-ku, Tokyo 100. (03) 212-7111, Fax (03) 214-8417

Kobe Steel Co., Ltd., Hyogo-ken, Chuo-ku, 1-3-18 Wakihama-cho, Kobe-shi 651. (078) 251-1551, Fax (078) 232-3459

Mitsubishi Heavy Industries, 2-5-1 Marunouchi, Chiyoda-ku, Tokyo 100. (03) 212-3111, Fax (03) 284-19272

Nippon Steel, 2-6-3 Otemachi, Chiyoda-ku, Tokyo 100-71. (03) 242-4111, Fax (03) 275-5607

Nissan Motor Co., 6-17-1 Ginza, Chuo-ku, Tokyo 104. (03) 5565-2148, Fax (03) 546-2669

Sanyo Chemical Industries, 11-1 Hitotsubashi, Nomoto-cho, Higashiyama-ku, Kyoto 605. (075) 541-4311, (075) 551-2557

Toyota Motor Corp. 1, Toyota-cho, Toyota-shi, Aichi-ken 471. (0565) 28-2121, Fax (0565) 80-1116

ADVERTISING

Advertising companies hire foreign copywriters, account executives, graphic designers, translators, rewriters, and proofreaders, both from overseas and within Japan.

DAIKO Advertising Inc., 3-39 Miyahara 4-chome, Yodogawa-ku, Osaka 532. (06) 392-8111, Fax (03) 392-8130

Dentsu, Inc., 1-11 Tsukiji, Chuo-ku, Tokyo 104. (03) 544-5599, Fax (03) 546-2967

Hakuhodo, Inc., Tokyo Bldg., 7-3, Marunouchi 2-chome, Chiyoda-ku, Tokyo 100. (03) 240-7700, Fax (03) 240-7073

J. Walter Thompson, 1-4-10 Takanawa, Minato-ku, Tokyo. (03) 280-9595, Fax (03) 440-48-48

McCann-Erickson-Hakuhodo, Shin Aoyama Bldg, E-23, 1-1 Minami Aoyama 1-chome, Minato-ku, Tokyo 107. (03) 748-8001, Fax (03) 746-8017

Kyodo Advertising, Hibiya Chunichi Bldg., 2-1-4 Uchisaiwaicho, Chiyoda-ku, Tokyo 100. (03) 503-1311, Fax (03) 580-9065

Standard Advertising, Sumitomo Higashi-Shimbashi Bldg., 1-1-11 Hamamatsucho, Minato-ku, Tokyo 100. (03) 434-8181

MARKETING

ASI Market Research, Yoneda Bldg., 6-17-20 Shimbashi, Minato-ku, Tokyo 105. (03) 432-1701

Dodwell Marketing Consultants, G.P.O Box 297, Tokyo 100 (03) 211-4451, Fax (03) 211-2154

Infoplan, Jichiro Kaikan Bldg., 1-Rokuban-cho, Chiyoda-ku, Tokyo 102. (03) 265-5411, Fax (03) 265-5419

Marketing Intelligence Corp, Ikebukuro Aoyagi Bldg, Ikebukuro 2-43-1, Toshima-ku, Tokyo 171. (03) 5376-0456, Fax (03) 971-8300

PUBLIC RELATIONS

Burson Marsteller, Sogo No.3 Bldg., 1-6 Kojimachi, Chiyoda-ku, Tokyo (03) 264-6701

Cosmo Public Relations, Isehan Bldg., 8-3-7 Ginza, Chuo-ku, Tokyo 104. (03) 572-3661

Dentsu PR Center, 2-16-7 Ginza, Chuo-ku, Tokyo 104. (03) 542-2374

IBI Inc, Izumiya Bldg, 3-1-1 Kojimachi, Chiyoda-ku Tokyo 102 (03) 230-1835, Fax (03) 234-8634

Japan Counselors Inc., Mita 43 Mori Bldg., 3-13-16 Mita, Minato-ku Tokyo. (03) 457-0311, Fax (03) 452-5200

Universal Public Relations, BR Shinagawa 2 Bldg, 1-20-9 Kita Shinagawa, Shinagawa-ku, Tokyo 140. (03) 5479-5001, Fax (03) 5479-5218

TRADING COMPANIES

The Japanese trading companies (*sogo shosha*) have been doing international business longer than just about any other organization in Japan. They hire foreigners in a variety of positions, from lawyers to researchers to translators to international liaison personnel. One woman working at one of the large trading companies considers herself a "fluid asset"—she flows wherever they need her.

Mitsui and Co., 1-2-1 Otemachi, Chiyoda-ku, Tokyo 100. (03) 285-1111, Fax (03) 285-9819

Mitsubishi Trading Co., 2-6-3 Marunouchi, Chiyoda-ku, Tokyo 100. (03) 210-2121, Fax (03) 210-8071

C. Itoh & Co., 4-1-3 Kyutaromachi, Chuo-ku, Osaka 541. (06) 241-2121, Fax (06) 241-3167

Marubeni Corporation, 2-5-7 Honmachi, Chuo-ku, Osaka 541-88, (06) 266-2111, Fax (06) 266-42893, or 4-2 Otemachi, 1-chome, Chiyoda-ku, Tokyo 100. (03) 282-4866, Fax (03) 282-7259

Sumitomo Shoji, 5-15 Kitahama, Chuo-ku, Osaka 541. (06) 220-6000, Fax (03) 217-7860 or 2-2 Hitotsubashi 1-chome, Chiyoda-ku, Tokyo 100. (03) 217-5000, Fax (03) 217-7860

Nissho Iwai Corp., 4-5 Akasaka 2-chome, Minato-ku, Tokyo 107. (03) 588-4038, Fax (03) 588-4854

HOTELS & DEPARMENT STORES

Many hire foreigners for international customer relations purposes, but there are also jobs in sales and other areas.

Century Hyatt Hotel, 2-7-2 Nishi-Shinjuku, Shinjuku-ku, Tokyo 160. (03) 349-0111

The Keio Plaza Hotel, 2-1 Nishi-Shinjuku, 2-chome, Shinjuku-ku, Tokyo 160. (03) 344-0111

Hotel Okura, Toranomon 2-10-4, Minato-ku, Tokyo 105. (03) 586-7400, Fax(03) 582-3707

Hotel Seiyo, Tohka Bldg, 1-16-1 Ginza, Chuo-ku, Tokyo 104. (03) 535-1111, Fax (03) 535-1123

Sheraton Grande Tokyo Bay Hotel and Towers, 1-9 Maihama, Urayasu, Chiba 279. (0473) 55-5555, Fax (0473) 55-5588

Tokyo Hilton International, 6-6-2 Nishi-Shinjuku, Shinjuku-ku, Tokyo 160. (03) 344-5111

Tokyu Hotel Chain, 6-6 Kojimachi, Chiyoda-ku, Tokyo 102 (03) 264-0111, Fax (03) 264-0225

Hankyu Dept. Stores, 8-7 Kakuta-cho, Kita-ku, Osaka 530 (06) 361-1381, Fax (03) 311-5680

Isetan Department Store, 3-14-1 Shinjuku, Shinjuku-ku, Tokyo 160. (03) 352-1111, Fax (03) 225-2464

Mitsukoshi Dept. Store, 1-4-1 Nihonbashi Muromachi, Chuo-ku, Tokyo 103. (03) 241-3311 Fax (03) 245-0949

Seibu Department Stores Ltd., Sunshine City, 3-1-1 Higashi-

Ikebukuro, Toshima-ku, Tokyo 170. (03) 989-0111, Fax (03) 988-9696

Tokyu Store Chain, 1-21-12 Kami-Meguro, Meguro-ku, Tokyo 153 (03) 711-0109, Fax (03) 791-6521

MODELING AGENCIES

Foreigners already in Japan who want to do some part-time modeling should take their portfolios to:

Askew Japan, 3-10-7 Minami Aoyama, Minato-ku, Tokyo 107. (03) 478-1232 or Shinseifu Bldg., 1-2-19 Nakatsu, Oyodo-ku, Osaka. (06) 373-1524

Boa Agency Co., 2-1-1021 Udagawacho, Shibuya-ku, Tokyo. (03) 476-1516

Fame Promotion, Inc, Gaien House 326, 2-2-39 Jingumae, Shibuya-ku, Tokyo. (03) 478-5541

Japan Model International Co., 3-5-3-405 Nishi-Shinjuku, Shinjuku-ku, Tokyo 106. (03) 345-7671

K & M Promotion Co., 2-10-25 Kita Aoyama, Minato-ku, Tokyo. (03) 404-9429

GALLERIES

Hillside Gallery, Daikanyama. (03) 476-4683 or 476-4874

Sagacho Exhibit Space, Monzen-nakacho (03) 630-3243

Hara Museum of Contemporary Art, Shinagawa. (03) 445-0651

Heartland Tsuta-Kan, Roppongi. (03) 404-3232 or (03) 791-7733

Gallery Lunami, Ginza. (03) 535-3065

The Seibu department store's **Foreign Customer Liaison Office** (03) 286-5482, and the Isetan department store's **Club Isetan** (03) 356-4311 may also be able to put you in touch with exhibit organizers or sponsors.

CLUBS

Body & Soul, Roppongi (03) 408-2094 Some of the best Japanese musicians play here, and visiting foreign jazz artists often drop by late to jam.

The Carnival, Shinjuku, Kabukicho (next to the Koma Theater). (03) 200-1261 Jazz club with a lot of vocalists.

Crocodile, Halfway between Harajuku and Shibuya stations, on Meiji-dori. (03) 499-5205 Rock house. The manager is friendly to foreign musicians, and many play here.

Inaoiza, Koenji. (03) 336-4480 Folky coffee house with late sixties/early seventies atmosphere.

La Petite Rue, Harajuku. (03) 400-9890. The American manager books small rock/folk/blues acts on Saturday nights.

Romanisches Cafe, Roppongi, on TV Asahi-dori. (03) 405-6122. Owner likes eclectic jazz and improvisation. Live only on Saturday night.

Someday, near Shin Okubo station, on Meiji-dori. (03) 207-1818. Jazz, fusion, bossa nova, and the like are played here.

Club Z, Koenji, within the Lazy Ways club. (03) 336-5841. A group of foreign rock musicians leases out the Lazy Ways club in Koenji every Saturday from 11 P.M. till morning. For details, call Alan Kidd at (03) 310-9598.

HOSTESSING jobs are sometimes advertised in the English-language daily newspapers, but most are passed on by word of mouth. It is best to know someone who has worked in the bar before you sign up since many of the entertainment establishments have ties to the underworld of organized crime and there have been cases of things getting nasty.

SUGGESTED READING

GENERAL BACKGROUND

Japan Periodicals: A Guide to Business and Economic Periodicals in English Published in Japan Keizai Koho Center, 3rd edition, 1989

Tokyo, A Bilingual Atlas Kodansha International. An invaluable guide for both the newcomer and longtime resident. Includes 19 maps showing museums, hotels, embassies, hospitals, etc.

Your Life in Tokyo: A Manual for Foreign Residents The Japan Times, 1987. A comprehensive guide to everything from taxes and housing to pets and garbage.

Living in Japan American Chamber of Commerce in Japan, 1987

This Country, Japan Edward Seidensticker, Kodansha International, (Tokyo) 1979. Brilliant essays on miscellaneous topics from Japanese literature to porn movies.

The Chrysanthemum and the Bat Robert Whiting, Permanent Press, (Tokyo), 1977. A very readable account of Japanese baseball which tells more about the Japanese character and values than most books on those topics.

You Gotta Have Wa Robert Whiting, Macmillan Publishers, (New York), 1989. Whiting's in-depth update of his first book is, again, an instructive and entertaining look at Japan–U.S. relations through baseball.

Womansword Kittredge Cherry, Kodansha International, (Tokyo), 1987. A glimpse into Japanese customs and culture via the use and meaning of words relating to women.

The Japanese Mind, the Goliath Explained Robert C. Christopher, Linden Press, Simon and Schuster, (New York) 1983. A good overview of Japanese society and business.

Japan As We Lived It: Can East and West Ever Meet? Bernard Krisher. Yohan Publications, (Tokyo), 1989. Seven "old Japan hands" tell of their experiences over the past few decades.

A Japanese Mirror Ian Buruma, Penguin, (London), 1985. A perceptive, well-written, endlessly entertaining account of the peculiarities of the Japanese. Buruma examines popular culture to elucidate modern-day Japan.

The Japanese Century: Challenge and Response Thomas R. Zengage and C. Tait Ratcliffe, Longman Group, (London), 1988. An in-depth look at what the future holds for Japan and the world.

The Enigma of Japanese Power Karel van Wolferen. Macmillan Publishers, (London), 1989. An incisive, comprehensive analysis of how the Japanese "system" really works in all facets of Japanese life.

JAPANESE COMPANIES AND DOING BUSINESS IN JAPAN

Kaisha: The Japanese Corporation James C. Abegglen and George Stalk, Jr. Charles E. Tuttle Co., (Tokyo) 1985. A down-to-earth, practical view of the strengths and weaknesses of *kaisha*.

The Sogo Shosha: Japan's Multinational Trading Companies Alexander K. Young, Charles E. Tuttle Co., (Tokyo) 3rd printing, 1986. An in-depth look at how the huge Japanese trading companies do business in Japan and abroad.

Hidden Differences: Doing Business With the Japanese Edward T. Hall and Mildred Reed Hall, Anchor Press, Doubleday (New York) 1987. A good introduction to Japanese customs and culture and how these relate to business.

Japanese Business Etiquette Diana Rowland, Warner Books, (New York) 1985. A must if you want to avoid embarrassing yourself in any business or social setting in Japan.

Polite Fictions: Why Japanese and Americans Seem Rude to each Other Nancy Sakamoto and Reiko Naotsuka, Kinseido, (Tokyo) 1982. Explains through illustrations and examples exactly what the title says it does.

FOREIGN FIRMS IN JAPAN

Directory of Foreign Capital Affiliated Enterprises in Japan Takashi Kubo. Japan Times (Tokyo), 1988. Provides detailed information on business and tax planning for foreign corporations operating or intending to operate in Japan.

Labor-Management Relations in Foreign Affiliated Firms in Japan Business Intracommunication, (Tokyo) 1984.

Setting Up and Operating a Business in Japan Helene Thian. Charles E. Tuttle, (Tokyo), 1988. A comprehensive introduction to setting up your own business. Many examples from those who have done it.

Taking on Japan: How 18 Companies Compete in the World's Second Largest Market Look Japan Ltd. (Tokyo), 1988. Interviews with the CEOs of 18 foreign companies that have been successful in Japan.

Japan Company Handbook Toyo Keizai Inc. (Tokyo). Published quarterly. Lists all of the companies in the first section of the Tokyo Stock Exchange, giving characteristics of the company, their recent performance, future outlook, and a wealth of other information.

TEACHING

Jobs in Japan John Wharton, The Global Press, (Denver), 1983. A good introduction to finding jobs teaching English in Japan. Also has sections on living and traveling in Japan.

Teaching Tactics for Japan's English Classrooms John Wharton, The Global Press, (Denver), 1986. An overview of teaching methods; includes language games.

A Guide to Teaching English in Japan ed. Charles B. Wordell, Japan Times, (Tokyo), 1985. Detailed chapters tell you how to find, keep, and/or exchange jobs, plus how to design syllabuses and improve your teaching skills. Good advice for beginners and veterans alike.

LAW

Directory of International Lawyers in Japan Survey Japan. Lists both Japanese and non-Japanese lawyers and their specialties and languages handled. Can be ordered from Survey Japan, Suite 61, No. 6, Kojimachi, Bldg., 4-5 Kojimachi, Chiyoda-ku, Tokyo 102. Cost: US$160 or ¥18,000.

The Japan Law Journal Survey Japan. A bi-monthly on legal affairs in Japan. Same address as above. (03) 262-7476 Fax 262-7453. A one-year subscription is US$87 or ¥15,000.

VISA INFORMATION

A Guide to Residence and Registration Procedures in Japan for Foreign Nationals Japan Immigration Association, 1988. The official word on immigration regulations and procedures. Updated regularly, available from government publications bookstores. One is on the corner next to the main immigration office in Tokyo.

Employment of Foreign Nationals: Questions and Answers Study Group Immigration Bureau, Ministry of Justice, 1988. A list of frequently asked questions along with the official answers. Updated regularly and available at government publications bookstores.